Education and Modernity

About the Author

Kocheril Chackappan Sabu is a Ph.D. in Education from Bangalore University. He has done Master of Arts (M.A.) in Sociology from the University of Kerala as well as from Barkatullah University, apart from Master of Education (M.Ed.) from Bangalore University. Further, Sabu holds a Post-Graduate Diploma in Human Resource Management (PGD-HRM) from Indira Gandhi National Open University (IGNOU).

Sabu started his career as Lecturer in Education at Sri TVV College of Education, Madhugiri, Karnataka. He also worked as Lecturer in Education as Guest and on adhoc basis at NCERT-Regional Institute of Education, in Bhopal. Later on, he joined as Assistant Professor of Educational Administration in the College of Education at Eritrea Institute of Technology (EIT) in Eritrea, North East Africa. Sabu also served as the Principal of Noble International Indian School in Doha, Qatar.

Apart from his work in Education, Sabu has also done considerable work in the area of Social Development. He worked with various Research and Social Development Projects of DANIDA, Bangalore, Action Aid, Bangalore, Om Consultants, Bangalore, Society for Participatory Research in Asia (PRIA), New Delhi, Aide et Action, Bhopal and DeNovo Consultants, Bhopal.

He served as the Sub Editor of *Central Chronicle newspaper* in Bhopal. Currently, he is working as Area Manager of Advertising and Marketing with *Gulf Times newspaper* in Doha, Qatar.

Sabu has published several research-based articles on different themes in national and international publications. His novel *'KENDRAN'* in Malayalam (2014), won the Kanam EJ Novel Award 2015.

Email: sabukc2001@yahoo.co.in

EDUCATION AND MODERNITY

SABU K.C.

CONCEPT PUBLISHING COMPANY, PVT. LTD.
NEW DELHI-110059

ISBN-13: 978-81-8069-858-3

First Published 2016

Published and Printed by

Concept
Since 1974

Concept Publishing Company Pvt. Ltd.
A/15-16, Commercial Block, Mohan Garden,
New Delhi-110059 (INDIA)
Phones : 25351460, 25351794, *Fax* : 091-11-25357109
Email : publishing@conceptpub.com
Website: www.conceptpub.com

Editorial Office: H-13, Bali Nagar, New Delhi-110 015, India.

Cataloging in Publication Data—DK Courtesy: D.K. Agencies (P) Ltd. <docinfo@dkagencies.com>

Sabu, Ke. Si., 1959- author.
Education and modernity / Sabu K.C.
pages cm
Includes bibliographical references and index.
ISBN 9788180698583

1. Education—India—Kerala—History. I. Title.

LA1151.S23 2016 DDC 370.95483 23

Dedication

This book is dedicated to my parents,
KV Chackappan
and
Mariamma Chackappan.

Foreword

Modernization is a process of social change. Indian society has been in the grip of modernization since the times of Rajaram Mohun Roy, Swami Vivekananda and Swami Shivananda. Down the time-line, Mahatma Gandhi, Dr. Zakir Hussain, Dr. Baba Saheb Ambedkar, Jawaharlal Nehru and scores of other distinguished sons of the soil championed the values of modernization. Still, the observed impact on individual lives of commoners in India has been minimal. Modernity, a mind-set for rational acceptance of tradition is the expected impact. Rationality is understood as Universality in thinking. It is characterized by respect for individual dignity, openness to new ideas, empathy with the lowly which is tempered with humanism. Two words summarily describe all these qualities Tolerance and Compassion. Education on modern lines, ought to develop modernity in the products of the system. This study has demonstrated that secondary education is critical for achieving a social state wherein individual members are modern.

The mean level of education in India, as per the 2009 estimates of Lee and Barro is well within 5.5 years. India has to travel a long distance to reach a minimum level of 10 years. This is the challenge. But this goal should not be insurmountable as there has been a fresh initiative in India for Universalisation of Secondary Education through the Rashtriya Madhyamik Shiksha Abhiyan since 2009. National efforts at access and participation should be complemented with continuous curricular scrutiny using a Modernity Search Light. Classroom processes should be reflecting the concerns of modernity while teacher empowerment for this purpose is to be addressed. Assessment standards should follow suit. The tool developed in this study to assess modernity should serve handy for the purpose.

In sum, this study will be useful as a basis for policy and practice for Indian education. The researcher did an excellent piece of work in an impassionate way. My compliments on this feat will always be there.

A.S. Seetharamu
Professor of Education (Rtd.), ISEC,
and Senior Consultant,
Sarva Shiksha Abhiyan,
Government of Karnataka.

Preface

This book is based on a study set in Cochin Taluk of Kerala covering 700 respondents with diverse levels of education and even no formal education, selected using quota sampling.

Modernity has been conceived at the individual level as consisting of Democratic orientation, Scientific orientation, Secular orientation, Achievement orientation and Change Proneness as reflected in eight areas of life, viz. Education, Employment, Marriage and Family, Religious life, Political life, Social life, Health and Hygiene, and Economic life. This wholistic conception synthesises two classes of theories namely: the Structure Function model and the Process model, as well as the Sociopsychological model. Herein modernity is a transitional state of a network of attitudes and behaviour which have been influenced by the given social structures and ongoing processes. This research proposed to study modernity as a Sociopsychological state of the individual, taking into account the effect of given social structures and ongoing processes.

In this study, Education, defined in terms of levels of completed formal schooling, is the independent variable. Modernity defined in terms of attitudes, and behaviour and convergence between the two is the dependent variable. The intervening variables considered are Sex, Marital Status, Religion, Occupation, Income, Type of schooling, Place of residence, Migration status, and Exposure to Mass Media.

In the course of the research, an Attitudinal scale of modernity was constructed and standardised using Thurstone and Chave Technique. Attitudinal responses were analysed using ANOVA and Duncan's Multiple Range Technique. Other data were analysed using percentages.

The study found that there is significant relationship between Education and Total Modernity. As level of Education rises, modernity of the person in General also rises. This is true in the case of all dimensions of modernity except Change Proneness, and in all areas of life. All respondents have recorded a moderately high score on Change Proneness.

It was furhter revealed that Sex, Place of residence and Type of Schooling did not affect the relationships between education and modernity. However, Marital Status, Religion, Occupation, Income, Type of schooling and Exposure to mass media affected the relationships. Maximum variations in the relationships were observed in case of occupation as an intervening variable followed by income.

According to this study, Secondary Education appears to have high potential as a Critical Level for modernity, though significant changes begin even after Upper Primary Level. Lower Primary Education appears to be critical as regards Democratic orientation and in the area of Marriage and Family Life. Upper Primary Education appears to be critical with regard to scientific orientation and in the areas of Health and Hygiene as well as Economic Life apart from General Modernity.

It is expected that this book will be a useful resource in the process of decision making, especially on Education and Human Resource Development. It is also expected that findings of this study will promote further explorations in explaining the linkages between Education and Modernity.

Doha-QATAR
27-8-2015

Sabu K C

Acknowledgements

I am extremely grateful to Dr. A.S. Seetharamu, Professor and Head, Education Unit, Institute for Social and Economic Change, Bangalore, for having kindly guided and supervised my research work. He took immense pains in reading my several drafts and improving therein both language and organisation of materials. But for his expertise, concern and generous encouragement, it would have been difficult for me to complete this research work. I only hope that I have been able to conform to the rigorous standards of research expected by my supervisor.

I place on record my sincere gratitude and indebtedness to the Institute for Social and Economic Change (ISEC), Bangalore for providing me the opportunity and facilities to undertake and complete this research. I am also thankful to several members of the faculty at ISEC with whom I have discussed my research work at various stages and profited from such discussions. Mr. V.S. Parthasarathy was a constant source of encouragement for me right from the formative stages of the research. Dr. C.S. Nagaraju and Dr. J. Acharya helped me in analysing the data using SPSS. I am also indebted to several experts in Education and Social Sciences who have contributed to this research by way of their opinions and suggestions, especially during the preparation of the research tool.

I am indebted to all my fellow researchers at ISEC who were sources of support and encouragement. I am immensely grateful to S.V. Anita, H.S. Shylendra, N. Rajasekaran and A.D. Gouri Shankar who always stood by me, especially in times of difficulty.

I take this opportuntiy to place on record the role of my friends during the different phases of the research, particularly Christy Daniel, Baby Joseph, Advocate C.P. Udayabhanu, Dr. Bino George and S.S. Induchoodan. Meetings, discussions and interactions with my friends have always been encouraging in broadening my perspectives.

I am grateful to the Indian Council of Social Science Research (ICSSR) for granting me Doctoral Fellowship without which this research would not have been possible. I sincerely thank the Department of Education, Bangalore University for their continued support and encouragement to me. I am extremely grateful to Concept Publishing Company for undertaking the publication of this research.

The field work for the study was conducted in Cochin Taluk of Ernakulam district in Kerala. I place on record my gratitude to the 700 respondents of Cochin taluk without whose patient and enthusiastic cooperation, the study would not have been possible.

I am grateful to Project Officer of National Literacy Mission's Ernakulam Literacy Project, Mr. C.G. Shanthakumar, for allowing me to access the survey records of the Project to identify the illiterates.

It is my pleasure to place on record, my gratitude to all the Literacy volunteers and activists of the Ernakulam Literacy Project on the field for helping me to meet the 'Illiterate' category of respondents. Mr. Girish Palluruthy, Mr. Kripal Kuzhuppilly, Ms. Sheeba Xavier Fishermen Colony, Mr. Koya Mattanchery, and Mr. Shaji Kumbalangi, were among the many volunteers who kindly dedicated considerable duration of their time to help me in identifying and meeting the respondents.

The Ernakulam District Employment Exchange was the major source for me to collect details of potential respondents with different levels of education. I am extremely grateful to the Employment Officer and members of the staff for allowing me access to the records.

It is very important for me to record my deep sense of gratitude to the Elected representatives of the people as well as officials of Municipal Corporation and Village Panchayats of Cochin Taluk for cooperating with me for the field study. I am deeply indebted to late T.M. Mohammed for supporting me to complete the field visits in the Corporation areas of Cochin.

I must also place on record the opportune support of Danish International Development Assistance (DANIDA) assisted Integrared Rural Sanitation and Water Supply Project, Karnataka, by taking me on board as Assistant Social Scientist of the project. I am indebted to Dr. Shyamala Abeyratne, Chief Advisor of the project, for all the encouragement and support extended to me during the final stages of the research report.

My parents were extremely happy when I embarked on this research. My father, late K.V. Chackappan, who had to discontinue schooling after the initial 4 years of excellence in studies, was always ready to support me with additional resources, especially for my prolonged stay in the field. My mother Mariamma Chackappan, who was also my teacher at the Upper Primary level, constantly encouraged me during the study. My brothers Shibu, Ashok and Eldho were supportive to me while doing this research. Eldho, my youngest brother, was keenly involved in this research by assisting me in the data compilation and coding. Ashok, expressed his moral support by way of periodic visits to the Institute. Shibu, went out of his way to support me. I find it difficult to choose words for expressing my happiness and gratitude to my parents and brothers for their crucial role in supporting me in this research.

I am indebted to my life partner Lipsy for her highly supportive role during the preparation of the manuscript for publication and the proof reading. My daughters, Arunima, Ananya and Arya, played a crucial role in keeping me happy throughout the period of preparing for the publication of this research.

I thank Mr. K.S. Narayana and Mr. Amarnath who have taken pains to type the manuscript. There were many occasions when even on short notice, they have obliged to put in extra efforts to do the requested work without any displeasure.

I place on record my gratitude to Gulf Times, Doha Qatar, for all the direct and indirect support I received during the final stages of preparing this book. Mr. James John, AGM Gulf Times, was always a source of encouragement for me. I am extremely grateful to Mr. James John for the constant moral support and encouragement.

I am indebted to Dr. N. Sudip, Editor, Gulf Times, for his support in the final stages of editing the proof. In spite of his busy schedule, Dr. Sudip wholeheartedly obliged to go through the requested sections and suggest refinements. I am extremely grateful to Dr. Sudip.

There are a number of other persons who have helped me directly and indirectly in completing this research study. They are definitely a part of my indelible memory in life though I have not mentioned each of them by name.

Doha-QATAR **Sabu K C**
27-8-2015

Contents

List of Tables, Map and Diagram

LIST OF MAPS

LIST OF FIGURES

1

Introduction

Education is conceived as a significant social institution through which every society develops its young members in accordance with its goals and aims. From a sociological perspective, education is a process of socialization. By planning the curriculum and structuring the methods of teaching, education helps the individuals to acquire desired values, attitudes, skills, behaviour, etc., enabling them to become efficient members of a society.

Apart from the universally common function of socialization, education has also to cater to the specific requirements of particular societies, which vary from society to society and from time to time. This is of relevance in the context of the difference in the pace at which the societies have developed across the world. While some societies have achieved remarkable progress in the social, economic and political spheres of life, the others are lagging behind. Majority of the developing countries belong to the latter category, i.e. they are developing. Similarly the immediate necessities of the societies also are different at a given point of time.

The significance of education in catering to the changing needs of the societies, however, has attracted the concern of social scientists and national leaders of different countries across the world. In a cumulative way, this concern got reflected in the United Nations' Declaration of Human Rights (1948). Article 26 of the UN's Declaration of Human Rights, declared education to be a human right. This, according to Keith Watson, "... was to have far reaching consequences for the shape of educational development throughout the world" (Watson, 1988:137).

The UN's declaration occurred at a historic point of time, when most of the Third World Countries were beginning to emerge as independent states. During the post-Second World War decades of 1950s and 1960s, most of these developing countries (as they are called), which were under the colonial regimes, attained political independence. There was a wide range of problems to be solved by these countries in the process of their nation building. Problems such as high rate of illiteracy and non-enrolment in schools, lack of adequate nutrition due to shortage of food, paucity of adequate medical and health care, sub-standard sanitation, high rate of population growth, slow rate of economic growth, and low per capita income, were characteristic of the emerging Third World countries. However, the gravity of these problems was felt differently by these countries. In spite of these handicaps, people of the Third World countries maintained the hope that "... there would be rapid progress all-round and that in a matter of a few years they would join the ranks of the industrialized affluent" (Jayasuriya, 1981:4). Such wishes and aspirations to modernize themselves were reflected in the goals set by these societies. Thus, for the developing countries, the attainment of political freedom was not an end in itself; rather it was a means for modernization and development, i.e. "... the rational transformation of their social, economic and political infrastructure of society to raise their national status on the world map" (Jindal, 1984:1). In the deliberations that followed thereafter in the developing countries, education was considered as the chief means for rapid social and economic progress.

> "For the past forty years educational investment in the countries of the Third World has been high on the political agenda" (Watson, 1988:137). The expansion of 'educational systems and educational provisions' that took place during the period 1950-80 was 'unprecedented'. "During those three decades more students enrolled in formal education than at anytime in all of the previous history put together" (Coombs, 1985).

At this juncture, i.e. towards the end of the twentieth century, it is time now to examine whether due consideration and importance given to education was really fruitful in achieving the social and economic goals set by these developing countries.

In this connection, more specific issues like: Has education accelerated economic growth?, How far has education helped the process of social change?, What are the areas of life in which education has contributed to national development?, etc., require attention of social scientists. In particular it is worthwhile to examine the contribution of education in modernization of developing countries.

An examination of the Indian experience in this context is relevant, since India happens to be one of the early beginners among the Third World Countries. "India is a developing country marching ahead on the road to modernization" (Sharma, 1979:13).

Education and Modernization—The Indian Context

India is currently in the process of 'modernization' (meaning of the word Modernization and the theoretical perspectives will be discussed in the following chapters). Modernization in India began with the advent of the British. During the British period modernization began with a proposal for Western education and promotion of Western culture. The freedom movement in India since the days of Raja Ram Mohun Roy, Annie Besant, Vivekananda, Gandhiji and others as well as the Arya Samaj and Brahmo Samaj, did not accept full scale westernization as a model of modernization. They wanted to integrate the rational aspects of Indian culture with the learning of English and science education. The net result, by the time India became independent was a model of modernization which integrated the best aspects of both Western culture and traditional Indian culture.

The distinguishing feature of independent India's desire for modernization is reflected in its decision to become a democratic republic. The nation wants to secure to all its citizens: Justice-socio-economic and political, Liberty of thought, expression, belief, faith and worship, Equality of status and of opportunity and Fraternity, assuring the dignity of the individual and the unity of the nation.

For the realization of the above goals, education was considered as an important avenue. It is to be noted that provision for free and universal primary education for all children till the age of 14 was included in the Directive Principles (Article 45) of the Constitution of India. Accordingly constant efforts were made by the Government of India in order to spread education. During the past four decades of Independence, literacy rate has increased in the country though not to the level of satisfaction.

In its effort to promote education the Government of India has made periodic attempts to take stock of the Indian education with a purpose of identifying the problems of education and to take corrective measures. Different Commissions and Committees have appraised the government in this regard. The Education Commission (1964-1966) has made significant contributions in this respect.

The Education Commission was appointed to advise the Government on the national pattern of education and on the general principles and policies for the development of education at all stages and in all respects. In its report, the Commission has expressed the need for drastic changes in the Indian education. The recommendations of the Commission touched upon all levels of education (except medical and legal education as these were not in the purview of the Commission).

The Commission has emphasised the relevance of education for modernization in the Indian context. "The progress of education will... be directly related to the pace of educational advance and the one sure way to modernize quickly is to spread education, produce educated and skilled citizens, and train an adequate and competent intelligentsia' (NCERT, 1971:33).

More than two decades have passed since the Commission submitted its report in 1966. During this period different States in India made different degrees of progress in the spread of education. The latest achievement to be mentioned in this context is that of Kerala State, which is the first State in India to attain total literacy.

At this juncture, It is essential to know whether the spread of education has made any useful contribution to the process of modernization.

As the development of the individual personality is an important concern of education, it is vital to know whether education has contributed to such aspects of individual development like attitudes, behaviour, values, etc., in the context of India's modernization.

If India is to become a nation, if the fundamental values of the constitution are to be realized in everyday life, if India is to be a strong, stable, dynamic and progressive society, then it is possible to do so with the large scale diffusion of modern attitudes and values among the common people, virtually a 'man in the street'. An enlightened civil society is the need of the hour. There can be no second opinion on the role of education in the creation and sustenance of such a civil society. Any effort in this direction should begin with a review of past performance and an examination of ongoing efforts. The research here falls in this genre. In other words it is to be known whether education has made any contribution at all towards individual modernity (in terms of attitudes, behaviour, etc.).

It is not only essential to know the contribution of education to modernity but also worthwhile to examine the relative differentials among levels of education in such contribution. Apart from education several other correlates of life such as religion, caste, occupation, place of residence, etc., may also influence the modernity of a person. Hence, the contribution of education to the promotion of modernity has to take into account the interplay of all these variables.

It is with these assumptions that a study was proposed to examine the relationship between levels of education and individual modernity (in terms of attitudes and behaviour). The problem considered for the study is as follows:

Relationship between Education and Modernity—A Study in Kerala State

Setting of the Study

The task of the study is to examine the relationship between education and modernity. While such a study could be conducted in any of the states in India, it was felt that it would be appropriate to choose a state which has made adequate progress in education. In view of this consideration, Kerala, which is a unique case in the Indian context, was found to be the most appropriate State.

Kerala State

Kerala is situated on the south-west corner of the Indian subcontinent (Map 1.1). The north and north-east boundaries of the state are marked by Dakshina Kannada, Kodagu and Mysore districts of Karnataka state.

The eastern side of the state is marked by Nilgiris, Coimbatore, Madurai, Ramanathapuram and Tirunelveli districts of Tamil Nadu and the south by the Kanyakumari District of Tamil Nadu. The western boundary of the state is marked by Lakshadweep sea. The state has an area of 38,863 square kilometers. The population of Kerala state during the years 1981 and 1991 was 25,453,680 and 29,011,237 (provisional) respectively and the decadal growth rate during 1971-81 and 1981-91 was 13.98.

Kerala has a unique place with reference to the educational advancements made by various states in India. It has remained at the apex of all the major states in terms of literacy. By the time this research was proposed, the literacy rate of Kerala was as high as 70.42 per cent (1981 Census). "Kerala with 90.6 per cent literacy in the age group 7 and above continues to be much above any other State or Union territory in the Indian Union.... On April 18, 1991 Kerala has been declared a fully literate state covering all persons in the age group 6-60" (Premi, 1991:68).

Another feature that distinguishes Kerala from the rest of India is the fact that there exists in this state only narrow differences between literacy rates of men and women and of rural and urban areas (Nair, 1984: 50).

Apart from the high rate of literacy which is widespread in Kerala, a notable feature of the state is that its population growth is quite low, which is one of the least in the developing world. High rate of migration for jobs to other countries added with widespread occupational mobility from the primary to the secondary sector as well as several other factors make Kerala a unique case for the study.

Ernakulam District

According to 1981 census, Kerala had 12 districts. (As per 1991 census there are 14 districts. The new districts are Kasargod and Pathanamthita).

Eranakulam is a district in central Kerala, bounded by Trichur district on the north, Idduki district on the east, Alleppey and Kottayam districts on the south and Lakshadweep sea on the west. According to the 1981 census, the literacy rate of Ernakulam district was 76.83% which is much above the state average. It may be noted here that on 4 February, 1990, Ernakulam was declared as the first total literacy district in India.

Ernakulam district with its high rate of literacy, a low growth rate of population (lower than the state average), with a majority of the workers in the non-agricultural sector and with highest proportion (in the state) of urban population, formed a unique case—among the districts of Kerala—for drawing the sample.

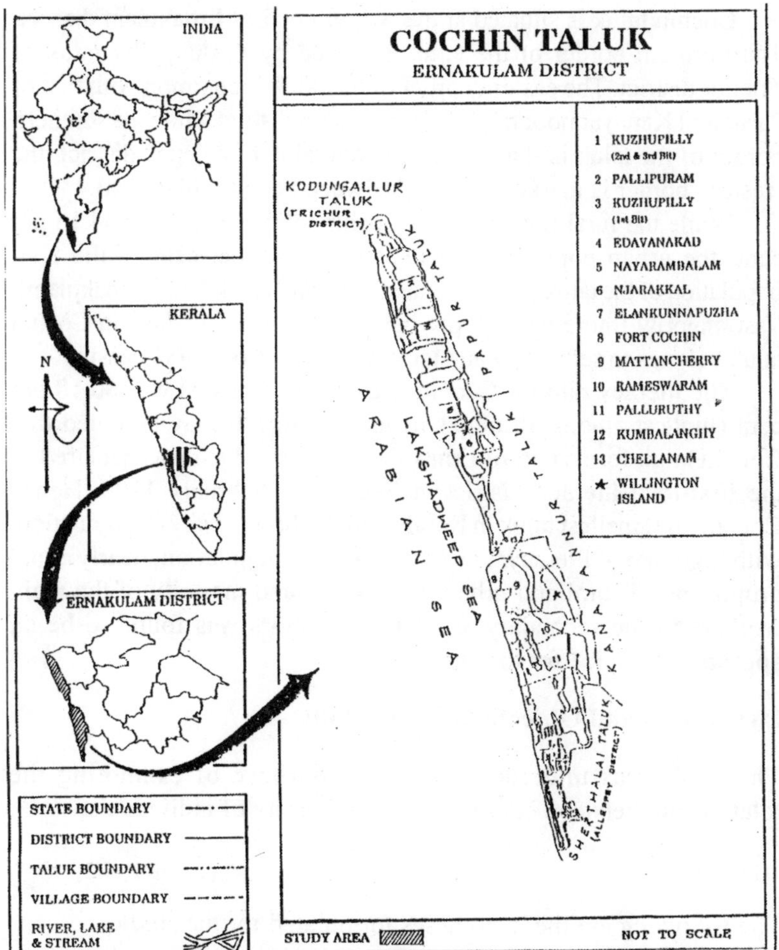

Map 1.1

Cochin Taluk

Ernakulam district has seven taluks in it. For the study, it was decided to draw sample from only one taluk of Ernakulam district. Accordingly Cochin taluk was selected. This selection was made after considering several indicators. The major characteristics of the taluk are as follows:

Cochin taluk is situated at the western end of Ernakulam district. The northern border of the taluk is shared by Kodungallur taluk of Trichur district. The eastern border of the taluk is common with that of Parur and Kanayannoor taluks of Ernakulam district while the southern border of the taluk is shared by Shertalai taluk of Allepey district, the western border is marked by Lakshadweep Sea (Arabian Sea).

While the rural population of Cochin taluk account for 44.16 per cent, the urban population account for 55.86 per cent of the total population of the taluk (District Statistical Hand Book 1986, Ernakulam). Vast majority (more than 95 per cent) of the main workers in Cochin taluk belongs to secondary and tertiary sector, as per 1981 census.

The literacy rate for Cochin taluk (1981 Census) was 80.18 per cent (highest among all taluks of the district). It may be noted that Cochin taluk forms part of Ernakulam district which was declared as the first total literacy district in India on 4 February 1990. Hence Cochin, the smallest taluk in Kerala with highest density of population, with high rate of literacy, low growth rate of population, nearly equal proportion of rural and urban population, and majority of the main workers in the secondary and tertiary sectors was found to be an appropriate choice for the study.

Hypotheses and Objectives of the Study

The study was undertaken with the purpose of examining the relationship between education and modernity of individuals.

Hypotheses

The following are the hypotheses formulated for the study:

1. There is no significant relationship between levels of education and modernity in terms of attitudes of respondents.
2. There is no significant relationship between levels of

education and modernity in terms of behaviour of respondents.

3. Differences in levels of education do not affect the relationship between education as well as attitudinal and behavioural modernity.
4. Variables such as sex, marital status, religion, place of residence, migration, occupation, income, type of schooling and exposure to mass media do not influence the relationship between levels of education and modernity of respondents.

Objectives were set for the present study keeping in view the hypotheses. They are classified under general and specific objectives.

General Objectives

1. To study modernity of individuals with regard to attitudes.
2. To study modernity of individuals with regard to behaviour.

Specific Objectives

The above general objectives were specified as follows for the study:

1. To study the relationship between levels of education and modernity in terms of attitudes of respondents.
2. To study the relationship between levels of education and modernity in terms of behaviour of respondents.
3. To study the cognitive dissonance defined as convergence/divergence between attitudes and behaviour of respondents with respect to modernity and in relation to levels of education.
4. To study the relationship between levels of education and modernity in terms of attitudes and behaviour of respondents while accounting for variables such as sex, marital status, religion, place of residence, migration, occupation, type of schooling and exposure to mass media.

Variables

As the study focuses on the relationship between education and modernity, the variables considered are as follows:

Independent Variable

Level of schooling/education is treated as the independent variable for the present study. The different levels considered are:

1. *Illiterate*: Those who did not have any exposure to formal education and who do not know reading and writing are included in this group.
2. *Lower Primary (LP)*: This includes individuals who have completed the first four years of school education.
3. *Upper Primary (UP)*: Those who have completed the first 7 years of school education.
4. *SSLC*: This category includes individuals who have completed 10 years of school education.
5. *Pre-degree (PDC)*: This includes individuals who have completed 12 years of education. It also includes persons who have completed Diploma/Certificate courses after SSLC, other than Graduation.
6. *Graduation*: This includes individuals who have completed three-year degree course i.e. B.A./B.Sc./B.Com. This does not include those who are graduates in professional courses.
7. *Post-Graduate and Professional*: Such of those who have completed the two-year master degree courses, i.e. M.A./ M.Sc./M.Com. and those who have completed a professional degree course after P.D.C./12th standard, i.e. BE, M.B.B.S. LLB, B.Pharm, B.Sc., Nursing, B.V.Sc., B.D.S., D.H.Ms., B.Ed., etc. It includes professional post-graduates also.

Dependent Variable

Modernity as reflected in attitudes and behaviour of individuals, is considered as the dependent variable in the study.

Modernity in Terms of Attitude (Attitudinal Modernity)

Modernity in this context is measured in terms of the 'score' obtained by individuals on the attitudinal modernity scale used for the study. The 'modernity score' depends on the nature of response (Agree/

disagree) expressed by the respondents for the attitudinal statements given in the scale.

An attitudinal modernity scale was developed and standardised for the study. It consists of 112 statements pertaining to 8 major areas of human life, viz., 1. Education, 2. Employment, 3. Marriage and Family, 4. Religious Life, 5. Political Life, 6. Social Life, 7. Health and Hygiene, and 8. Economic Life.

The modernity scale measures the attitudes of respondents with regard to the following dimensions:

1. Change proneness as well as openness to new experiences and innovations,
2. Scientific orientation (with an emphasis on rationality).
3. Democratic orientation,
4. Secular orientation, and
5. Achievement orientation.

Modernity in terms of Behaviour

Modernity in behaviour is understood as the specific act carried out by an individual in one of the 8 areas of life referred to earlier. It includes both covert (e.g., decision making) and overt acts (e.g., observable behaviour). The five dimensions of attitudinal modernity also serve as bases for interpreting behavioural modernity.

Intervening Variables

Apart from formal schooling/education there are a number of other factors that are likely to influence the modernity of an individual. Examples of such variables are sex, marital status, religion/caste, place of residence, urban exposure, occupation, income, type of schooling, exposure to mass media, education of parents, occupation of parents, etc.

In order to know the influence of factors other than education, in the relationship between education and modernity, a set of variables have been selected for the study. The 'intervening variables' thus considered are as follows:

1.	Sex	—	Male/Female
2.	Marital status	—	Married/Unmarried
3.	Religion	—	Hindu/Christian/Muslim
4.	Place of residence	—	Rural/Urban
5.	Migration	—	Migrant/Non-migrant
6.	Occupation (as classified by the National Classification of Occupations)		1. Professional, technical and related workers. 2. Administrative, Executive and managerial workers. 3. Clerical and related workers. 4. Sales workers 5. Service workers 6. Farmers, fishermen, hunters, loggers and related workers. 7. Production and related workers, transport equipment operators and labourers.
7.	Income (Income of the family to which the respondent belong to)	—	1. Poor—Less than Rupees 6,000 per annum,
		—	2. Low income—Rs. 6,000 to 12,000 per annum.
		—	3. Lower middle income—Rs. 12,000 to 24,000 per annum.
		—	4. Upper middle income—Rs. 24000 to 36000 per annum.
		—	5. High income—Above Rs. 36,000 per annum

(Per capita income of Kerala State, for the year 1985-86, at current prices, and at constant prices were Rs. 2140 and Rs. 646 respectively.)

8.	Type of schooling (Management of the school in which the respondents studied during UP)	—	1. Government
		—	2. Private
9.	Exposure to mass media	—	Mass media exposure is understood in terms of mass media index. Mass media index is a numerical figure attained for each respondent based on the frequency of exposure to the media, i.e. newspaper (reading/listening to oral/reading aloud); radio listening; TV-watching/listening; and film-seeing/watching.

Responses given by respondents are given (directional) weightages as follows:

Table 1.1

Item	*Response*	*Code*	*Weightage*
Newspaper (Reading/ listening to reading aloud)	Regularly	3	50
	Sometimes	2	20
	Never	1	0
	No response	0	0
Radio (Listening)	Regularly	3	25
	Sometimes	2	10
	Never	1	0
	No response	0	0
T V (Listening/watching)	Regularly	3	15
	Sometimes	2	5
	Never	1	0
	No response	0	0
Film (Watching/seeing)	Regularly	3	10
	Sometimes	2	5
	Never	1	0
	No response	0	0

The maximum a person can score would be 100. The weightages for all the media according to the response given by the individual are added up. This figure is referred to as mass media index. This was arrived at in consultation with several media personnel and experts.

A score of 50 and above in the mass media index is considered as high exposure to mass media and all scores below 50 are considered low exposure to mass media.

Methodology

For the study, Normative Survey method was adopted. The design is as follows:

Sources of Data

The study is aimed at an examination of the relationship between levels of education and modernity in terms of attitudes and behaviour of individual respondents. Hence, primary data, qualitative and quantitative, pertaining to the attitudes and behaviour of individual respondents constitute the major data source.

However, secondary data from relevant sources like census publications and other literature are also used at various phases of the study.

Tools of Data Collection

Data required for the present study were collected through three tools :

1. A general information schedule for collecting information regarding the independent and moderator variables;
2. An attitudinal modernity scale for measuring attitudinal modernity; and
3. A schedule for measuring behavioural modernity.

Tools 1 and 3 were presented in a schedule form in a sequential manner following a thematic order.

Attitudinal modernity scale was placed at the end of the schedule. Attitudinal statements pertaining to different areas of life were presented in a jumbled order.

Standardization of the Attitudinal-Modernity Scale

In the absence of a suitable scale for measuring attitudinal modernity as required for the present study, a scale was developed, following the method prescribed by Thurstone and Chave (Edwards, 1969: 83-119).

Accordingly, a number of statements, approximately 2000, belonging to the major areas of human life, i.e. education, employment, marriage, family life, religious life, political life, social life, health and hygiene, and economic life were collected (from different sources, like magazines, newspapers, books, journals, etc.), restructured and developed.

Each of these statements was subjected to a conceptual examination to test whether it would conform to operational definitions of modernity. The items should satisfy one of the following five descriptive dimensions of modernity.

1. *Change proneness and openness to new experience and innovations*: A state of readiness to accept new ideas and changes in social organisations, new ways of feeling and acting, etc.
2. *Scientific orientation*: A tendency to understand the world on the basis of rules of evidence and verification rather than just in terms of the wisdom of the past.
3. *Democratic orientation*: A love for an individual as a human being and respect for the dignity of the individual, i.e. love and respect for the person as such independently of his birth, religion, caste, race, language, status, etc.
4. *Secular orientation*: It refers to the acceptance of the withdrawal of authority of religion from various institutional spheres such as matrimonial, educational, economic, etc., with the result that religion ceases to extend its influence over interpersonal relations and corporate actions. A person is guided by reason for actions than tradition or custom or religious authority.
5. *Achievement orientation*: A tendency to achieve higher goals in the spheres of education, occupation, economic life, etc., through planning and hard work.

As a result of the modernity test, 213 statements were selected and were submitted to a panel of judges for their ratings, choices, judgements, comments and reactions on each item.

Based on the analysis of ratings (scale and Q values), judgement on each item, given by the judges, and insights from the pilot study, 112 statements were finally selected and included in the attitudinal modernity scale. Each statement was followed by two alternatives—agree and disagree. The respondent was requested to express his/her acceptance or rejection of the given statement. Clear instructions were also provided regarding the method of answering which was common for all statements. While neutrals could be one of the alternative responses, it was deliberately not provided in the scale as it could encourage respondents to be non-committal.

Distribution of Items

The final list of 112 statements in the attitudinal modernity scale are distributed among the 5 dimensions of modernity as well as the 8 areas of life considered for constructing the scale. However, the statements were arranged in random order while being presented in the final form.

Validity of the Scale

Construction of the scale was done following the prescribed procedure. The statements constituting the attitudinal modernity scale were collected from relevant sources like published literature. Opinion of experts was sought on each of the statements and on the scale as a whole. Experts included were mainly academicians specialised in education, psychology, sociology, economics and political science, from different parts of the country, including eminent scholars. There were senior citizens and at least one IAS officer. Age of these experts ranged from 28-70 years and above. The experts were requested to examine the statements in terms of adequacy, suitability, relevance, clarity, and balance. Later the scale was purged of several statements which were not found adequate by a majority of the experts. A coverage of 80 per cent approval and higher than that for an item qualified it for field selection. This is how consent validity of the scale was established.

Reliability of the Scale

The reliability coefficient of the scale was established by test-retest method. It was found to be 0.87.

Hence, the attitudinal modernity scale was found to enjoy high degrees of validity and reliability.

Modernity Score (Method of Scoring)

Based on the responses given by the respondents on the attitudinal statements, modernity scores are obtained for all individuals.

The score for any individual is obtained by taking the arithmetic mean of the scale values of all the statements which the respondent has agreed with. The statements with which the respondent has disagreed or has not responded to are not considered for arriving at the modernity score. It may be noted here that there is a balanced mix of positive and negative scales.

Following the above procedure, modernity scores are calculated for each of the eight areas of life as well as for each of the five dimensions. In addition to these, a composite score—general modernity score—is also calculated, taking into account all statements agreed with, irrespective of the areas of life or dimensions. Hence, 14 separate modernity scores are obtained for each individual.

Items on General Information and Behavioural Modernity

Items for measuring behavioural modernity, corresponding to the areas of life, considered for attitudinal modernity, are included in the tool. These items are subject to careful scrutiny and editing before inclusion in the tool. (The procedure followed for attitudinal modernity scale was, however, not followed in this case). Similarly, items for measuring general information are also included in the tool.

Statistical Techniques used for the Analysis of Data

Data collected for the present study belong to mainly three categories, i.e. (i) General Information on the background of the respondents, consisting of independent and intervening variables; (ii) Attitudinal modernity of respondents; and (iii) Behavioural modernity of the respondents.

Analysis of general information is done using percentages and verbal description.

Attitudinal modernity of respondents is subjected to Analysis of Variance and also Duncan's Multiple Range Test. This is supplemented by a verbal description of mean values of attitudinal modernity scores.

Percentage analysis is used for analysing data on behavioural modernity.

Cognitive dissonance defined as the convergence/divergence between attitudes and behaviour is analysed using percentages.

Sample

The sample drawn for the study consisted of 700 adults, residents of Cochin taluk, who were born between 1962 and 1964.

The age group was specified not only to get homogeneity in the sample but also to have some uniformity in the educational exposure of the respondents. It was expected that the selected group would have had their schooling during or after 1968.

1968 was the year in which Report of the Education Commission in which modernisation as an objective of education was stated explicitly was accepted by the Government of India.

Since then, modernization has been accommodated in the curriculum of school and college education to which the individuals in the sample have been exposed.

Using quota sampling, seven hundred individuals were selected for the study. The sample was selected in such a way as to have 100 respondents each under 7 levels of education, viz.,

1. Illiterate,
2. Lower Primary,
3. Upper Primary,
4. SSLC/Equivalent,
5. PDC/Equivalent,
6. Graduation/Equivalent, and
7. Post-Graduation and Professional/Equivalent.

Apart from level of education, quotas were fixed with reference to the following variables:

Sex	: Male = 48%, Female = 52%
Place of residence	: Rural = 50%, Urban = 50%
Religion	: Hindu = 60%, Muslim = 20%
	Christian = 20%
	(Hindus include 10% as SC/ST).

It may be noted that macro level distribution of population in Kerala State also corresponds to the distribution of the sample in this study on all these three variables.

These proportions were maintained at all levels of education in the sample. It was followed as a norm that only one individual from each household would be included in the sample.

Given the sample requirements, there was no single source which the researcher could have depended on in identifying the sample for the study, particularly in identifying individuals who are Illiterates and those who have not studied beyond Upper Primary level of education. Therefore, different sources were made use of. The major sources are as follows:

1. Voters list of Cochin taluk;
2. Live register of the Divisional Employment Exchange Ernakulam;
3. Registration record of the Medical Council, Trivandrum;
4. Registration record of the Dental Council, Trivandrum;
5. Registration record of the Nursing Council, Trivandrum;
6. Registration record of the Bar Council, Ernakulam;
7. Admission register of Colleges, Ernakulam; and
8. Survey records prepared for the Ernakulam district total literacy programme 1989.

Based on the above sources, a list of eligible individuals satisfying the requirements for the quota sampling was prepared. Nearly 2,500 individuals were thus included in this list. Name of the individual, sex, religion, educational qualifications and residential address were the information collected from secondary data in the list thus prepared. Residents of Chellanam Panchayat were not included in this list, as the pilot study was carried out in Chellanam which was a representative panchayat of Cochin Taluk. Using this list, sample was drawn, as per the quotas fixed.

Stages of the Study

In order to collect the required data from the sample selected for the study, fieldwork was conducted in Cochin taluk, Ernakulam district, Kerala State. The fieldwork was carried out in two stages—pilot study and the main study.

Pilot Study

A pilot study was conducted in Chellanam panchayat of Cochin taluk, on a sample of 70 individuals. Among the objectives considered for the pilot study, the important ones are as follows:

1. To understand the nature of the sample;
2. To try out the proposed tool for collection of data in order to know: whether the words used in the tool were simple enough for the respondents to understand; whether the statements were winding and long or whether they were brief and straight-forward; whether the translation of the tool into Malayalam, originally constructed in English, is true to its meanings; and to know the time normally taken by a respondent to answer the tool, which was separately noted for people with different levels of education;
3. To get an initial feedback on the hypotheses set for the study;
4. To examine the budgetary requirements regarding time and resources for the main study; and
5. To find out the difficulties if any that may arise during the main study.

Pilot study was conducted in Chellanam panchayat during the period 25th May to 2nd July, 1988. Chellanam was selected as a representative panchayat of Cochin Taluk. It was decided to have a sample size amounting to 10 per cent of the sample for the main study. Thus the sample for the pilot study was only 70.

Systematic random sampling was followed in drawing the sample for the pilot study. For this purpose, voters list of the panchayat was made use of.

Data were collected individually through household visits, using the tool designed for the main study. The tool consisted of selected items on attitudinal modernity, selected behavioural items and the general information schedule. Altogether there were 197 items on which information was gathered. The tool used was in Malayalam translated from the original English version.

Data thus collected were analysed using percentages.

Insights from the Pilot Study

Based on the fieldwork experiences during the pilot study and the results of the analysis of the data collected, certain insights emerged which were used for planning the final study. The most important among them are as follows:

1. Systematic random sampling was found to be unsuitable in drawing sample for the main study. It was felt that quota sampling would be more appropriate for drawing sample for the main study.
2. It was found that some of the items included in the schedule were difficult for the respondents to understand particularly in the case of illiterates and those who have studied only up to lower primary level. It was, therefore, felt that such items should be simplified.
3. Some of the items were found to be eliciting uniform responses from all the respondents. It was felt that such items should be dropped.

Based on the insights from the pilot study, necessary modifications were made in the tool for the main study.

Main Study

The main fieldwork for collecting data for the study was carried out in Cochin taluk, during the year 1989. Since Chellanam panchayat was already covered in the pilot study, only the remaining areas of the taluk were considered for drawing the sample.

Data were collected from 700 individuals, who satisfied the sample requirements, by canvassing the schedule through household visits. Interviews were held in the case of respondents belonging to Illiterate, Lower Primary and Upper Primary categories. In the remaining cases most of the respondents provided data pertaining to them, by filling in the schedule themselves. However, interviews were held in cases of necessity.

Most of the interviews were held at the residence of respondents during day time, i.e. 10 a.m. to 6 p.m. However, visits were made even late in the night, subject to the convenience or availability of the respondents (particularly in the case of fishermen, casual labourers, workers and employees).

During the initial rounds of the fieldwork, on an average 3 interviews were held per day. Each of these interviews took 45 to 50 minutes time. However, subsequently the number of interviews held per day increased to an average of 5-6 and the time consumed for each interview reduced to 25 to 30 minutes.

Building rapport with the respondents during the field visits was easier as the researcher knew the local language.

Scope of the Study

Education is an instrument in bringing about desired attitudinal and behavioural changes among individuals. Even in India, education is expected to play an important role in realising the national goals. The nation wants to secure to all its citizens JUSTICE, social, economic and political; LIBERTY of thought, expression, belief, faith and worship; EQUALITY of status and of opportunity; and to promote among them all FRATERNITY assuring the dignity of the individual and the unity and integrity of the Nation. For the realisation of these goals, education was considered as an important avenue.

This study is essentially interested in the role of education in promoting individual modernity. However, it is not intended to study modernity exclusively in this research. An attempt is made in this research to study modernity in terms of attitudes and behaviour only of individuals in the context of their educational level.

Attitudinal modernity in five dimensions are included in the study. Similarly, eight major areas of life are also considered in studying attitudinal modernity.

Behavioural modernity reflected in selected areas of life are examined in the study. It is essential to know whether there is any variation in the level of modernity of individuals, as educational attainment increases. For this purpose modernity—attitudinal and behavioural—of individuals with different levels of education, starting from illiterate to post-graduate and professional level through SSLC is compared.

An attempt is also made in order to identify whether there is any 'critical level' of education with reference to attitudinal modernity of individuals.

An attempt is made in the study to know whether there is any influence of other variables in the relationship between education and modernity. For this purpose, variables such as sex, marital status, religion, place of residence, migration, occupation, income, type of schooling and exposure to mass media are considered in analysing the relationship between education and modernity. Such analysis is, however, followed only in the case of attitudinal modernity.

It is also essential to know whether attitude and behaviour of individuals move in similar directions. An effort is made to this effect in analysing cognitive dissonance, defined as convergence/divergence of attitudes and behaviour of individuals.

Limitations of the Study

The study is essentially interested in the role of education in promoting modernity and not modernity as such.

It is confined to attitudes and behaviour of individuals in measuring modernity. The study does not cover such aspects of modernity like beliefs, values, etc.

While attitudinal modernity is measured (with the help of an attitudinal modernity scale) in terms of five dimensions as well as eight areas of life, behavioural modernity here is limited to some areas of life to only—Education, Marriage and Family, Religious Life, Social Life, Political Life, and Health and Hygiene.

The sample taken for the study consists of 700 individuals. It is difficult to observe modernity of individuals in real life contexts of behaviour, more so with a large sample size. Hence behaviour as reported by individual respondents is taken for studying behavioural modernity. This is a limitation of the survey method.

There are a number of variables that are likely to influence modernity of individuals. Education is only one of those variables which is considered for the study. It is not planned to examine the relationship between the variables other than education and modernity separately. It is the influence of variables other than education on the relationship between education and modernity that is studied here. For this purpose, only variables which are considered significant on the basis of review of literature are included. Such analysis, of course, is confined only to attitudinal modernity.

Chapterization

The study is organized in eight chapters, as follows:

Chapter One deals with the introduction, need for the study, setting of the study, objectives, hypotheses, methodology and the scope and limitations of the study.

Chapter Two provides theoretical perspectives on the relationship between education and modernity, discusses the meanings of the key terms used, outlines the process of modernization and educational development in India as well as presents the perspective followed in the study.

An attempt is made in Chapter Three to review the empirical studies on education and modernity. This review aims to arrive at inferences that may have a bearing on the hypotheses of the study, as well as the selection of sample, method of data collection and selection of statistical techniques.

Chapter Four presents a general description of respondents in the sample, with reference to demographic particulars, food and nutritional habits, the skills possessed by the respondents, membership in social organizations, family background, and details of married respondents.

Chapter Five discusses the role of formal education in bringing about attitudinal modernity in three sections: levels of education and modernity in terms of attitudes; critical levels of education with reference to modernity in terms of attitudes; and the relationship between levels of education and modernity in terms of attitudes as moderated by different intervening variables.

Chapter Six deals with the relationship between levels of education and modernity in terms of behaviour. An attempt is made to analyse whether differences in levels of education will be reflected in differences in the pattern of behaviour.

Chapter Seven deals with the consistency between attitudes and behaviour reflecting modernity of respondents across different levels of education.

Chapter Eight presents the summary of the work done, findings and conclusions.

2

Theoretical Perspectives

In the previous chapter, introduction to the problem, need for the study, setting of the study, objectives, hypotheses, methodology, scope and limitations of the study were presented.

The present chapter deals with theoretical perspectives with regard to the relation between education and modernity and the position adopted for the present study. Meaning and characteristics of modernization, meaning of modernity, characteristics of modernity, a brief account of education and modernization in India, operational definitions of other key terms used in the study are also presented.

Meaning and Characteristics of Modernization

In common parlance, the word 'modernization' implies "something new". The dictionary meaning of modernization refers to 'the process of becoming modern', 'adapting modern ways', etc. The etymology of the word is from the Latin root *modo*, which means 'just now'. 'Modernization' as a concept gained currency in the social sciences by nineteenth century following the industrial revolution.

Modernization as a process began in Western countries of Europe in the nineteenth century. It started with the advent of industrialisation and commercialization, which ushered in the following fundamental changes in the Western societies:

(a) Ever-increasing new technology,
(b) Ever-increasing use of inanimate power and technology in competitive market situations,

(c) Ever-increasing rate of trade and voyage,
(d) A scientific world view against traditional world view; and
(e) Fall of traditional-feudal structure and rise of democratic and totalitarian system.

The process of modernization thus brought in its wake many new ideas and concepts which were utilized for collective action for change. Concepts like equality, freedom, justice, democracy, *laissez faire* economy, etc., determined the ethos of the time. The course of modernization, it cannot be denied, began with the decline of medieval conditions of life and thought (Srivastava *et al.,* 1976 : 20). Indeed, since the Renaissance, there has been a visibly identifiable process of modernization in the Western World. It has had different phases. The growth of oceanic commerce, manufacturing, industrial and finance capitalism, steel, electric and atomic technology and power, are some of its external characteristics. At the ideological level, modernization has been marked by the growth of scientific scrutiny, rational enquiry and the spirit of humanism in place of ecclesiastical theology and creedal denominationalism. At the political level, modernization has symbolized the growth of the notion of individual rights, liberty, equality, participant citizenship, pluralistic associational structure and interest groups, dynamics of political parties and social justice in place of patriarchal authority, power, regimentation and control. Furthermore, modernization has meant a future-oriented valuational adherence in place of a nostalgic longing for a primitive paradise (Varma, 1976: 36).

It will be recalled that the most dramatic changes took place during the middle and closing decades of the nineteenth century, although, the origins of modernization can be traced back to fifteenth and sixteenth century Europe. Early in the twentieth century Japan, the first Asian country to do so, joined the race for industrialization. Later, the USSR, as well as some other countries, achieved modernization in varying degrees (Dube, 1988: 17).

Ever since the industrial revolution, modernization, both as a pattern and a process, has attracted the attention of social scientists. Modernization has been discussed as 'collective' as well as 'individual' form of behaviour. Numerous definitions, interpretations and explanations are available on the concept of modernization. These conceptualizations vary according to the discipline and approach of the concerned authors. Some of them are presented here.

To take an example, modernization has been considered as "a general term which describes the process of rapid social change and used recently for the understanding of social phenomenon" (Tripathi, 1976: 121).

It has also been stated that "... modernization is a process that first characterised the societies which changed from primarily agricultural to primarily industrial economies. As this happened these societies simultaneously underwent other changes in their social practices and value premises which have been recorded, discussed and analysed by social scientists and literary men. These changes have been identified as constituting the process of modernization" (Gore, 1982: 7).

On the other hand, there are those who hold that "Changes in the proportion of people holding modern values, or changes in the extent to which individuals have gone 'modern' constitute modernization.... whereas the terms 'development' and 'industrialization' are used to describe mainly economic growth, and 'urbanisation' is used to describe shifts in population disposition and concentration, the concept of modernization has to do with a transformation of culture and of personality in so far as it is influenced by cultural rather than by some aspect of social organisation or human ecology. The idea of modernization is that there is an alteration or movement of something from a more traditional state to a more modern state from one point in time to another" (Stephenson, 1969: 265-6).

According to Levy, modernization is "the ratio of inanimate to animate source of power" (Levy, 1986: 3).

It has also been noted that "Structurally, modernization is often employed as a synthetic term for urbanization, literacy, a democratic polity, industrialization, and overall economic development" (Portes, 1973: 16).

"Modernization is nothing but availing of increased opportunities of systematic inquiry and subjecting our life more and more to rational examination" (Murty, 1987: 8).

According to Damle, "It is important to realise that the concept of modernization is multi-dimensional, incorporating economic development, technological and industrial revolutions, rationality and scientific temper, emphasis on achieved status, equality, social justice, individualism and so on" (Damle, 1974: 34).

Damle goes on to state that modernization is generally expected to favour nuclear family types and promote democratic relationships within the family. Achievement, orientation and a high level of aspiration are regarded as important components of modernization. Manipulation of physical and social environment is another important indicator of modernization. Modernization is again expected to promote rationality and to dispel blind faith in supernatural forces (Damle, 1974: 35-9).

It, therefore, appears that "modern" generally means a national state characterised by a complex of traits including urbanization, high levels of education, industrialization, extensive mechanization, high rates of social mobility, and the like. When applied to individuals, it refers to a set of attitudes, values and ways of feeling and acting, presumably of the sort either generated by or required for effective participation in a modern society (Smith and Inkeles, 1966).

Dube explains that modernization... is essentially a process—a movement from a traditional order to certain desired types of technology and associated forms of social structure, value orientation and motivations and norms....Modernization thus is not just superficial acquisition of some isolated traits and elements, characteristics of the more advanced countries. Their selection in a logical order and sequence, and integration into the cultural pattern in a widely ramifying manner is essential. A great deal of value change is involved, and some significant institutional modifications are essential (Dube, S.C., 1967).

> "The concept of modernization refers to the process of social change in which the individual imbibes certain attitudinal-cum-personality traits conducive to socio-economic and political development as well as individual self-actualisation" (Singh, 1984B : 6).

According to Everette M. Rogers, "modernization is the process by which individuals change from a traditional way of life to a more complex, technologically advanced, and rapidly changing style of life. Modernization at the individual level corresponds to development at the societal level" (Rogers, 1969: 14).

B.V. Shah, attempting a comprehensive definition, holds that modernization is a multi-dimensional process. It is not merely an economic process concerned with maximization of physical power and improving of tools to increase the productive potential and thereby increase the levels of living of a given society. It is a political, social and cultural process as well. It is a complex process which frees the potential in them in various spheres of their lives and maximizes their ability to share in defining the goals of their society, to internalize them and to participate creatively and effectively in their realization in the wider society.

In the economic sphere it results in industrialization which brings in large-scale organization of men, money and materials, mechanization, monetization and urbanization. It emphasizes distinctions between private and corporate property and separates place of work from place of residence. It provides individual's freedom of choice of occupation and requires them to be rational and mobile. It expects them to develop new attitudes to earning, purchasing, saving and investing in consonance with the goals of society. In the political sphere, it develops a secular and welfare state with enlarged functions to include concerns such as education, health, housing, employment, etc. It establishes the rule of law and provides to all equality before law. It gives freedom to people in choice of rulers and form of government as well as freedom to change them and requires their conscious participation in the political process. In the social sphere it necessitates an open system of stratification and emphasises achieved status rather than an anscriptive one. It emphasizes equality of opportunity for all and lays stress on individual freedom in matters of family, marriage, occupation, religion, etc. In the individual sphere, it emphasizes change as a value and encourages individuals to have faith in the efficacy of human effort for bringing about desirable social changes. It expects them to be secular, cosmopolitan, rational, scientific and universalistic in their outlook and approach to life and its problems, egalitarian and democratic, in their relationship with others, and innovative and creative in their contribution to societal problems and development (Shah, 1971: 240-1).

Drawing up on the works of many eminent scholars including Weiner, Apter, Lerner, Black, Inkeles, Bendix, Marion Levy, Smelser,

Nettl and others—A.R. Desai has summarised the characteristic features of modernization as follows:

The shift from use of human and animal power to inanimate power, from tool to machine, as the basis of production, and its implications in terms of growth of wealth, technical diversification, differentiation, and specialisation leading to a novel type of division of labour; and industrialization and urbanization are... accepted by all scholars as features of modernization. The shift of the sanction behind the state from the supernatural to secular, the extension and increasing diffusion of power to a wider strata of population and the supremacy of law over the regulative systems are also recognised as basic features of modernization. Similarly, a shift in the social structure based on allocation of roles on the principle of ascription to one based on the principle of achievement and merit, thus qualitatively transforming the very basis of role recruitment and, therefore, of the social structure, is accepted as a trait of modernization. The major shift in the principle of social solidarity from a 'mechanical' one built on a precontractual, diffused and particularistic basis, is also recognized. Scholars also recognize that the modernization process implies a shift from sacred, other-worldly, change-resistant outlook to a secular, this-worldly, forward-looking change-prone outlook. Similarly scholars implicitly or explicitly acknowledge that rationality, humanism, and feasibility and necessity of improvement in the conditions of life of the human beings in this world and not in the other world constitute the hallmark of the cultural outlook of modernization [Desai, 1971(A): 463].

Defining modernization as 'the transition of societies from traditional to the modern model', Frank Tachau described the characteristics of modern society (compared to traditional society) as follows:

Modern society, by contrast, is a mass society. Cash, commercial credit, advanced technology, and specialized production underlie an extensive market economy based on mass production and consumption. Mass media of communication and universal public education help to instil a common set of values, a common ideology, and common aspirations among all groups in the society. Mass transportation enables individuals to become mobile in physical as well as psychic sense, and thus to associate with members of social groups who might be culturally alien and physically far removed. Election of government officials means mass participation in the political system, whether there are actually meaningful choices among alternate sets of leaders or merely plebiscites which legitimize the rule of those already in power. In sum, modern society is geographically extensive—often of continental proportions—possessed of a large and diverse population, but highly integrated in terms of values and communications. The bulk of the population identifies closely with the symbols of political authority. Governments impinge visibly on the lives of the members of the society; governments demand and usually receive overt signs of active support and allegiance from the bulk of the population. Finally, the predominant world view is secular and rationalist; natural and social forces are typically viewed as subject to purposeful human control (Tachau, 1974: 2-3).

An analysis of different interpretations and definitions available in the literature on modernization leads one to the following understandings:

(i) Modernization is an ongoing complex process which covers all areas of human life. It emerged as a concomitant effect of industrialization, urbanization and related processes.

(ii) Modernization represents a move towards more complex, technologically advanced and rapidly changing life styles.

(iii) Modernization is a relative term (when considered as a continuum between tradition and modernity).

(iv) Modernization can be understood at two levels, i.e. at the societal level and at the individual level. At the societal level modernization is indicated by:

1. Increased rate of industrialization and urbanization.
2. Development of transport and communication facilities.
3. Advancement in science and technology.
4. A rational administration and democratic power system.
5. Growth oriented economy.
6. Controlled growth of population.
7. High level of participation by the members of the society.
8. High rate of literacy.
9. Increasing social mobility, and so on.

At the individual level, modernization is indicated by literacy, empathy, mobility, high participation, rationality, new attitude towards wealth, work, savings, moderate risk taking, etc. Faith in the desirability and possibility of change, social, political and economic discipline, high level of aspiration, high level of need achievement, adapting small family as the norm, a balanced self-image, etc.

(v) There are certain prerequisites for the process of modernization. These include factors like literacy and education, scientific outlook, attitudinal and value changes, dynamic and determined leadership, etc.

(vi) The concept of modernization includes time dimensions and change.

As can be observed from the discussion above, "Modernization cannot be described adequately as it has come to be associated with many diverse dimensions of change. This has also led to many interpretations. It is at times treated as a process of change, while in other contexts it is considered as a goal towards which every society is moving or will strive to move. Neither as a process, nor as a goal, has it been described in precise terms" (Saksena, 1972: 92).

Meaning of Modernity

Before presenting the meaning of modernity and its relationship with modernization that are understood in this study, it would be worthwhile to understand the same from the existing social science literature.

In social science literature, modernity has been referred to as an aggregate of certain attitudinal and personality traits conducive to social and economic development.

"Modernity is a psychological prerequisite of development. The economic backwardness and failure of democracy in several Third World countries have been explained on the basis of a paucity of modern socio-political attitudes and personality characteristics" (Jayaswal, 1985).

"Modernity denotes the common "behavioural systems" historically associated with the urban, industrial, literate, and participant societies of Western Europe and North America as well as those of USSR and Japan" (Dube, 1967: 35).

"Modernity, when conceived at the individual level, refers to a complex of certain psychological dispositions, attitudes, values and behaviour that promote development and help people to cope with changes brought about by the development process" (Mahajan, 1989: 399).

"Modernity is an aggregate of certain personality-cum-attitudinal traits which facilitates individual growth and development with social responsibility and makes the individual an effective agent of socio-economic and political development" (Singh, 1984B: 7).

It refers to "a set of attitudes, values and ways of feeling and acting presumably of the sort either generated by or required for effective participation in a modern society" (Smith and Inkeles, 1966).

Characteristics of Modernity

Some of the most important characteristics of modernity at the individual level are as follows:

A modern person is rational, is open to change, is committed to work and has aspirations. He/she is not fatalistic, and he/she believes that hardwork and ability, not luck, determine success. He/she is willing to work even if he/she can live comfortably without doing any work. A modern person is liberal in his socio-cultural attitudes. He/she supports women's rights, social equality, and family planning. He/she opposes casteism and orthodox social customs. He/she disapproves of the customary practice of wife giving better food to her husband than what she takes herself. He/she supports widow-remarriage and birth-control. The social liberalism of a modern person is matched by his/her political liberalism. He/she supports democracy, civic rights and secularism. He/she believes that every citizen should have full freedom to criticise the government. He/she realises the political usefulness of opposition parties. He/she is not limited within the narrow boundaries of family, caste and religion. He/she is conscious of his/her wider socio-political responsibilities. He/she is rational and has scientific attitudes towards health and disease, diet and nutrition. He/she does not believe that the cure of illness depends on the mercy of God; nor that mental illness is caused by evil spirits. He/she is against overeating because he/she knows that it is as harmful as inadequate eating. He/she believes that women, like men, also need physical exercise. These are only a few illustrations of the mental make-up of a modern person. He/she is scientific, rational, liberal, humane and effective (Singh, 1984B: 9).

Modernization and Modernity

'Modernization' and 'Modernity' are two words which are quite often used interchangeably in social sciences literature. Though related, these two are distinct concepts.

Modernization is essentially a process—a process of becoming modern. Modernization is a macro-level, all-pervading, diffusive process of social change that cuts across the economic, social, and political life of a society. It may include technological changes in the fields of agriculture, industry, infrastructural development and support services. It may include the emergence of economic institutions such as those of banking, commerce and trade, and the setting up of political institutions for decentralised planning and development of a sophisticated bureaucracy as well as a complex network of institutions for management of the state. There may be changes in social institutions, marriage and kinship, family structure, status of religion in social life, etc. Similarly, large scale structural changes as well as phenomenal expansion of formal and non-formal educational systems may also be part of this modernizing process.

It is felt that the end state of these processes of modernization may be considered to be the creation of a sustainable enlightened civil society, whose tool is 'universal reason' and whose goal is 'human welfare'. The creation of such a society implies a metamorphic change in the lives of the people, a large scale change in their habits of social life, thinking processes. attitudes and values. This contemplated end state of change may be conceived of as 'modernity'. However, for any given point of time modernity can be considered to be a set of attitudes and behaviours that are commensurate with this end state.

Perspectives on Modernization

Modernization as a process has attracted the attention of scholars across various disciplines. Scholarship on Modernization is increasingly becoming specialised, as each discipline approaches the subject from its own perspective (Saksena, 1972: 92).

According to Holsinger (1987), it is possible to see, to some degree, in the research literature on Modernization, the distinctive theoretical stamp of several social science disciplines. Economists see Modernization in terms of the application of technology to the control of resources in order to produce growth in per capita production and consequent economic growth or development. Sociologists have concerned themselves with the process of social differentiation that characterizes a society as it moves to ever-increasing levels of impersonal power. They observe and describe new structures with new functions and old structures with changing functions. They describe changes in the occupational structure and the rise in the interdependence of roles accompanied by an inexorable move to specialization.

Demographers and other students of human population have described Modernization in terms of the patterns of settlement that accompany urbanization and the impact on population size growth, density, and distribution of changing patterns in health care, hygiene, sanitation, and medicine.

Political scientists have concerned themselves with aspects of government and nation building during the process of Modernization and in some cases, have defined it in terms of the extent to which a society has developed the ability to adapt to change—how power is shared, how legitimization is achieved, how extensive a sense of national identification is, and so on.

Historians such as Black (1966) have produced theoretical models of Modernization through which, they assert, most nations have passed or are passing. It is not argued that all nations must move along this path and distinctive patterns have been noted. However, more recently, some students of modernization have written about the convergence of societies as they move from the uniqueness produced by centuries of relative separation and isolation into an era characterised by growing commonality. Thus, an emerging world social structure is described.

New scholarship on Modernization has not only become more specialized as the several social science disciplines have applied their respective theoretical paradigms to its study, but it has also become more explicitly comparative and rigorously empirical.

In their attempt to explain the process of Modernization, scholars have put forth several models–which vary in their foci. According to Abraham (1977) they may be classified into four general models of Modernization:

1. Structural models:
   (a) Social system model,
   (b) Cultural system model,
2. Process model;
3. Conflict model; and
4. Social-Psychological model.

Social System Model

In this approach, social system is taken as the unit of analysis and values are relegated to the background.

Smelser (1969), Rostow (1960), Apter (1965), Marion Levy (1966 and 1972), Eisenstadt (1966), Nettl and Robertson (1968), Hunter (1969), and Huntington (1968) have all used some form of macro-sociological approach to explain the process of modernization as it alters and articulates the institutional arrangements, systemic attributes and structural concomitants of a given society. Smelser (1966) identified four distinct but inter-related processes of modernization in the areas of technology, agriculture, industry and ecological arrangements. Marion Levy (1966) has presented a holistic approach to modernization touching on a whole gamut of structural variables and functional prerequisites which differentiate between relatively modernized and relatively non-modernized societies—a general taxonomy he developed.

Cultural System Model

The cultural system model portrays the dynamics of Modernization in terms of changes in the normative structure of the community. Following the Weberian thesis on protestant ethic and the rise of capitalism, several generations of sociologists have sought to determine a set of cultural values that are crucial to modernization. Of course, these values are the abstracted quintessence of the normative system of modern industrialized societies of the West.

Exponents of the model argue that traditional societies can be modernized only by the diffusion of those values and cultural traits that characterize contemporary advanced societies.

Hoselitz (1963) used Parsonian pattern variables (Affective *vs.* Affective neutrality, Self-orientation *vs.* Collective Orientation, Particularism *vs.* Universalism, Quality *vs.* Performance, and Specificity *vs.* Diffuseness) to differentiate between traditional and modern societies and contend that the former is characterized by the norms of ascription, particularism and emphasize the norms of achievement, universalism and specificity. Lipset (1967: 6) considers the combination of universalism and achievement "most favourable to the emergence of an industrial society since it encourages respect of deference towards others on the basis of merit and places emphasis on achievement." Cochran (1959), Fillol (1961), Richard Morse (1958) and Willems (1953) show how strong kinship ties and the tendency to view business property very much like a family estate tend to impede growth of technological efficiency and a rational bureaucracy in Latin America.

Process Model

Process model seeks to explain Modernization in terms of certain pervasive processes like secularization, communication, industrialization, urbanization and westernization which set in motion a chain of consequences in developing countries.

One of the most important process model analyses is the communication theory of modernization exemplified in the works of Lerner (1958), Pye (1963), Pool (1967). Rogers (1969), Schram (1964), Lerner and Schram (1967), Deutchmann (1963), Doob (1961), and Frey (1966). Mass communication is deemed to be a catalytic agent in the process of modernization. Rogers (1969: 37) has termed mass media as the 'magic multiplier'. "Attendance to the mass media is a broadener of horizons, an informer, and a persuader for change." The conceptual model underlying Rogers' (1969: 102) communication theory of modernization is the paradigm that certain antecedents like literacy, education, social status, age and cosmopolitanism are mediated and processually articulated by mass media exposure which transforms these antecedent variables into traits of modernity such as empathy, agricultural and home innovativeness, political knowledge, achievement motivation and educational aspirations.

Srinivas (1966) analyses social change in modern India in terms of four universal processes: Westernization, Sanskritization, Secularization and Politicization. Secularization is, perhaps, the most effective single process underlying socio-cultural change in developing societies. This assertion is supported by Fals Borda's (1962) evidence from the Colombian rural community and Halpern's (1963: 19) report from the Middle East which has witnessed "the disintegration of a social system founded in God's final word". whereas Hoselitz and Moore (1963) and Moore (1965) find industrialization as the prime mover of modernization, Breese (1966) treats urbanization as the key to social change in the developing areas. Finally, the numerous sociological treatises that deal with developmental change or planned social change, community development and rural extension, may be considered to be variants of the process model.

Conflict Model

Conflict theories seek to analyze the processes of Modernization in terms of dissensions, disequilibrium or revolutionary upheavals. Marx is undoubtedly a pioneering theorist of social conflict who developed the evolutionary theory of revolution to explain how various socio-economic systems like feudalism, capitalism and socialism emerge and transform themselves. He made extensive use of class struggle as a tool for the analysis of change in total societies and argued that the economic system of production and distribution could determine the social, cultural and political structure of the society.

Barrington Moore (1966) has made a seminal contribution to our understanding of change in contemporary societies through a systematic analysis of class antagonisms and class alliances. Moore has sought to identify the historical constellations and structural concomitants which produce or prevent peasant revolutions. And Di Telia (1969: 68) has singled out three bases for social revolutionary movements in underdeveloped countries: (1) Elements drawn from the poorly organized urban working class, (2) Poorer sections of the peasantry, and (3) Discontented segments of lower middle class and intelligentsia who constitute an elite of professional revolutionaries. He explains how demonstration effect, revolution of rising expectations and status incongruence produce discontent among various classes leading eventually to types of social movements.

The potentials of a conflict model as a tool for the analysis of modernization cannot be overemphasized. Speaking in broad terms, the areas of conflict in the developing societies could be outlined as follows:

1. *Conflict of Classes*: The landless peasantry, landed aristocracy, commercial and industrial middle classes, incongruent groups among the salaried professionals and bureaucrats, and the political and military elites represent possibilities of revolution and counter-revolution through expedient alliances and bitter class struggles.
2. *Conflict of Values* : The cultural system of every developing society is a perpetual battle-field, where the forces of modernity and tradition meet. The conflict of values creates structural strain, dissensions, disequilibrium, and the erosion—if not the complete breakdown—of some of the old normative structures and facilitates the emergence of new norms and value-orientations.
3. *Conflict of Personality* : The concepts like. demonstration effect, revolution of rising expectations, status incongruence, relative deprivation and achievement motivation, illustrate variations of personality conflict within the individuals. Educational revolution, gap between aspirations and achievement, conflict of loyalties and the absence of adequate opportunities would increase frustration leading to widespread social discontent.

Social-Psychological Model

According to this perspective, favourable change in the personality structure of social actors is the key to modernization of a given social system. Here the emphasis is on changing life styles, belief systems and personality attributes.

McClelland (1961) explains not only the dynamics of modernization but also the rise and fall of empires in terms of child-rearing practices which induce or inhibit achievement motivation and consequent entrepreneurial ability leading eventually to national economic development. This theory of modernization may involve numerous conceptual and methodological problems. According to McClelland, achievement motivation is inconsistent with the concern for affiliation and for power. In other words, if a man "worries a lot" about his family and friends, or speculates on power, instead of spending his time thinking about doing things better, he is low on achievement motivation. This assertion is heavily loaded with the cultural bias of the Western social system where family and kinship ties are weak. Only in highly individualistic societies is it possible to measure achievement motivation in terms of an individual's personal ambitions without reference to his family obligations. Yet Rogers and his associates Prodipto Roy (1968), Fliegel *et al.* (1968) have used such a crude index of achievement motivation in their study of modernization among Indian farmers. They operationalized the concept of achievement motivation on the basis of peasants' responses to three statements of which this one deserves particular mention here: "One should succeed in one's occupation even though one has been neglectful of one's family". Kumar (1970) and Abraham (1973) used the same data to study the dynamics of modernization in India and found little relationship between 'n' achievement scores and other variables of modernization.

> "The socio-psychological approach to modernization treats it mainly as a process of change in ways of perceiving, expressing and valuing. The modern is defined as a mode of individual functioning, a set of dispositions to act in certain ways" (Inkeles and Smith, 1974: 16).

It may be understood that the focus in the social-psychological approach is on the individual, rather than society. Accordingly, the concept of modernization may be understood as the "... process of social change in which the individual imbibes certain attitudinal-cum-personality traits conducive to socio-economic and political development...." (Singh, 1984: 6).

Approaching from this perspective, it could be understood that modernity—at the individual level—consists of certain "psychological qualities necessary for socio-economic and political development" (Singh, 1984: 6). These qualities are reflected in the attitudes and behaviour patterns of the individual.

Education and Modernization in India

India is one of the early beginners, among the developing countries, on the road to modernization. Modernization began in the Indian subcontinent with the advent of British rule. This does not mean that Indian society has existed without change till the British period. At different stages of its evolution it has adapted itself to the changing milieu by a highly selective permutation and combination of elements from a fluid fund of beliefs and approaches broadly characteristic of the Indian tradition.

India has been subject to a number of invasions right from the Persian invasions in the sixth century BC to that of Ahmad Shah Abdali in 1761. It has gone through long periods of foreign rule each varying in its complexion and cultural legacies. A number of socio-religious movements have affected the life of people and changed their value systems. All these influences have left their mark on the family life, religious beliefs and practices and social structure in India over many centuries. Added to all these was the impact of Islamic and British cultures (Sachidananda, 1976). Though social change is not alien to traditional Indian society, "Social Change in the form of modernization was ushered into India by the British rulers" (Desai, 1967). The initial stage of modernization in India—during the colonial period—was oriented more towards Westernization. Traditional Indian society underwent several changes during this period of history. Among other things, these changes included the rise of bureaucracy, money and market economy, universalistic legal system, and formal Western education organised by the Christian Missionaries.

The transformation of Indian society based upon new ideas took place under the British regime (Srivastava, H.C., 1976). The most powerful effect and enduring result of British rule in India is the intellectual development of the people on an entirely new line, and the consequent changes in their political, social, religious, and economic outlook.

Western liberal education introduced the supremacy of reason, critical attitude to religion, and a new concept of social and political justice. The upper classes of India were the first to be influenced by English language, literature, journalism and ideas of Western society. There are several individuals whose efforts have contributed to the process of modernization in India. The works of Raja Ram Mohun Roy, Swami Dayananda, Annie Besant, Lokmanya Bal Gangadhar Tilak, M.K. Gandhi, and Jawaharlal Nehru need to be mentioned.

Major contributions of Raja Ram Mohun Roy (1772-1833) to the process of modernization are as follows:

(i) his attack on the existing form of religion; and
(ii) his conception of religion through the Brahmo Samaj (1828)—a theistic society.

He revolted against idolatory practices and other degenerated Hindu institutions like caste system, Kulin Brahmin polygamy, child marriage, *suttee* practice, etc. He fought against these evils through propaganda, press and vigilance committee. Through their newspapers educational institutions and personal contact, the Brahmo Samaj spread enlightenment among the people and lifted them to new consciousness. They advocated modern social values like personal freedom, social equality of man and religion without any distinction of caste or creed, discarded idol worship, and campaigned against subjugation of women.

Swami Dayanand (1824-1883), the founder of the Arya Samaj, sought to reform Hindu society by reviving Vedic rituals and institutions. The Arya Samaj organized relief work during social disaster, organized English education, accepted *suddhi* (reconversion) and Hindu universalism. The intellectual idea system of Arya Samaj resisted against the 'inferiority complex' from aggressive Christianity and Islam, and aroused a new national consciousness.

Annie Besant, through the Theosophical Society, contributed to the revival of the Eastern faith in her own intellectual potentials. The society provided an Indian ideal of education and a liberalizing effect on Indian intellectuals through its doctrines.

It was Lokmanya Bal Gangadhar Tilak (1893) who championed the cause of freedom when he opposed the conciliatory attitudes with the British by proclaiming that "Freedom is my birthright, I shall have it" rather than believing that we should persuade the British to grant us freedom. The origin of Congress, founded by A.O. Hume, gave an intellectual content to the discontent of the masses in India. Hume's attempt was to link the alienated intellectuals to the economic suffering of the masses. His purpose was to promote the mental, moral, social and political regeneration of the people of India.

The National Congress rallied the "high intellectual brilliance of a great galaxy of eminent leaders". The Congress represented the "thinking portion of the Indian people". Contemporary India is considered in large measure as the work of its idea systems under the Gandhi-Nehru leadership.

Gandhi's special contribution lies in arousing national consciousness as a crusader of total freedom and an apostle of equality and justice. He worked for the rejuvenation of Indian society, and for its freedom not only from British rule but also for economic, cultural and spiritual freedom. He combined social reordering and the fight for political *swaraj* in a non-violent type of struggle. He tackled problems of untouchability, child marriage, uplift of Harijans and women, basic education, economic self-sufficiency, rural reconstruction and non-cooperation with the foreign rule and a movement against them 'to quit India'. Gandhi's success lay in unifying the diverse forces in India. The unique modernizing effect of Gandhi was to create, through his ideas and practice, human conscience as a social institution, a prerequisite for modernization if it is conceived in terms of moral values.

Nehru introduced elements in Indian political thinking which were outside of the mainstream of orthodox Hindu thought. He made experiments with certain forms and ideas "to be realised through a synthesis of the surviving traditional values of India and some of the techniques of the west". His pragmatic and undefined humanism inspired an intellectual era from different realms. Nehru's concept of democracy implies rational consent. For him, freedom and democracy require responsibility, self-discipline, self-reliance, having no room for violence. He believed in welfare-statism that has no place for individualism. Nehru wanted people to develop cooperative attitude against acquisitive attitude. He proclaimed faith in socialism/planned development, institutional and technological modernization, etc., as the only way for economic freedom.

Way down in Mysore, Sir M. Visweswariah had given a long-term plan for the development of modern Mysore as early as 1917. Modern University Education which began in 1857 gained momentum in the beginning of this century.

> "Led by these intellectuals, the urge for change to modernization—beginning with the life and work of Raja Ram Mohun Roy, continuing through the period of freedom movement, culminating under the actual and (later) moral leadership of Mahatma Gandhi—found final expression in the Constitution of the Indian Union under the leadership of Pandit Jawaharlal Nehru" (Roy, 1976: 75).

The course and direction of modernization which was set in motion by the British towards Westernisation turned out eventually to be a unique blend of indigenous and Western cultures. The prominent facets of independent India's desire for modernization are reflected in its decision to become a democratic republic. The Constitution of India promises to all its citizens, Justice—socio-economic and political liberty—of thought, expression, belief and worship, equality of status and fraternity, assuring the dignity of the individual and the unity of the nation.

These in short "... seek to modernize the political, economic and social institutions of Indian society with a view to securing a better standard of life for all citizens" (Shah, 1971: 241).

Committing itself to the task of creating a new social order marked by the key values of liberty, equality and fraternity, as enshrined in the Constitution, the government of free India chose to accelerate the process of modernization and made stupendous efforts in that direction. On the political side, it set to itself the task of nation-building based on the values of secularism, democracy, and socialism. On the economic side, it vigorously pushed forward the process of industrialization, urbanization, and mechanization, and also launched important development schemes such as the Community Development Programme. On the social side, it enthusiastically embarked upon social legislation, mass media development, and educational expansion as instruments of social transformation (Sharma, 1979: 14).

The impact of all these efforts on the process of modernization cannot be doubted. Changes have been observed in several facets of Indian society.

With the advent of the Five Year Plans and the rapid growth of industrialization and urbanization, many changes are taking place in the lives and activities of people. Literacy has gradually improved and, coupled with this, communication facilities have also shown considerable development as can be seen from the large increase in newspaper circulation, the large volume of letters and telegrams sent, and the growing number of radios and TVs in use. People migrate from State to State in search of employment and for higher studies, and one finds that the trains and buses are always crowded. Airways are becoming a popular means of quick conveyance. Private cars, taxis and scooters have steadily grown in number. The pattern and mode of home furnishings and fashions in dress are also undergoing rapid change. In many villages and towns, bicycles and sewing machines can be seen in many households. There is rapid growth in the number of cities as revealed from census to census, and the size of cities too has been increasing. Growth of population and rural-urban migration are taking place almost continuously. In the sphere of agriculture, use of hybrid varieties of seeds and demand for fertilizers are growing with the cultivators' desire to step up crop-output. Increased use of pumpsets for irrigation and of tractors for cultivation is displacing the traditional methods (VVD and CGG, 1970: 1850).

Modernization as a continuing planned process has gathered momentum in contemporary India. There were a number of diverse factors which have contributed historically to the beginnings of Indian model of modernization. In giving an impetus to the process of modernization, one of the most important instruments considered is education. Hence, the role of education in bringing about the desired results as expected by the nation needs special attention in the Indian context.

For the realization of the national goals of independent India, education was considered as an important instrument. Widespread literacy was thought of as a factor that would help the process of modernization. It is to be noted that provision for free and compulsory education for all children up to the age of 14 was included under Article 45 of the Constitution of India enacted in 1950.

In the post-independent period the Government of India and the State governments have paid considerable attention to education as a factor vital to national progress and security. The opening of teachers' training institutions, for creating a cadre of qualified and professionally competent teachers, launching of incentive schemes of offering scholarships, midday meals, free text books, free school uniforms, etc., are only some of the steps taken towards the promotion of school education. Setting up of UGC, NCERT, ICSSR, ICMR, CSIR; opening of IITs, etc., are some of the landmarks of Indian education in the post-independence period. In the post-independent India, particularly since the inception of the Five Year Plans, an education explosion has taken place. While there were 1,72,661 primary schools in 1947, their number rose to 5,28,730 in 1986. Similarly, the number of upper primary schools increased from 12,843 in 1947 to 1,39,016 in 1986. The number of secondary schools increased from 5,297 to 52,560 during this period. The number of universities and institutions of higher learning deemed to be universities has increased from 17 in 1947 to 189 in 1990.

The overall enrolment has also recorded a manifold increase in India. While in 1947 the total enrolment in the age group 6-11 was 33 per cent of this age group, it rose to 75 per cent in 1986. The corresponding figures for the age group 11-14 are 9 per cent in 1947 and 51 per cent in 1986 respectively. More than 4 per cent of the population of the age group 17-23 are in universities and colleges. On the whole, literacy increased from about 14 per cent in 1947 to 52 per cent in 1991.

In all, the Indian education system produced the third largest professional class in the world, an asset that distinguishes India from the developing and even some developed countries. The education network is one of the largest in the world. This massive expansion was possible due to rapid increase in investment in education. During the First Five Year Plan 1.2 per cent of the GNP was invested in education, which increased to around 4 per cent by the end of the Seventh Plan.

While the overall expansion of Indian education appears impressive, it is to be noted that there are some hard realities which reveal a darker side of education. The most important observation to be made in this regard is that nearly half of India's population—48 per cent—is still illiterate. The number of illiterates has increased, the number reaching more than 400 million. As per the Census figures of 1991, there are at least five major States in the country with more than 60 per cent of the population unable to read and write. These are Andhra Pradesh, Madhya Pradesh, Uttar Pradesh, Bihar, and Rajasthan. India, according to World Bank estimates, will enter the twenty-first century leading the world in the number of people who cannot read and write. Provision for free and compulsory primary education for all children below the age of 14 years was accepted as a constitutional responsibility as far back as in 1950. Even after four decades, the percentage of illiterates below 14 years of age continued to remain high.

However, in spite of a large chunk of illiteracy in the country the efforts to eradicate it are still wanting as reflected in the expenditure patterns on Indian education. Even now, the importance given to primary and adult education is disproportionate to the needs therein. On the other hand, higher education, which has been alleged to be 'irrelevant' to needs of the masses, is highly subsidised. For instance, in one analysis of 1984-85, Professor Seetharamu (1992) has reported that "Looking at the expenditure pattern in the country as a whole wherein 91.68 per cent is contributed by the States and Union territories, it is observed that expenditure on primary education is hardly 45.61 per cent of the total. Rs. 2,913.985 crore is spent on a level where the enrolment is 93 million, while Rs. 843.610 crore is spent on a level (higher education—general) where the enrolment is hardly 4 million" (Seetharamu, 1992: 81).

It is thus clear that the expansion of education and spread of literacy have not reached evenly across various sections of Indian society.

Notwithstanding these glaring inequities, the post-independence period has been marked by considerable progress in quantitative terms in the field of education. Indeed, the progress made is all the more appreciable given the formidable odds which have had to be overcome. However, what is of significance here is not so much the quantitative expansion of education but the more important question of the relevance of this progress to national goals. Education in India has always been seen as an integral component of our efforts towards freedom, as a modernizing influence, and as an agent of social change. The extent to which education has fulfilled these responsibilities, is as much important as the concern for its quantitative expansion which is crucial in assessing the development of education after independence. The present research aspires to base its assessment of the progress of education in post-independent India on an analysis of these qualitative aspects of education.

Perspectives on Relationship between Education and Modernity

Regarding the nature of the relationship between education and modernity/modernization there are different perspectives among the social scientists.

One such view, termed as functionalist perspective, is that education promotes modernization. Within this school of thought, there are two approaches, i.e. economic approach and sociological approach (Sharma, 1979).

According to the economic approach, education promotes modernization in several ways, such as:

1. By providing the necessary knowledge for the effective manipulation of the environment, i.e. to find new economic resources and better tools;
2. By providing necessary skills so as to generate qualified manpower for modernizing the country; and
3. By providing an ideology favourable to economic growth.

The sociological approach focuses on the psychosocial potential of education for modernization. Accordingly, education helps the individuals to inculcate appropriate values, attitudes, behaviour patterns, etc., that are considered as requirements for the process of modernization. This is made possible through rewards and punishments, modelling, exemplification, generalization, etc. by way of planning the curriculum and structuring the methods of teaching.

In contrast to above school of thought, there is another view among the social scientists that education impedes modernization. (This is termed as Radical Perspective). It is argued that the existing educational system acts as a subversive force in the legitimization of existing power relations and perpetuation of structural oppression. Perspectives of this kind are reflected in the works of Bourdeiu (1972), Boudon (1973), Freire (1972), Illich (1971), Reimer (1971), Goodman *et al.* (1971).

Perspective followed in the Present Study

In the present study, modernity has been conceived at the individual level as consisting of five dimensions, viz. Change Proneness, Democratic Orientation, Scientific Orientation, Secular Orientation, and Achievement Orientation as reflected in 8 Areas of life, viz. Education, Employment, Marriage and Family, Religious Life, Political Life, Social Life, Health and Hygiene, and Economic Life. This conception is holistic in nature, as it synthesises two classes of theories, namely: (i) the structure function model as well as (ii) the socio-psychological model. Modernity is a socio-psychological transitional state, in a person, of a network of attitudes and behaviour which has been influenced by the given social structures and the ongoing processes.

Modernity has been studied here as a socio-psychological state in an individual taking into account the effect of given social structures and ongoing social processes.

Operational Definitions

Modernity in the present study is conceived at the individual level. It is understood in terms of five dimensions of modernity such as,

1. *Change proneness and openness to new experience and innovations* : A state of readiness to accept new ideas and changes in social organizations, new ways of feeling and acting, etc.

2. *Scientific orientation*: A tendency to understand the world on the basis of rules of evidence and verification rather than just in terms of the wisdom of the past.
3. *Democratic orientation*: A love for and dignity of the individual, love and respect for the person as such independently of his birth, religion, race, language, status, etc.
4. *Secular orientation*: It refers to the withdrawal of authority of religion from various institutional spheres such as matrimonial, educational, economic, etc. with the result that religion ceases to extend influence over interpersonal relations and corporate actions. A person is guided by reason for actions than tradition or custom or religious authority.
5. *Achievement orientation*: A tendency to achieve higher goals, occupational, educational, economic, etc., for oneself through planning and hard work.

These dimensions of modernity closely correspond to the conceptualisations of modernity in the works of Inkeles and Smith (1974), Sharma (1979), and Jindal (1984).

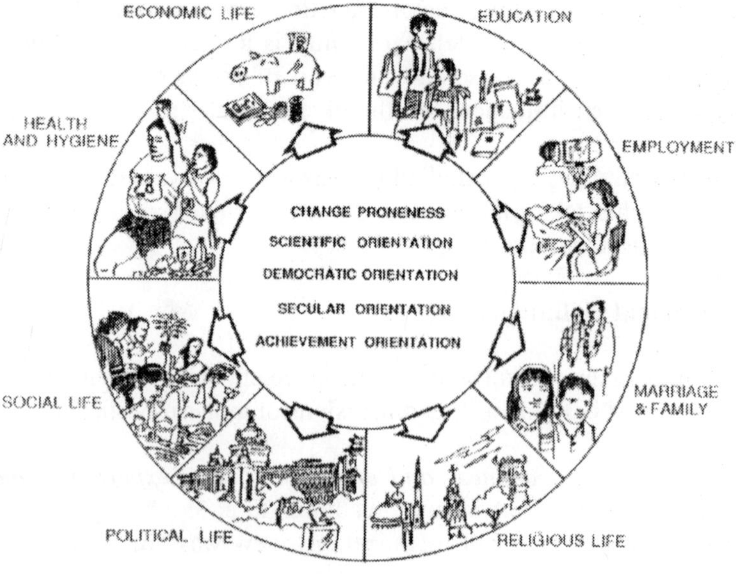

Fig. 2.1: Dimensions of Modernity and Areas of Life

The five dimensions of modernity can be observed in eight major areas of human life (Fig. 2.1). These are: 1. Education, 2. Employment, 3. Marriage and Family, 4. Religious Life, 5. Political Life, 6. Social Life, 7. Health and Hygiene, and 8. Economic Life.

Attitudes and behaviours of individuals are considered as indicators of modernity here.

Modernity in terms of Attitudes

In quantitative terms modernity is understood, in the study, in terms of the 'score' obtained by individuals on the attitudinal modernity scale used for the present study. The 'modernity score' depends on the nature of responses (agree/disagree) expressed by the respondents on the attitudinal statements given in the scale.

Modernity in terms of Behaviour

Behaviour is understood as the specific act carried out by an individual in a given context. It includes both covert acts (e.g. Decision making) and overt acts (e.g. Reading newspapers).

Modernity in terms of behaviour is taken to be based on the proportion of respondents at any given level of education who have demonstrated positive or negative behaviour for the given behavioural items in selected areas of life.

3

Review of Related Literature

The importance of formal education as a variable in understanding individual modernity has attracted the attention of researchers across nations. Researchers have examined the relationship between these two variables in different social contexts and with cross-cultural perspectives. These studies began in the 1960s and have continued to grow in number. They differ with respect to design and approach, conceptualisation, choice of variables, etc., in the study of the relationship between education and modernity.

An attempt is made in this chapter to review the empirical studies related to the study of education and modernity. Studies conducted abroad and those in India are presented separately. It is to be noted that the review made here is rather representative of the hypotheses of this study rather than being exhaustive of the whole field of modernity.

In a review of literature which examines the relationship between education and modernity and the interplay of variables therein, it may not be necessary to have a classification of studies conducted abroad and studies conducted in India. However, keeping in view that modernity/modernization is time-specific, it was felt that it would be better to group together all studies whose samples are societies outside India and group other studies for which the samples are within Indian society. Hence such a classification is followed here.

Studies Conducted Abroad

Lerner (1963) made a pioneering empirical study of the relation between education and psychological modernity.

Using data from adult samples of Six Middle Eastern countries, Lerner asserted that literacy is the basic skill underlying the whole modernization process.

Lerner hypothesised that geographic and social mobility gave rise to the formation of empathic individuals, empathy being the psychological mechanism which underlies and is reinforced by urbanization, literacy and mass media participation. Based on the data gathered from residents of Santiago, Chile, Briones and Waisanen (1966) suggested that there is a point of "modernization take-off" in such attitudinal variables as aspirations when the individual has more than five years of schooling, while respondents with two or three years of schooling are not much different in attitudes from those with no education, with further education, indicators of modernization also rise proportionately.

In his attempt to develop a scale for measuring modernism, Kahl (1968) studied data drawn from Mexico and Brazil. The study provided the first convincing empirical evidence of the strong association between formal education and modernity.

Kahl postulated that common institutions are developing In countries all over the world in response to pressures to industrialize, bureaucratize and rationalize, and that societies are responding in similar ways to these pressures.

The data revealed a "core modernism" which consisted of activism, independence, urbanism, individualism, low community stratification, mass media participation, and efficacy,

The results of the study showed that level of schooling correlated with modernity scores in Mexico as well as Brazil (0.55 and 0.57 respectively).

Based on data from six developing countries including India, Alex Inkeles studied different aspects of individual modernity (Inkeles: 1969, 208-25).

Data were gathered from 6,000 young men belonging to different categories such as cultivators, migrants to urban areas, non-industrial workers, experienced industrial workers, secondary school and university students. Data pertaining to attitudes, values, opinions and behaviour were collected through interviews.

Results of the study revealed that the amount of formal schooling a man has is the single most powerful variable in determining his modernity. Further it was found that for every additional year a man spent in school he gains somewhere between two and three additional points on a scale of modernity scored from zero to 100.

It was also found that a man's occupational experience particularly in factory is one of the strongest variables in explaining a person's modernity. Factory workers were found to be more modern than cultivators. Similarly those factory workers who have more experience were found to be more modern than those who are less experienced.

Findings of the study further revealed that individuals who are modern in their attitudes are also modern in their behaviour.

Rogers (1969) studied modernization among peasants, using data from Columbia, India and Kenya.

Findings of the study emphasised the importance of literacy in individual modernization. It was found that literacy is positively related to mass media exposure, empathy, innovativeness, achievement motivation, social status, cosmopolitan outlook, political knowledge and sociometric opinion leadership.

Using data of 255 Columbian respondents, with more than 4 years education, Rogers also observed that a Modernization take-off occurs at about four years of formal schooling. However, Rogers admitted that the sharply rising part of the aspiration curve "has an inadequate data base" (1969: 80).

Saunders (1969) in his study examined education and modernization in Brazil. It was found that education, instead of promoting, undermines modernity. He remarks: "Brazilian schools, especially at the primary level where their impact on personality development is greatest, tend to stifle rather than develop the personality traits on which modernization depends, and from which the society must draw its innovators."

Williamson (1970) undertook a study focusing on modernism and related attitudes of university students in four nations (United States, Germany, Japan and Columbia), using Kahl's rationalism-traditionalism scale.

It was found that Americans and Columbians are at the conservative end of the scale compared with Germans and contrasted to the Japanese who are at the other end of the scale.

Thus students in national cultures (Japan and Germany) which have undergone a social revolution are found more rationalistic and critical towards their social institutions than in those countries with less violent social change.

Armer and Youtz (1971) in their study examined the relationship between formal education and individual modernity.

Sample consisted of 591 seventeen-year old males in Kano, Nigeria. Data were gathered using structured interview.

Educational level of respondents was treated in three categories such as those who have no formal education, those who have attended one to seven years of primary school and those who have gone beyond primary school to at least one year of secondary school.

The dependent variable—individual modernity—was measured in terms of different modern value orientation dimensions.

Results of the study indicated a strong positive association, (largely independent of alternative modernising forces) between educational level and individual modernity.

Findings of the study revealed substantial variations in the magnitude and pattern of associations between formal education and separate value orientations. Clear positive association with formal education was observed in the case of seven dimensions. These are: independence from family, empiricism, futurism, ethnic equality, mastery, openness to new ideas and experiences and inter-personal trust.

There was no strong association with formal education in the case of receptivity to change, secularism, and women's equality.

A negative relationship was also observed in the case of secular orientations by level of schooling.

Waisanen and Kumata (1972) conducted a study on adult Samples, aged 20 and above, drawn from the USA, Finland, Japan, Mexico, and Costa Rica.

They assumed that man learns to be modern, and education as a social experience facilitates the learning process.

Findings of the study revealed curvilinearity in the relationship between education and various indicators of modernity.

The causal link between schooling and increased modernity was further proved by Holsinger's Brasilia study (Inkeles and Holsinger: 1974).

Holsinger hypothesized that schools because of their peculiar structural arrangements and the behaviour patterns of teachers, provide pupils with certain experiences largely unavailable in other social settings, and that these experiences represent conditions conducive to the acquisition of modern values (Holsinger: 1987).

The study conducted by Korllos (1977: 5383) examined how values and characteristics of male secondary students in Athens, Greece during a period of economic growth affected their selection of types of education such as traditional or emergent secondary schools.

Data was collected from a sample of 1,021 male secondary school students, enrolled in 4 types of secondary schools, in Athens and categorized by curriculum (general/vocational); administration (private/public); modernity (modern/traditional); and status (high/low).

It was found that students attending private schools had more modern values than public schools even with curriculum type controlled.

Students attending modern and higher status schools were more modern in values than students attending traditional and lower status schools.

Students attending private schools perceived higher openness towards change than students attending public institutions.

A major conclusion of the study was that students with more modern values are more likely to be enrolled in private general and vocational schools representing emergent educational forms.

Findings of the study indicate that the modernity in terms of values and the selection of type of schools are highly related.

Based on the data collected by Inkeles and Smith for their study (1974), a study was undertaken by Lachman (1977: 7329) which dealt with the impact of the process of modernization on the individual.

Data from 300 respondents of India and 812 of Argentina were analysed for the purpose of the study.

Findings of the study indicated that early socialization has a strong impact on Personal modernity (e.g. urban origin, education etc.). It directly influences core modernity and indirectly influences peripheral modernity.

Late socialization (e.g. work in industry) was found to have an effect mainly on peripheral modernity. But when the effects of early socialization were controlled, late socialization was found to have no independent effect on modernity.

The observed effect of late socialization on periphery scale is mostly due to the indirect effects of early socialization.

One of the major conclusions drawn in a study conducted by Farrell (1977: 2881-82) in Guatemala was that participation in a development programme accelerates individual modernization, but the primary variable in the modernization is exposure to alternative models of behaviour through various media and personal experience.

Elarabi (1985) conducted a study on a sample of 250 (through multi-stage sampling) employees of Sudanese public sector in Sudan.

The purpose of the study was to examine the relationship among level of education, sex and age, and a cluster of Sudanese values believed to be inversely related to modernization. The values thus considered include Rigidity, Fatalism, Apathy and Parochialism.

Data was collected through self-administered questionnaire and was analysed using chi-square coefficients.

It was found that education and modernization were positively correlated in the case of Sudanese bureaucrat, regardless of his or her sex.

Findings of the study also indicated that in terms of sex and age, modernization differed in the case of Sudanese bureaucrat.

A major conclusion of the study was that "The modernized system of education in Sudan seems to be a powerful change agent" (Elarabi, 1985: 126).

A study was conducted by Ghaban (1987) to profile the individual modernity of the Saudi students and to investigate the impact of a set of independent variables (level of education, experience of studying and length of stay in the United States, Mass Media exposure, urban experience, father's education, and age) upon the dependent variable of individual modernity of Saudi students in both Saudi Arabia and the United States.

Data were collected using questionnaire, which included a scale to measure individual modernity in terms of attitudes and values, constructed for the purpose of study.

The study made use of data from 900 Saudi male students, consisting of secondary and college students in which 300 Saudi students were college students in the United States.

Factor analysis and Regression analysis were used in analysing the data.

Results of the study showed that level of education positively and significantly influenced overall modernity of Saudi students in both United States and Saudi Arabia.

Mass media exposure was found to be positively affecting the overall modernity, and half of its dimensions in Saudi Arabia, especially the dimension of family modernism.

Age, father's education and urban experience were found to have no significant contributions to overall modernity.

Hasan (1987: 4277) conducted a study, in order to: (a) clarify the concept of modern development oriented persons in the Indonesian context so as to devise a measuring scale of individual development oriented modernity (IDOM); and (b) investigate major forces promoting the IDOM among students at four teacher training colleges in Malang, Indonesia.

Using a questionnaire including a scale to measure individual development oriented modernity which was constructed for the purpose of study, data were collected from 536 students, drawn randomly from four teacher training colleges.

Results of the study supported the proposition that education is a powerful force promoting modern development oriented values.

Students' parents' education and students' mobility were the other variables promoting individual development oriented modernity.

The study conducted by Soepangat (1987: 4353) examined a schooling process that is aimed at producing responsible citizens and modern individuals who can participate in the national process of growth and development of Indonesia.

Focus of the study was on the enculturation through elementary schooling of the tribal children into the mainstream of Indonesian social and cultural life.

The study made use of data collected from pupils, teachers, parents and community leaders, through participant observation, structured and unstructured interview.

Results of the study showed that the teaching learning process in Pikhe Aikima elementary schools fails to realise the citizenship and modernity goals that the government has laid out for schools to realise.

A cross-national study on economic development, economic

dependency, cultural dependency, and internal structural mechanism: modernization or dependency was carried out by Kim (1987: 229).

The study made use of data from 70 non-socialist countries with colonial experiences, independent before 1965, and more than one million population. The time period covered was 1965 to 1980.

It was found that primary education is the most important factor in determining economic development, including foreign investment, and structuring internal social, economic and industrial structure.

Mehdi (1988: 2468) used survey data, consensus and historical resources in examining the family structure and family modernization beliefs in three Egyptian settlements that varied in their development.

The data showed that living in a more technologically advançed community exposed the individual to more institutional forces of modernization.

Findings of the study revealed that level of modernity achieved by men and women varies. Women hold more modern family beliefs than men when equally exposed to modernizing forces.

Acheampong (1988: 1892) examined structural change, individual modernity and fertility preference in Taiwan.

Data were gathered by interviewing 973 Taiwanese women aged 15-44 years and who have at least one child.

Individual's attitudes, perception about the costs associated with child bearing, her knowledge of contraceptives and her ownerships of consumer durables were conceptualized as determinants of her position on the tradition-modernity continuum.

Of all the structural variables examined, education appeared to have the strongest direct impact on individual modernity.

Khatun (1991: 162-63) made a comparative study of two villages of Bangladesh to examine the role of education as an agent of modernization. Sample consisted of 300 individuals, including heads of households, school-going students as well as non-school-going adolescents.

Studies in India

Data was collected, through interview schedules and Attitudinal Modernity Scale developed by Sharma, and were analysed using Chi-square and ANOVA.

It was found that education affected modernity in terms of attitudes, beliefs and behaviour.

The school-going respondents were found significantly more modern than the non-school-going respondents in rural setting.

Education up to secondary stage significantly influenced student modernity.

Extra curricular activities especially the academic among them (debates and declamation contests) and cultural (music and dramatics) had a potential for inculcating higher levels of modernity among the students.

Education seemed to have greater effect on universalistic achievement and scientific orientation whereas it was found less conducive to the growth of secular and civic orientations. The educational variables were found more powerful for facilitation of modernity whereas the familial variables were found to be subordinate to the education variables as they prepared the ground for the students entry into the school.

Exploration in understanding the nature and relationship between education and modernity began in India also in the 1960. Both Indian scholars as well as researchers from developed countries were involved in these efforts.

Cormack (1961) conducted a study on a sample of 404 students drawn from over a dozen colleges located in various parts of India.

Findings of the study revealed that college education is ineffective in changing the values and attitudes of students.

Shah (1964) studied a sample of college students from Gujarat, by classifying them into three categories, namely: traditional, partially deviated and non-traditional.

The study revealed that college students were traditional in the areas of caste endogamy, joint family, and gainful employment of women. They were partially deviated in such areas as boy-girl relationship, caste commensality, the selection of bride, place, livelihood and occupation.

Damle (1966) made a study on a sample of 26 academically and intellectually gifted college youths in Pune. He found some positive evidence of individuation (modernization).

Sullivan (1968) in his study tried to examine whether the teacher training programme contributes to the remoulding of traditional values, beliefs and practices by comparing students of four training colleges in India.

It was found that factors other than experience at a particular training college are operative in changing the student's outlook towards traditional social practices.

Pareek and Kothandapani (1969) used data from a study on modernization, collected in Bihar, in an attempt to determine relationships between family size preferences and attitude towards birth control with several variables including caste, ethnicity, occupation, and education.

The sample consisted of 1,300 farmers, factory workers and non-industrial workers.

Both formal education and membership in a work organization (factory) were positively (significantly) related to preference for small families (3 children or less).

Gore *et al.* (1970) in their study tried to identify some broad indicators of modernity such as secularism, activist orientation, optimism, achievement-orientation and civic sense.

The study revealed evidence of positive effects of education on student modernity. It was concluded that the state, sex, and educational level are important variables in determining student modernity.

V.V.D. and C.G.G. (1970) in their attempt to identify the major indicators of the process of modernization by examining a number of macro indicators of development found literacy as an important modernization factor.

Using a sample of 402 youths, Srivastava (1971) conducted a study to find out the role of education in modernization of two tribes in Chotanagpur. This study revealed that educated tribesmen are more modern than the uneducated ones. The educated tribesmen, compared to the uneducated ones are more mobile spatially, occupationally and socially. Their emphathetic capacity has increased and they are capable of choosing new individuals' roles and situations, and participating in socio-economic and political activities. Education has also made the tribesmen more competent to take interest in public matters and to express opinions thereon.

Based on field research in Uttar Pradesh in India, Vajpayi (1971: 3396) conducted a study to investigate the relationship among empathy, mass media exposure, political participation and modernization.

The theoretical framework provided in Daniel Lerner's 'Passing of Traditional Society' and current conceptualizations of the modernization process in India were used in the study. Data were collected from 926 respondents of Uttar Pradesh.

Results of the study indicated a positive relationship between empathy and other variables of modernization such as political participation, higher education, mass media exposure and achievement orientation,

Malik and Marquette (1974) in their study on college students in Punjab found that education is an agent of attitudinal change.

Sharma (1975A : 7409-7410) studied the psycho-social modernism and its implications for a programme of planned social change. Focus of the study was on psycho-social aspects of traditionalism and modernism at the individual level. Sample consisted of 239 individuals (heads of households) drawn from two villages in Punjab. Data were gathered using a research schedule and Likert type attitudinal scales.

Results of the study revealed that mass media participation and extra community contacts of the respondent are the most important predictors of psycho-social modernism as well as of positive attitudes towards programmes for planned social change. Age and formal education of the respondent were the next important predictors.

It appeared from the findings of the study that psycho-social modernism is helpful for the planned developmental efforts. Psycho-social traditionalism on the other hand appeared to be a hindrance to such efforts.

Sinha (1977: 2398) conducted a study in two villages in Bihar, India, with the purpose of examining the role of mass communication in the modernization process.

Data were collected using participant-observation and focused interview techniques. It was found that mass communication can successfully play a role in modernization. The study also substantiated the earlier findings that literacy is not a precondition to mass communication playing an influential role in modernization.

In their study, Thorat, Patil and Sawant, focused on Change-proneness, Educational levels, Aspirations and Achievement motivations of farmers (Thorat, S.S. *et al.,* 1978).

The independent variables considered for the study were: Educational levels (illiterate, those with primary education and those with secondary education and above); Aspirations level and Achievement motivation. The dependent variable was change-proneness.

Data were gathered from a sample consisting of 180 farmers, who are adopters of dry farming technology from two villages of Ahmednagar district in Maharashtra. Data were analysed using percentages and Chi-square.

Findings of the study revealed a strong positive association between the educational level of the farmers and change-proneness. The higher the educational level the greater was the change-proneness.

Vlassoff (1978) studied the effects of female education on rural adolescents in a Maharashtrian village. The sample consisted of 88 girls aged 13-18 years.

Findings of the study revealed that education of rural girls was significantly related to modern attitudes.

Mishra (1979: 15) conducted a study in order to examine the mass media use patterns and modernization process among slum dwellers. Data were collected using questionnaire from 406 slum dwellers selected from four slums in Delhi.

The most important pattern of relationships that emerged from the study was a systematic pattern of association among education, mass media use, empathy and political participation.

Sharma (1979), in his attempt to study the modernising effects of university education, used a sample of 770 students of Punjab University. Data were collected by means of a specially devised "Attitudinal Modernity Scale" and interview schedules. The modernity scale comprised six dimensions—secular, scientific, universalistic, achievement, independence and civic orientation.

The principal independent variable of the study was higher education which was operationalized in terms of five components: class, faculty, teacher, extra curricular activities and residence in hostel. The intervening variables included age, sex, family socio-economic status, urban exposure, Chandigarh exposure, mass media exposure, contact with other cultures and type of schooling, etc.

Findings of the study revealed a negative relationship between levels of education and modernity with each of the six dimensions of modernity.

Faculty variations were observed in student modernity with the highest percentage of modern in science faculty and the lowest in humanities.

Among the intervening variables, age was found to be negatively related to modernity.

Father's income was found to be positively associated with modernity.

Urban dwelling was found to be positively associated with modernity.

Sex-wise males were more modern than females.

Those with background of convent/public schools were more modern than those educated in government schools.

Mass media exposure as well as the extent of exposure to other cultures were found to be positively related to the level of modernity.

Chatterjee (1982) attempted comparing the attitudinal modernity of factory workers and farmers. The sample consisted of 300 individuals comprising farmers, first and second generation factory workers, drawn from Ranchi and Jamshedpur.

Data were collected using attitude scales measuring religious, familial, caste and social customs attitudes.

Results of the study indicated that attitudinal modernity increases by the increase in exposure to industrialisation and urbanisation. This was found true for high and low caste groups and for high and low levels of educational groups.

Singh, Upmanyu and Ramneek in their study (Singh *et al.,* 1982) investigated the structural relationship of modernity and its opposite traditionality with motives, values and temperamental factors as well as the relevance of sex differences on formation of modern-traditional attitudes.

The sample consisted of 211 post-graduate students including males and females. Data were collected using different tools, including traditional-modern attitude scale.

Findings of the study indicated that respondents with high score on modernity tended to be enterprising, matured, achievement oriented, interested in academic pursuits, dominated by matching and somewhat less in mysticism.

It was also found that the males and females differ qualitatively as well as quantitatively on modernity.

Murty and Rao (1983) conducted a study on female education, modernity and fertility. Data were collected from a sample of 150 wives of readers and professors at Andhra University, with the help of an interview schedule.

Data were analysed using correlation and regression. Findings of the study revealed that education was significantly related to modernity. It was also found that education is negatively related with fertility.

A study was conducted by Meera Jayaswal on women of South Bihar (Jayaswal, 1985). The main aims of the study were: to measure the extent of health modernity in women of South Bihar, and to examine the variations in relation to such sociological factors as religion and ethnicity, rural-urban residence, age and SES, including education.

A quota sample of 640 women were selected from Ranchi district for the study. The main tool for collecting data was the Health Modernity Questionnaire. Data were analysed using percentage and ANOVA.

Findings of the study indicated that Health Modernity was significantly influenced by SES (a combination of caste/tribe + education, occupation + income) and religion ethnicity. SES was more influential than religion/ethnicity.

The study conducted by Singh (1986) focused on impact of education on social change among tribals of Ranchi in Bihar.

Data were collected from 100 subjects belonging to different educational levels viz. illiterate could read and write, education up to middle level, education up to secondary level, education up to intermediate or higher secondary level, education up to graduate and post-graduate level.

It was found that the educated tribals had changed their ways of living, thinking and doing. They had gained consciousness towards modernization and Westernization.

The study concluded that education had proved to be an instrument of social change among the tribals.

Srivastava (1986: 223-24) conducted a study with a purpose of examining the process of modernization among educated rural youth in India. Formal education and modernity—attitudinal and behavioural were the key variables in this study.

It was found that there was a consistent pattern of positive association between formal education and individual modernity.

Using data collected from 1,032 respondents from 10 backward villages of Malabar in Kerala, Sudhirkumar, (1996: 226) studied the influence of education on social attitudes.

Findings of the study revealed a positive relationship between levels of education and modernity in terms of attitudes. It was found that the mean score on modernity attitude scale increased with every increase in the level of education of the group, with the college educated serving the highest. The "college educated' were found to be significantly (positive) different from all other groups in terms of mean score on modernity attitude scale.

Similarly significant opinion variance was marked in the response of the respondents belonging to different levels of education towards the select social issues.

A study was undertaken by Jindal (1986: 141) with the following objectives: (1) to examine the modernizing effects of school education on the rural setting and to compare it with the modernizing effects of urban schools, (2) to determine the contribution of education towards modernity, (3) to analyse modernizing effects of high-ranking schools in contrast with low ranking schools, (4) to specify the conditions under which school education promoted or crippled modernity, and (5) to identify those variables which affected modernity in general.

Sample for the study included 465 secondary school students, (male and female) between the age range of 12-16 years, chosen from rural and urban schools; and 72 male adolescents of the same age range who had never attended school.

Tools used for collecting data included the modernity scale of Sharma, school organisational description questionnaire and interview schedule. Data were analysed using t-test, z-test, Chi-square, and product moment correlation.

It was found that the school-going male adolescents were significantly more modern than non-school-going respondents in the rural setting.

The level of education, when considered independently was positively related to student modernity, irrespective of the setting (rural/urban).

The students of urban schools were significantly more modern than their counterparts in rural schools.

In terms of medium of instruction, English medium students were moie modern when compared to Hindi medium students.

Boys were found to be more modern when compared to girls.

Participation in extra-curricular activities particularly in academic and cultural activities, father's high income and parents' English medium schooling were positively related to the students' modernity scores.

Mass media was not found to have any significant effect on the students' modernity.

Gandhi (1986) conducted a study on a sample of 200 rural students and youth. One of the objectives of the study was to ascertain the extent to which modern values of achievement and social mobility were developed (among the rural youth).

Data were collected using structured interview and quasi-participant observation.

Findings of the study indicated lack of convergence between the modern values accepted and the behaviour of the rural youth. "Modern values were accepted because they represented the dominant norms and helped one to attain status. As long as the results of such acceptance were impersonal they accepted them without being committed."

It was also reported that the life of rural youth were "found to be guided by the customs and tradition of the family and caste. Individuality and options were few".

Sahay and Singh (1989) in their study examined modernity in tribal Hindus, using a sample of 480 tribal Hindus (adults) in Chotanagpur and Santhal Pargana region of South Bihar.

The study aimed at finding out the level of modernity in the tribal Hindus. The relationship of age, sex, rural-urban residence and SES with modernity was also examined.

Modernity was measured using a modernity scale with the dimensions of personality, socio-cultural, political and health.

Findings of the study revealed that among the different variables considered, SES (education, income and occupation) was the most powerful influence on modernity.

SES and modernity scores were found to be positively correlated.

Jayaswal and Singh (1989) studied Health Modernity in tribals of South Bihar. The sample consisted of 800 rural tribal males and females.

Data on attitudes and behaviour in relation to physical and mental health, diet and nutrition, family planning, child care and breast feeding, and health habits were measured using health modernity scale.

It was found that the extent of health modernity varied from zero to two per cent. The near absence of health modernity was attributed to poverty and illiteracy.

The study conducted by Ramana (1991:187) focused on Modernistic Orientation and Role Performance of Lady Teachers of Visakhapatnam Municipal schools.

A sample of 225 female teachers including primary and secondary school teachers was selected for the study. Data were collected with the help of an interview schedule.

Findings of the study revealed that education, socio-economic status, religion, marital status and level of school classes taught significantly determined levels of modernity of respondents.

There was significant relationship between socio-economic status and modernity among lady teachers.

Religion had a positive effect on modernity. Hindus were more modern than Muslims and Christians.

Married teachers were more modern than the unmarried.

Secondary female teachers were more modern than the primary female teachers.

Drawing sample from Cochin in Kerala and Visakhapatnam in Andhra Pradesh, Verghese (1991) studied Modernization and Alienation, their empirical structure and relationship with education.

Students (800) belonging to matriculation, intermediate, graduate and post-graduate levels of education were included in the sample. Equal number of boys and girls were selected. Half of them were arts students and the other half were science students. Only from urban areas the samples were drawn with equal number from Cochin and Visakhapatnam.

Data were collected using questionnaire. Modernisation was measured through attitudes.

Findings of the study revealed that there was significant relationship between modernization and education. There were consistently higher modernization scores for every progressive level of education.

Of all the independent variables (culture, sex, science, arts, education level) level of education was found to be highly associated with modernization.

Among the environmental variables (Region, Religion, Caste and Class), only Region and Caste were found to be significantly associated with modernisation.

Among the parental and family variables, mothers occupation, number of siblings and geographical mobility were found to be associated with modernization. Mother's occupation and geographical mobility were found to be positively associated with modernity.

Sex was found to be associated with modernity. Females were negatively associated with modernity.

Educational aspiration and occupational aspiration were negatively associated with modernity, indicating that these two variables were not core constituents of modernity.

Insights from the Review

The studies reviewed here lead to inferences that have a bearing on the hypotheses of the present study. Findings of majority of the studies indicate that formal education is an important variable that influences individual modernity. Most of the studies reviewed here converge towards a positive relationship between education and modernity. The general observation is that as education increases, modernity also increases. However, there are studies which do not support this finding. For example Saunders (1969) in his study found that education, instead of promoting modernity, undermines it. Armer and Youtz (1971) observed a negative relationship between level of schooling and secular orientations. Similarly Sharma (1979) found a negative relationship between levels of education and modernity with each of the six dimensions of modernity considered for the study.

Contradictory to the general observation that formal education is positively related to modernity, some researchers have found that there is no relationship between education and modernity. For instance Cormack (1961) found that college education is ineffective in changing the attitudes and values of students. Armer and Youtz (1971) observed that there was no strong association between formal education and receptivity to change, secularism, and women's equality. Khatun (1991) found that education is less conducive to the growth of secular and civic orientations. Sullivan (1968) found that factors other than experience at a particular training college are operative in changing the students' outlook towards traditional social practices. Seopangat (1987) observed that the teaching learning process in Pikhe Aikima (Indonesia) elementary schools fails to realise the intended goals of citizenship and modernization.

It is thus clear that there is no consensus among the researchers in the area of relationship between education and modernity.

Another aspect which is to be noted is that, while a number of studies have concluded that formal education is positively related to modernity, there is hardly any study that tries to examine the relation between differentials in individual modernity with the differential in levels of education. To some extent the studies by Briones and Waisanen (1966), and Rogers (1969) are exceptions to this observation. Briones and Waisanen suggested that there is a point of "modernization take-off" in such attitudinal variables as aspirations when the individual has more than five years of schooling. Rogers observed that a modernization take-off occurs at about four years of formal schooling. Rogers, however, admits that the sharply rising part of the aspiration curve "has an inadequate data base". It should be noted that even these studies are confined to the role of primary education in promoting modernity. The marginal contributions of increasing levels of education to modernity are not covered.

Hence, it is clear that in the available literature there is a near absence of studies which aim at identifying the relation of various levels of education with individual modernity.

While there are good number of studies focusing on modernity in terms of attitudes and values, the behavioural aspect has remained practically left out. Among the exceptions to this are studies by Inkeles (1969), Sullivan (1968), Srivastava (1986) and Gandhi (1986), Even these studies do not throw much light into the nature of relationship between education and behavioural modernity as well as the relationship between attitudes and behaviour.

Absence of studies focussing on behavioural aspects of modernity, in the literature reviewed, is prominent. Further it should be noted that in regard to the samples drawn, the studies under review are proliferated with student samples. Majority of the studies concentrate on the school effect or college/university effect on modernity. Taking into account all these limitations in the previous studies the following insights for the present study are drawn:

1. The relationship between formal education and individual modernity needs to be examined further.
2. Relationship between education and behavioural modernity needs to be explored.
3. Relationship between modernity in terms of attitudes in relation to behaviour is to be studied keeping education as an intervening variable.
4. The take-off levels of education for different components of modernity as well as total modernity needs to be identified.
5. Such of those studies which examine the above aspects should not be confined only to students at any level of education. Persons with different levels of completed education should be covered in the sample.

Based on the insights from the above research studies present study has been planned. The review of studies was also helpful in guiding the selection of sample, selection of tools, method of data collection, and selection of statistical techniques for anlaysis of data for the present investigation.

4

Profile of the Sample

In this chapter, a general description of the characteristics of respondents in the sample is presented in six sections.

Section I deals with the demographic particulars of the respondents. The variables considered are age, sex, religion, etc. Section II deals with food and nutritional habits of the respondents. In Section III, the skills possessed by the respondents, and in Section IV their membership in social organisations are presented. Section V deals with the family background of the respondents. Variables such as education of parents, occupation of parents, family income, etc., are included herein. Details of married respondents are dealt with in Section VI. Tabular representation of data is provided, wherever necessary, followed by narrative interpretation.

This chapter on profile of respondents is intended to serve as a backdrop for analysis of data on the theme of the present study.

I. Demographic Particulars

The sample drawn for the present study, through quota sampling, are residents of Cochin taluk, Ernakulam district, Kerala. Quotas were fixed on the basis of levels of completed education, sex, religion and place of residence.

Respondents' Age

Age was treated as a control variable in the selection of the sample. Accordingly, only those who were born during the years 1962, 1963 and 1964 were included in the sample in the proportion of 34.29 per cent, 28.14 per cent and 37.57 per cent respectively.

Sex

There are 336 males and 364 females in the ratio of 48 and 52 per cent.

Religion

The respondents of the present study belong to three religions, i.e. Hindu, Muslim and Christian in the proportion of 60 per cent, 20 per cent and 20 per cent of the sample. This ratio is uniformly maintained at all levels of education. Census figures of 1981 for Kerala State were used as the universe of the study. Hindus constitute 58.15 per cent while Muslims constitute 21.25 per cent and Christians constitute 20.56 per cent of the population.

Mother Tongue of the Respondents

Malayalam is the mother tongue of nearly 93 per cent of the respondents.

Number of Languages known by the Respondents

Those who know three or more languages are in a majority constituting 53.86 per cent of the sample. While 14 per cent of the sample know two languages, 32 per cent of them know only their mother-tongue, i.e. Malayalam.

Education of the Respondents

Educational level of an individual was the primary variable used in selecting the sample for the present study. The respondents were selected from 7 different levels. These are:

1. Illiterate – Those who had no schooling.
2. Lower Primary – Those who had completed four years of schooling, i.e. up to IVth standard.

3. Upper Primary – Those who had completed 7 years of schooling, i.e. up to VIIth standard.
4. SSLC (Secondary School Leaving Certificate) – Those who had completed 10 years of schooling, i.e. up to SSLC.
5. PDC (Pre-degree) – Those who had completed 10 years of schooling and 2 years of college education, i.e. up to PDC.
6. Graduate – Those who had completed graduate level of (Degree) college education.
7. Post Graduate – Those who had completed post and professionals graduate course of general education or graduate or post graduate course of professional education.

For the present study, an equal number of 100 respondents constituting 14.29 per cent was selected under each of the above 7 categories.

Occupation

Information about the occupation of respondents was recorded in accordance with the National Classification of Occupations (NCO, 1968). Out of 700 respondents, only 335 reported to have some occupation. Among these, only 102 reported as having salaried jobs. The occupational pattern of the sample is shown in Table 4.1.

It may be observed from Table 4.1 that the highest concentration of respondents in terms of occupation is in the category of production and related works, transport equipment operators and labourers. It is followed by service workers' category with 68 respondents; administrative, executive and managerial workers' category with 55 respondents; professional, technical and related workers with 36 respondents; and sales workers with 31 respondents.

Farmers, fishermen, hunters, loggers and related workers, and clerical and related workers, are the two categories with a very low representation. While in the former category there are only 7 respondents, the latter accounts for only 6.

It may also be noted that the concentration of respondents belonging to the occupational categories 1, 2, 3 and 4 is more in SSLC.

Table 4.1: Distribution of respondents by Level of Education and Occupational Category

Level of Education	*Occupational Category**								*Total*
	1	2	3	4	5	6	7-9	N R	
Illiterate	0	1	0	1	3	23	31	41	100
Lower Primary	1	l	0	4	1	13	41	39	100
Upper Primary	0	3	0	3	2	14	33	45	100
SSLC	1	12	0	5	1	7	13	61	100
PDC	6	10	2	9	0	3	6	64	100
Graduate	15	14	4	4	0	4	3	56	100
PG and Professional	13	14	0	5	0	4	5	59	100
Total	36	55	6	31	7	68	132	365	700
Percentage	5.14	7.86	0.86	4.43	1.0	9.71	18.86	52.14	100.00

* Occupational categories (according to the NCO, 1968).
NR = Not response

1: Professional Technical and related workers.
2: Administrative executive and managerial workers.
3: Clerical and related workers.
4: Sales workers.
5: Service workers.
6: Farmers, fishermen, hunters, loggers and related workers.
7, 8, 9: Production and related workers, transport equipment operators and labourers.

and higher levels of education, whereas in the case of respondents belonging to occupational categories 6, 7, 8 and 9, the higher concentration is in the levels of education below SSLC.

Marital Status

Information on marital status (Table 4.2) has been recorded based on whether the respondent was never married before, i.e. unmarried, or currently married, married, widowed, separated, divorced or deserted.

As may be observed from Table 4.2, 99.43 per cent of the respondents are either married or unmarried. Entries in other categories are marginal and negligible. Majority of respondents are unmarried.

Place of Residence

The sample consists of individuals who reside in rural as well as

Table 4.2: Distribution of Respondents by Marital Status

Marital Status	*Frequency No. of persons*	*Percentage*
Unmarried	410	58.57
Married	286	40.86
Widowed	1	0.14
Separated	1	0.14
Divorced	2	0.29
Deserted	0	0.00
Religious (Priests, Nuns, etc.)	0	0.00
Total	700	100.00

urban areas of Cochin taluk. It was decided to have 50 per cent of the sample from rural areas and 50 per cent from urban areas. This distribution is by and large observed in the general population distribution as represented in the 1981 District Census. Accordingly, 350 respondents belong to rural areas and 350 respondents belong to urban areas of Cochin taluk, where rural-urban ratio (1 : 1) is uniform at all levels of education.

Migration

Data, regarding the migration status of the respondents were sought through information pertaining to the place of birth. It may be recalled that all the respondents selected for the present study were residents of Cochin taluk at the time of data collection. For the purpose of the present study, a migrant is defined as a person whose place of birth is different from his/her place of residence at the time of data collection. The minimum unit considered as a place in this context is either a division of a corporation/municipality or a panchayat.

According to the above definition, 222 respondents out of 700 are migrants whereas 476 respondents are non-migrants, in the case of two respondents, Information is not available in this respect. Data on migrants relating to their place of origin is analysed separately.

Among the 222 migrants, more than 70 per cent are female respondents. Table 4.3 shows the distribution of migrants by level of education and sex.

It may be observed from Table 4.3 that the proportion of female migrants is very high at all levels of education. The highest proportion of female migrants is at the SSLC level of education.

Table 4.3: Distribution of Migrant Respondents by Level of Education and Sex

Level of Education	*Sex*		*Total*
	Male	*Female*	
Illiterate	10 (33.33)	20 (66.67)	30 (100.00)
Lower Primary	11 (29.73)	26 (70.27)	37 (100.00)
Upper Primary	12 (30.77)	27 (69.23)	39 (100.00)
SSLC	5 (18.52)	22 (81.48)	27 (100.00)
PDC	7 (24.14)	22 (75.86)	29 (100.00)
Graduate	9 (30,00)	21 (70.00)	30 (100.00)
P G and Professional	10 (33.33)	20 (66.67)	30 (100.00)
Total (Percentage)	64 (28.83)	158 (71.17)	222 (100.00)

Among the 158 female migrants, large majority (81.01%) are married. It is likely that these respondents migrated to their present place of residence after marriage.

Based on the location of the place of birth (place of origin), five categories of migrants are identified for the present study. These are intra-taluk, intra-district, intra-state, inter-state and international.

Table 4.4: Distribution of Migrant Respondents by their Level of Education and Place of Birth (Place of Origin)

Level of education	*Place of birth (Place of origin)*						*Total*
	Within Coohin Taluk	*Outside Coohin taluk but within Ernakulam district*	*Outside Ernakulam district but within Kerala*	*Outside Kerala but within India*	*Abroad*	*No response*	
Illiterate	17	3	9	1	—	—	30
Lower Primary	24	4	8	—	—	1	37
Upper Primary	22	6	10	—	—	1	39
SSLC	17	3	4	—	—	3	27
PDC	12	2	10	1	—	4	29
Graduate	17	2	4	3	—	4	30
PG and Professional	8	1	11	3	1	6	30
Total	117 (52.70)	21 (9.46)	56 (25.23)	8 (3.60)	1 (0.45)	19 (8.56)	222 (100.0)

It is clear from Table 4.4 that as high as 52.70 per cent of the migrants were born in different places of Cochin taluk itself. Migrants from outside Ernakulam district (but within Kerala State) account for 25.23 per cent of the migrants. By and large, these respondents are from Alleppey and Trichur districts, which are neighbouring districts of Ernakulam.

Of all the 222 migrants, only 1 respondent was born abroad and 8 respondents were born in other States of India. It may also be observed from the table that the concentration of migrants who were born within Cochin taluk but migrated from one panchayat/corporation division to another is high at all levels of education except at the P G and Professional level of education.

II. Food and Related Habits

Food Habits

Of the total sample, 93.71 per cent consume fish; meat eaters account for 89.14 per cent and those who eat egg constitute 92.14 per cent. Hardly 6.29 per cent are pure vegetarians.

Only 51.86 per cent of the sample are punctual in taking their food whereas 328 respondents (46.86 per cent of the sample) are not punctual in taking their food. It is likely that they may not be in regular occupations.

Smoking and Consumption of Alcohol

Majority of the respondents do not smoke or consume alcohol (66.71 and 66.86 per cent respectively). One out of four respondents smokes and consumes alcohol.

By and large alcoholic and smoking habit is observed among respondents with lower levels of education.

Tobacco/Narcotics

When compared to the habit of smoking, chewing tobacco/consuming narcotics is not a practice among the respondents. Only 55 out of 700 respondents chew tobacco or consume narcotics.

III. Skills

In order to know the spread of skills, associated with industrial modernisation in the sample, information was sought on respondents' skills in cycling, two-wheeler driving, car driving, using calculator, typewriter and computer.

Cycling, Two-Wheeler Driving and Car Driving

The proportion of respondents in the sample who do not know cycling is 49.43 per cent. The corresponding figures in the case of two-wheeler driving and car driving are 73.86 and 85.29 per cent respectively.

Those who know cycling, account for 49 per cent of the sample. This figure is consistently observed across levels of education.

Ability to drive two-wheelers is reported only by 20.43 per cent of mostly belonging to higher levels of education, i.e. SSLC and above. Only 7.71 per cent of the respondents are able to drive a car. These respondents, however, belong to all levels of education including illiterates.

Ability to use Calculator, Typewriter and Computer

More than 53 per cent of the respondents in the sample are not able to use calculator. In the case of typewriter more than 67 per cent of the respondents do not know typing. The corresponding proportion for computer is 89 per cent.

Those who are able to use calculator as well as those who are able to type, are in a minority. They are mostly concentrated at the higher levels of education, i.e. SSLC and above. A negligible number of respondents, belonging to higher levels of education, know how to use a computer.

IV. Membership in Social Organisations

The extent of participation and involvement of the respondents in the social organizations was gauged through information, their membership, in the local library, a political party, a trade union, recreation club and other organizations. More than 80 per cent of the respondents are not members of these organizations.

Membership in library, political party, trade union, recreation club as well as any organization other than these, is observed only in a minority (less than 18%) of the sample.

Such of those who are members of the library and recreation clubs by and large belong to higher levels of education, i.e. SSLC and above.

Membership of trade union is concentrated at the lower levels (below SSLC) of education while membership of political parties is fairly distributed across levels of education.

V. Family Background

Household size, parents' education and occupation, relatives holding jobs abroad, family income, possession of houses and land, etc., constitute information collected regarding family background. They are converted into a living standards index for comparative purposes.

Household Size

Nearly 3 out of 4 respondents are from medium sized (4-6 members) or large households (7-9 members), Respondent belonging to small (having 1-3 members) as well as very large households (having 10 or more members) are very few.

Education of Parents

In Table 4.5, the distribution of respondents by parents' level of education is presented.

It may be observed from Table 4.5 that a large majority (more than 70%) of parents have studied only upto SSLC. The proportion of parents who have studied beyond SSLC account for only 8.72 per cent in the case of fathers and only 5.57 per cent in the case of mothers. Differences between father's and mother's education is quite large only at the level of illiteracy. Otherwise, they are quite low except at graduate and PG and Professional levels.

Educational Mobility

Education is considered as a key variable in analysing the process of 'Social mobility'. Mobility in terms of education could be understood

Table 4.5: Distribution of Respondents by Parents' Level of Education

Level of education	*Education of Father*		*Education of Mother*	
	Frequency	*Percentage*	*Frequency*	*Percentage*
Illiterate	90	12.86	162	23.14
Lower Primary	202	28.86	192	27.43
Upper Primary	118	16.86	100	14.29
SSLC	102	14.57	102	14.57
PDC	21	3.00	29	4.14
Graduate	27	3.86	8	1.14
PG and Professional	13	1.86	2	0.29
No response	127	18.13	105	15.00
Total	700	100.00	700	100.00

as the movement of individual/s from one level of education to another. The direction of this movement could be either positive, i.e. upward, or negative, i.e. downward.

Based on the data available pertaining to the parents' education and respondents' level of education, an attempt is made to find out whether there has been any mobility in terms of educational attainment of the respondents from that of their parents.

For the purpose of understanding, male and female respondents have been treated separately in examining mobility in terms of education. Educational mobility is worked out based on the proportion of respondents who have moved upward or downward in their educational attainment from the level of education of their parents. For male respondents, father's level of education and for the female respondents, mother's education are considered as bases for identifying the mobility in terms of education.

Inter-generation matrices were prepared (using frequencies) by respondents' level of education and parents' level of education, separately for male and female respondents. From these matrices, the proportion of cases at each level of education showing upward/ downward mobility are worked out for drawing educational mobility.

Educational Mobility among Male Respondents

Using the data pertaining to father's educational category and male respondents' level of education, an inter-generational matrix has been generated, as shown in Table 4.6.

Table 4.6: Intergenerational Matrix: Distribution of Male Respondents by Level of Education and Father's Educational Category

Respondent's Level of education	*Respondent's father's educational category*							*Total*
	1 Illiterate	*2 LP*	*3 UP*	*4 SSLC*	*5 PDC*	*6 Graduate*	*7 PG & Professional*	
1. Illiterate	19	15	7	1	—	—	—	42
	45.24	35.71	16.67	2.38				100.00
2. LP	10	20	5	—	—	—	—	35
	28.57	57.14	14.29					100.00
3 . UP	6	23	11	2	—	1	—	43
	13.95	53.49	25.58	4.65		2.33		100.00
4. SSLC	5	17	13	2	1	—	—	38
	13.16	44.74	34.21	5.26	2.63			100.00
5. PDC		15	12	10	2	—	1	40
		37.50	30.00	25.00	5.00		2.50	100.00
6. Graduate	3	2	8	19	2	6	—	40
	7.50	5.00	20.00	47.50	5.00	15.00		100.00
7. PG & Professional		11	6	14	4	9	3	47
		23.40	12.77	29.79	8.51	19.15	6.38	100.00
Total	43	103	62	48	9	16	4	285

Note: Cases of no response (information not available) are excluded.

From this matrix, the proportion of cases showing either upward or downward or no educational mobility from that of the fathers has been calculated as presented in Table 4.7.

Table 4.7: Distribution of Male Respondents by Level of Education and Educational Mobility

Level of Education	*Educational mobility category*			*Total %*
	Upward mobility %	No mobility %	Downward Mobility %	
Illiterate	—	45.24	54.76	100.00 (42)
LP	28.57	57.14	14.29	100.00 (35)
UP	67.44	25.58	6.98	100.00 (43)
SSLC	92.11	5.26	2.63	100.00 (38)
PDC	92.50	5.00	2.50	100.00 (40)
Graduate	85.00	15.00	—	100.00 (40)
PG & Professional	93.62	6.38	—	100.00 (47)
Total	66.32 (189)	22.11 (63)	11.58 (33)	100.00 (285)

*Excluding the cases of no response.
Note: Figures in parentheses indicate actual number.

It may be observed from Table 4.7 that among the male respondents, 66.32 per cent have moved at least one level upward from that of their fathers.

The proportion of downward mobility is 11.58 per cent. Whereas in the case of 22.11 per cent of the respondents there is no educational mobility, i.e. they have remained at the same level of education of their fathers.

It is also clear from Table that the proportion of respondents showing upward educational mobility steadily increases from 0 at the illiterate level to 93.62 per cent at the PG and Professional level, with the exception of Graduate level of education. When compared to PDC, the Graduate level shows a slight decrease in the proportion of respondents who have attained upward educational mobility.

An interesting observation to be made is the steep increment in the proportion of respondents showing upward educational mobility from upper primary level with 67.44 per cent, to SSLC level with 92.11 per cent.

The proportion of male respondents showing no mobility is relatively quite high among illiterate, LP and UP levels of education. However, among the higher levels, SSLC and above, this proportion is quite low. Downward mobility among Illiterates is the highest, i.e. 54.76 per cent. Though the proportion is low, the occurrence of downward nobility at all levels of education except Graduate and PG and Professional levels is notable.

Educational Mobility among Female Respondents

As in the case of male respondents, an inter-generation matrix was prepared in the case of female respondents, using data pertaining to mothers educational category and respondents' (female) level of education.

From this matrix, the proportion of cases showing upward, downward, or no educational mobility was worked out as presented in Table 4.8.

It may be observed from Table 4.8, that majority of the female respondents (71.25%) have moved at least one level upward in terms of educational level from that of their mothers. [This is relatively high when compared to that of male respondents where it is only 66.32% (Table 4.7)].

While 20.45 per cent of female respondents have remained at the same level of education of their mothers, most of them being at the illiterate level, 8.31 per cent have moved at least one level below than that of their mothers which is mostly at the primary level.

It may also be observed that upward educational mobility increases from zero at the illiterate level to 97.88 per cent at the P G and professional level of education, through SSLC. (The respective percentages at different levels of education are relatively high when compared to that of male respondents, except in the case of SSLC where the males have an edge over females).

Table 4.8: Inter-generational Matrix: Distribution of Female Respondents by Level of Education and Educational Mobility

Level of Education	*Educational mobility category*			*Total %*
	Upward mobility %	No mobility %	Downward Mobility %	
Illiterate	—	60.42	39.58	100.00 (48)
LP	40.91	47.73	11.36	100.00 (44)
UP	85.11	10.63	4.26	100.00 (47)
SSLC	91.67	8.33	—	100.00 (36)
PDC	92.85	7.15	—	100.00 (42)
Graduate	95.92	4.08	—	100.00 (49)
PG & Professional	97.87	2.13	—	100.00 (47)
Total	71.24 (223)	20.45 (64)	8.31 (26)	100.00 (313)

Note: Figures in parentheses indicate actual number.

It is also apparent from Table 4.8 that the proportion of cases with no mobility and downward educational mobility steadily decreases as the level of education goes up.

Unlike in male respondents, downward educational mobility is visible only among illiterates, Lower Primary and Upper Primary levels in the case of female respondents.

As in the case of male respondents, upward educational mobility has occurred (at least one level above) in the case of female respondents at all levels of education. Upward educational mobility appears to increase as the level of education goes up.

On the other hand, the incidents of no mobility and downward educational mobility decrease, as the level of education goes up.

The incidents of downward educational mobility, though marginal, observed in the sample is surprising considering the demand for education that prevails in Kerala. The researcher enquired about the reasons behind this phenomenon. The reasons reported by the respondents, as well as their parents, include the following:

1. The respondent was ill and hence was not able to go to school.
2. The respondent had to cross river/stream to reach the school and hence the parents discouraged him/her.
3. The respondent had to look after younger siblings (this was mostly in the case of female respondents).
4. The respondent was not interested in studies.

Occupation of Parents

Information on the occupation of parents was recorded, as reported by the respondents or their parents. Father's and mother's occupations were classified separately following the NCO, 1968.

Father's Occupation

In Table 4.9. the distribution of respondents by level of education and father's occupational category is presented.

It may be observed from Table 4.9 that fathers of the respondents belong to al! occupational categories. However, among the occupational categories, production and related workers, transport equipment operators and labourers have the highest concentration (194 out of 700), followed by farmers, fishermen, etc. (118 out of 700), and sales workers (93 out of 700).

Fathers of respondents belonging to Illiterate, LP, UP, and SSLC levels of education, by and large belong to the occupational categories, i.e. production and related workers, transport equipment operators and labourers, farmers, fishermen, hunters, loggers and related workers, service workers and sales workers. In the case of respondents at PDC above, fathers belong to almost all occupational categories.

An interesting observation to be noted from Table 4.9 is that the number of respondents whose fathers belong to the occupational categories 7, 8 and 9 steadily decreases from illiterate to PG and professional levels. A similar trend is observed in the case of occupational category 6 from illiterate to graduate level of education. Fathers belonging to occupational categories 1, 2 and 3, by and large, are with respondents at PDC and higher levels of education.

Mother's Occupation

A large majority of respondents reported that their mothers are housewives. This accounts for nearly 85 per cent of the sample.

Those respondents whose mothers have any occupation, account for 15.57 per cent of the sample. These are distributed across all occupations, except occupational category 2, i.e. administrative, executive and managerial workers.

Overseas Employment of Family Members

It is expected that the presence of a family member who is employed abroad can lead to notable impact in the economy of the dependents in the native country. Apart from the influence on the economic aspect, they are exposed to certain new practices and views of life. Examples of such influences could be: exposure to more modern technology through access to modern gadgets brought in by the outmigrant, awareness of foreign culture by listening to the experiences narrated by the outmigrant, etc.

In order to know whether the respondents of the present study are exposed to influences of any family member employed abroad, the information regarding this aspect, i.e. 'whether the respondent has any family member or relative employed abroad, was collected.

It was found that vast majority of the sample (91.29%) did not have any family member or relative employed abroad. Such of those respondents with family member/relative employed abroad 7.57 per cent are spread over all levels of education including illiterates, with UP and PG and Professional levels of education having the highest number, i.e. 14 respondents each.

Income of the Family

Information about the annual income of the family (to which the respondents belong) was estimated through a number of items upon which data were collected. Using information about agricultural production, animal husbandry, poultry, fish rearing, business, industry, wages or salaries of the family members, an aggregate figure of annual family income was worked out (Rates of commodities used in this procedure were fixed at par with that of market rates as on June 23, 1990).

Table 4.9: Distribution of Respondents by Level of Education and Father's Occupation

Respondent's level of education	*Father's Occupational Category*								*Total*
	1	2	3	4	5	6	7,8,9	NR	
Illiterate	—	—	1	13	3	29	40	14	100
LP	3	—	—	16	4	25	39	13	100
UP	—	—	1	12	10	23	38	16	100
SSLC	—	—	5	8	4	15	34	34	100
PDC	7	4	4	18	1	10	26	30	100
Graduate	11	8	6	17	3	5	13	37	100
PG & Professional	24	11	13	9	—	11	4	28	100
Total	45	23	30	93	25	118	194	172	700
Percentage	6.43	3.29	4.29	13.29	3.57	16.86	27.71	24.57	100

NR = No response

1 = Professional, technical and related workers

2 = Administrative, executive and managerial workers

3 = Clerical and related workers

4 = Sales workers

5 = Service workers

6 = Farmers, fishermen, hunters, loggers and related workers

7, 8, 9 = Production and related workers, transport equipment operators and labourers.

The income figure thus estimated was verified with that reported by the respondent and in cases of disparity the higher figure of the two was fixed as the annual income of the respondent's family.

On the basis of the annual income of the family, the respondents are classified into five groups, viz.,

1. Poor, i.e. annual family income being Rs. 6,000 or less than that;
2. Low income, i.e. annual family income between Rs. 6,001 and Rs. 12,000;
3. Lower middle income, i.e. annual family income between Rs. 12,001 and Rs. 24,000;
4. Upper middle income, i.e. annual family income between Rs. 24,001 and Rs. 38,000; and
5. High income, i.e. annual family income being Rs. 36,001 and above.

In Table 4.10, the distribution of respondents by level of education and annual family income is presented.

Table 4.10: Distribution of Respondents by Level of Education and Annual Family Income

Level of education	*Family Income Category*						*Total*
	1	*2*	*3*	*4*	*5*	*NR*	
Illiterate	20	50	24	4	—	2	100
LP	13	43	34	7	3	—	100
UP	10	38	39	10	1	2	100
SSLC	16	42	27	9	4	2	100
PDC	6	24	43	16	10	1	100
Graduate	5	24	27	23	21	—	100
PG & Profes.	—	1	32	33	34	—	100
Total	70	222	226	102	73	7	700
Percentage	10.0	31.71	32.29	14.57	10.43	1.0	100.00

N R = No response

1 = Less than Rs. 6,000 — Poor
2 = Rs. 6001-12,000 — Low income
3 = Rs. 12,001-24,000 — Lower middle income
4 = Rs. 24,001-36,000 — Upper middle income
5 = Above Rs. 36,000 — High income

It may be observed from Table 4.10 that majority of the respondents (64%) belong to either lower middle income or low income group.

While 10 per cent of the sample account for the poor, 10.43 per cent constitute the high income group.

In terms of levels of education, the poor are by and large concentrated among different levels of education below SSLC and SSLC whereas the respondents belonging to high income groups are concentrated more among the levels of education above SSLC.

Ownership of House

According to the "Survey on Housing and Employment, 1980, of Kerala, nearly 7 per cent of the households in the State do not own any house and are staying in rented houses."

In the case of the respondents of the present study, nearly 90 per cent of them belong to families owning houses. Those who belong to families living in leased/rented houses account for 9.29 per cent. These respondents, however, are distributed across many levels of education, including illiterates.

Ownership of Land

Majority (63.57%) of the respondents belong to families owning land. In terms of area, most of the landholdings are small, i.e. less than 50 cents.

Respondents who belong to families owning less than 10 cents of land account for 44.57 per cent of the sample whereas those who belong to families owning more than 100 cents account for only 3 per cent of the sample.

The fact that 44.57 per cent (312) of the respondents belong to families owning land areas of 10 cents or less has relevance to the Land Reforms Act of Kerala (1963). Kerala is the first State which implemented an integrated Land Reforms Act in India. As a result of this Act (which came into effect in 1964), a large number of landless agricultural labourers and tenants became land owners. Majority of the respondents who belong to families owning land areas of 10 cents or less revealed that the land which their families own came in as a result of the Land Reforms Act in Kerala. Most of these holdings are non-agricultural.

Living Standard Index

Apart from the data pertaining to the income of the family to which the respondents belong information pertaining to the availability of facilities at the household level (of the respondent) were also collected, in order to get a vivid picture of the level of living which the respondents have at home. In order to obtain a fairly clear indication in this respect, information on a set of 24 items was considered. These include essential facilities like drinking water, lavatory, electricity, etc., and also to the relatively luxurious facilities such as air conditioner, refrigerator, washing machine, etc.

Rather than considering each of these items separately, it was decided to have a comprehensive index, i.e. 'Living Standard Index'.

The Living Standard Index (LSI) is a numerical figure arrived at by summing up the weightages (given on an ordinal scale) for all the 24 items. Weightages are given to positive responses only, i.e. only if a particular item is reported by the respondent as available at home. In the case of negative response it is assigned 0 (zero).

As per the above procedure, the maximum that any respondent can obtain as 'Living Standard Index' is 100 and the minimum is 0 (zero).

Based on the scores obtained as Living Standard Index, the respondents are classified into four groups for purposes of comparison. Accordingly, respondents with "Living Standard Index' score of < 25 are classified as the lower group, 26-50 as low middle group, 51-75 as high middle group and those with LSI scores of 76-100 form the higher group.

The distribution of respondents by Level of education and living standard index is presented in Table 4.11.

It may be observed from Table 4.11 that almost all up to Upper Primary and more than two-third of SSLC belong to lower Living Standard Index group.

Further, the incidence of higher living standard index is quite low. Those who belong to high middle category are mostly from Graduate and PG and Professional levels.

Savings, Investment and Credit

Information regarding the respondent's habits of saving/investment as well as borrowing were sought from the respondents. Accordingly, information on holding of a bank account, membership in a chit fund, holding of shares/bonds/debentures and insurance policy as well as availing loan were collected.

Table 4.11: Distribution of Respondents by Level of Education and Living Standard Index

Level of Education	*Living Standard Index Category*				*Total*
	Lower (<25)	*Low Middle (26-50)*	*High Middle (51-75)*	*Higher (76-100)*	
Illiterate	97	3	–	–	100
LP	93	7	–	–	100
UP	91	7	2	–	100
SSLC	68	26	6	–	100
PDC	37	44	17	2	100
Graduate	27	38	30	5	100
PG and Professional	13	33	42	12	100
Total	426	158	97	19	700
Percentage	60.86	22.57	13.86	2.71	100.00

Majority (more than 66%) of the respondents do not have any bank account. Similarly 79 per cent of the respondents are not members of any chit fund organisation.

The corresponding figures in the case of respondents not holding shares/bonds/debentures as well as life insurance policy are 82.86 and 89 per cent respectively.

In Table 4.12 the distribution of respondents by their bank account, membership in chit fund, holding of shares/bonds/ debentures as well as insurance policy (across levels of education) is presented.

It may be observed from Table 4.12 that bank account holders, members in chit fund, share/bond/debenture holders are distributed across several levels of education, including illiterates. However, a majority of the life insurance policy holders are concentrated at higher levels—above SSLC—of education.

It was observed by the researcher at the time of data collection that almost all the share holders belonging to illiterate, LP and UP levels are holding shares of co-operative societies. (Mostly they are

Rs. 11 of value, shares required for benefits under development schemes). It was also noted that incidents of holding bonds/debentures were practically nil.

Table 4.12: Distribution of Respondents by Level of Education and Holding of Bank Account, Membership in Chit Fund, holding of Share/Bond/Debenture and holding of Insurance Policy

Level of education	*Category*							
	Holding bank account	*N*	*Member in chit fund*	*N*	*Holding share/bond/ debenture*	*N*	*Holding insurance policy*	*N*
Illiterate	25	100	25	100	30	100	4	100
LP	21	100	12	100	19	100	4	100
UP	21	100	17	100	21	100	7	100
SSLC	29	100	21	100	7	100	6	100
PDC	33	100	18	100	6	100	8	100
Graduate	45	100	21	100	11	100	17	100
PG and Professional	53	100	17	100	20	100	13	100
Total	227	700	131	700	114	700	59	700
Percentage	32.43	100	18.71	100	16.29	100	8.43	100

Credit

Majority (77.86%) of the respondents have not availed any loan from banks/cooperative banks.

Nearly 20 per cent of respondents at all levels of education have availed loans. Most of these loans were availed from nationalised banks or cooperative societies.

Other General Information

Passport

A general tendency prevailing among the people particularly the youth of Kerala is that passports are acquired with the intention of going abroad for employment or as a spouse. In many cases, passports are kept ready in anticipation of such a possibility. For most of the passport holders' desire is to go to Gulf countries or if possible to the United States of America.

Table 4.13 reveals the distribution of respondents by level of education and possession of passport.

It may be observed from Table 4.13 that a majority of the respondents do not have passport. Those who are passport holders account for only 10.86 per cent of the sample. The passport holders belong to all levels of education including illiterates.

However, a majority of the passport holders belong to SSLC and higher levels of education. Though the number is small, the presence of passport holders among UP, LP and even illiterates is notable. It was found that all these are male respondents (6 of them Muslims, 2 of them Hindus and 2 Christians).

Table 4.13: Distribution of Respondents by Level of Education and Possession of Passport

Level of Education	*Category*			*Total*
	Having passport	*Not having passport*	*NR*	
Illiterate	3	65	32	100
LP	3	42	55	100
UP	4	56	40	100
SSLC	17	75	8	100
PDC	17	80	3	100
Graduate	13	83	4	100
PC and Professional	19	78	3	100
Total	76	479	145	700
Percentage	10.86	68.43	20.71	100.00

VI. Married Respondents

Majority of the respondents are unmarried at the time of the study. Those who are married account for 40.86 per cent of the sample. Table 4.14 shows the distribution of married respondents by their level of education and sex.

It may be noted, from Table 4.14 that among the married respondents, majority are females at all levels of education. A majority of the married, both male and female, belong to lower levels of education, i.e. up to UP. It may further be noted that the number of married male respondents steadily decreases as the level of education increases, whereas no clear trend is observed in the case of females.

Table 4.14: Distribution of Married Respondents by Level of Education and Sex

Level of Education	*Male*		*Female*		*Total*	*Percentage*
	No. of persons	*Percentage*	*No. of persons*	*Percentage*		
Illiterate	28	41.79	39	58.21	67	100.00
LP	24	38.71	38	61.29	62	100.00
UP	17	30.36	39	69.64	56	100.00
SSLC	9	27.27	24	72.73	33	100.00
PDC	3	9.68	28	90.32	31	100.00
Graduate	2	13.33	13	86.67	15	100.00
PG and Professional	2	9.09	20	90.91	22	100.00
Total	85	29.72	201	70.28	286	100.00

*Excluding the widowed (1), Separated (1). and divorced (2) respondents.

Sources of Information for Choice of Marriage Partner

The most commonly observed sources of information regarding the choice of marriage partner in Kerala are either 'marriage brokers' or relatives. The matrimonial columns in the newspapers and magazines have not yet become a popular means of making marriage alliances. During recent years, even computers have entered the area of matrimony.

In Table 4.15, the distribution of married respondents by level of education and the source of information in choosing the marriage partner is presented.

It may be observed from Table 4.15 that for a majority (76.57%) of the respondents, relatives or marriage brokers are the source of information in choosing the marriage partner. This is more or less true at almost all levels of education.

A notable proportion (17.48%) of the married respondents have chosen their life partners by themselves. Majority of these individuals reported that they entered into a love marriage. These individuals mostly belong to lower levels of education, i.e. below SSLC. Entries in the remaining categories are very few and are negligible.

Decision Making in Selecting the Marriage Partner

Table 4.16 shows the distribution of married respondents *vis-á-vis* the decision makers who played a crucial role in selecting the marriage partner.

Table 4.15: Distribution of Married Respondents by Level of Education and the Source of Information in the Choice of Marriage Partner

Level of education	*Source of Information in the Choice of Marriage Partner*							*Total*
	Marriage broker	*Relatives*	*Friends*	*Colleagues*	*News-papers*	*Self*	*No Response*	
Illiterate	26	23	2	—	—	16	—	67
LP	21	23	1	1	—	15	1	62
UP	21	19	3	—	—	10	3	56
SSLC	5	21	1	—	—	6	—	33
PDC	8	20	—	—	—	3	—	31
Graduate	2	10	2	—	1	—	—	15
PG & Professional	1	19	—	—	1	—	1	22
Total	84	135	9	1	2	50	5	286
Percentage	29.37	47.20	3.15	0.35	0.70	17.48	1.75	100.0

It may be observed from Table 4.16 that slightly more than 55 per cent of the married respondents have reported that parents took decisions regarding their marriage.

Table 4.16: Distribution of Married Respondents by Level of Education and Decision-maker in Selecting the Marriage Partner

Level of education	*Decision-maker in selecting the marriage partner*					*Total*
	Self	*Parents*	*Self & Parents*	*Any Other*	*NR*	
Illiterate	19	37	10	1	—	67
LP	16	37	7	—	2	62
UP	10	27	17	—	2	56
SSLC	9	16	8	—	—	33
PDC	4	14	13	—	—	31
Graduate	1	10	4	—	—	15
PG & Professional	1	17	3	—	1	22
Total	60	158	62	1	5	286
Percentage	20.98	55.24	21.68	0.35	1.75	100.0

Considerable number of respondents at all levels of education have reported parents as the decision makers.

On the other hand, in selecting the marriage partner, 20.98 per cent of the married respondents took decisions by themselves. These individuals mostly belong to lower levels of education, i.e. up to SSLC. More than 21 per cent at the currently married respondents reported that in their cases the decision in selecting the marriage partner was made jointly by them and their parents.

Age at Marriage

Information regarding the age at marriage of the currently married respondents was recorded as reported by them. A majority among the married respondents married after attaining the prescribed minimum age for marriage (as per the Special Marriage Act of 1954, the minimum age fixed for marriage is 21 for males and 18 for females). While among the married male respondents 77.65 per cent married after attaining the minimum age prescribed, 78.12 per cent of the female respondents married after attaining the prescribed minimum age for marriage.

Table 4.17 presents the distribution of respondents who married before attaining the prescribed minimum age.

Table 4.17: Distribution of Respondents who married before attaining the Minimum Age Prescribed by Level of Education and Sex

Level of Education	*Male*		*Female*	
	No. of persons married before 21 years	*Total*	*No. of persons married before 18 years*	*Total*
Illiterate	1	28	9	39
LP	3	24	9	38
UP	2	17	7	39
SSLC	1	9	4	24
PDC	—	3	—	28
Graduate	—	2	—	13
PG & Professional	—	2	—	20
Total	7	85	29	201
Percentage	8.24	100.0	14.43	100.0

It may be noted from Table 4.17 that those who married before attaining the minimum age prescribed are minority both in the case of males and females and that they belong to lower levels of education, i.e. up to SSLC.

Spouse's Caste

A vast majority (91.61%) of the married respondents married from their own caste. The negligible number of cases of inter-caste marriage are spread among different levels of education up to PDC including illiterate.

Dowry

The practice of giving dowry to the groom/groom's parents in the form of cash, gold, house, land, car, other durable assets like refrigerator, T.V. almirah, etc. is still common in Kerala. However, gold and cash are the two items that are most frequently given when daughters are married off. Information pertaining to dowry were collected from the married respondents. It is found that gold and cash are the two major items that are given or taken during marriage. Incidents of giving or taking other items like household equipment are very few.

(i) Dowry among Males

Table 4.18: Distribution of Married Male Respondents by Level of Education and Gold/Cash received during their Marriage

Level of education	*Gold received*	*Total*	*Cash received*	*Total*
Illiterate	25	28	16	28
LP	18	24	16	24
UP	12	17	8	17
SSLC	6	9	2	9
PDC	3	3	—	3
Graduate	1	2	—	2
PG and Professional	1	2	1	2
Total	66	85	43	85
Percentage	77.65	100.00	50.59	100.00

It may be observed from Table 4.18 that over three-fourths and half of married male respondents have received gold and cash respectively during their marriage. These respondents belong to all levels of education though the incidence is low at higher levels.

(ii) Dowry among Females

Table 4.19: Distribution of Married Female Respondents by Level of Education and Gold/Cash given during their Marriage

Level of education	*Gold given*	*Total*	*Cash given*	*Total*
Illiterate	29	39	20	39
LP	30	38	27	38
UP	36	39	27	39
SSLC	17	24	4	24
PDC	21	28	11	28
Graduate	11	13	2	13
PG and Professional	12	20	3	20
Total	156	201	94	201
Percentage	77.61	100.00	46.77	100.00

It may be observed from Table 4.19 that a large majority (77.61%) of the married female respondents have given gold during their marriage. Cash was given by nearly one-half of them (46.77%). These respondents belong to all levels of education though the incidence is low at higher levels of education.

Number of Children

Among the married, a large majority (82.52%) of the respondents have children. Over two-thirds of these respondents have either one or two children.

Those who have more than two children belong to lower levels of education (Table 4.20).

Table 4.20: Distribution of Married Respondents by Number of Children they have

Level of education	*No. of Children*						*Total*
	1	2	3	4	5	*No response*	
Illiterate	20	26	8	3	—	10	67
LP	17	20	12	3	1	9	62
UP	13	20	12	2	—	9	56
SSLC	13	13	2	1	—	4	33
PDC	15	11	—	—	—	5	31
Graduate	10	2	—	—	—	3	15
PG and Professional	10	3	—	—	—	9	22
Total	98	95	34	9	1	49	286
Percentage	34.27	33.22	11.89	3.15	0.35	17.13	100.00

Birth Control

More than 46 per cent of the currently married respondents have reported as having adopted birth control measures.

As it can be observed from Table 4.21 a considerable number of those who have adopted birth control measures belong to illiterate, LP and UP levels of education. It was perceived by the researcher, during the fieldwork that there is a growing awareness among illiterates and those who are at the lower levels of education, that they 'cannot afford to have more children as children's health and nutritional care as well as school education is becoming more expensive these days'. A constead of one study on cost of rearing children and its relationship with family size in Kerala State (*Rayappa*, 1979) completed at ISEC has shown that cost considerations weigh very high and positively so in limiting family size. In most of the cases it is the women who volunteer to adopt birth control measures. They do so along with the child birth. This also helps them in not reducing the working days of their husbands, who are mostly daily-wage workers. The women also believe that vasectomy may adversely affect the man's health.

Table 4.21: Distribution of Married Respondents by Level of Education and Adoption of Birth Control

Level of education	*Category*			*Total*
	Adopted birth control	*Birth control not adopted*	*No response*	
Illiterate	31	27	9	67
L P	24	31	7	62
U P	33	16	7	56
SSLC	14	16	3	33
PDC	11	16	4	31
Graduate	8	5	2	15
PG and Professional	13	6	3	22
Total	134	117	35	286
Percentage	(46.85)	(40.91)	(12.24)	100.00

Among the methods, sterilization appears to be a popular method of birth control, as it is accepted by a majority (59.70%) of those who have adopted birth control. This is followed by contraception and natural methods of birth control (22.39 and 17.16% respectively).

Immunisation of the Child

Majority of the respondents were found to be aware of the need for immunisation of their children. More than 93 per cent of those who have children reported that triple-antigen injections were given to their children. Only a negligible number of respondents have reported that their children were not given such immunisation. These respondents are from lower levels of education.

Marital Harmony

More than 53 per cent of the married respondents reported that they 'never quarrel' with their spouses whereas 30.42 per cent of them quarrel with their spouses 'sometimes'. Quarrelling 'quite often' with the spouse is reported by 11 per cent of the married respondents. Those who quarrel with their spouses 'quite often' mostly belong to lower levels of education, i.e. below SSLC.

Cumulative Observation on the Profile of the Sample

Demographic Particulars

The sample drawn for the present study consists of 700 individuals and divided into seven levels of education. Including illiterate. with 100 respondents at each level. They are residents of Cochin taluk and were born during 1962 and 1964. While male respondents constitute 48 per cent of the total sample females account for the rest (52%).

A majority (60%) or the respondents are Hindus. Muslims and Christians account for 20 per cent each of the sample.

Malayalam is the mother tongue of more than 93 per cent of the sample. More than half of the sample know three or more languages, including Malayalam.

Salaried job is reported by only a minority of the sample. Among those who have some occupation, majority are production and related workers or transport equipment operators and labourers.

A majority (58.75%) of the sample is unmarried. While 50 per cent of the sample (belonging to all levels of education) reside in rural areas, the remaining 50 per cent reside in urban areas of Cochin taluk.

Among the respondents, a majority (68%) are non-migrants. Among the migrants to Cochin, females are in a majority. More than half of the migrants were born in Cochin taluk and they have moved from one panchayat to another, or from one part of the corporation to another.

Food and Related Habits

A majority of the respondents, nearly 90 per cent, are non-vegetarians. They eat fish, egg and meat. More than half of the sample (51.86%) are punctual in taking food. A majority of the respondents do not smoke or consume alcohol. Also they do not chew tobacco or use narcotics.

Skills

Nearly half of the sample (49%) are skilled in cycling. However, a vast majority of the respondents do not know two-wheeler driving and car driving. A considerable proportion (41.86%) of the sample are able to use calculators. A majority of the respondents do not know typing. Only a negligible number of respondents are able to use computers.

Membership in Social Organizations

A large majority of the respondents (more than 75%) are not members of libraries, political parties, trade unions, recreation clubs or any other organizations.

Family Background

A majority (73%) of the respondents belong to medium or large families having household sizes ranging from 4-9 members.

Parents of a majority (more than 73%) of the respondents have not studied beyond SSLC. Fathers of the respondents are better qualified than that of their mothers. Illiteracy is more common among mothers than fathers.

Upward intergenerational educational mobility has occurred in the case of male as well as female respondents belonging to all levels of education except among illiterates. Upward educational mobility was found to increase as the level of education goes up both in the case of male and female respondents. The incidents of no mobility and downward mobility were found to decrease as the level of education goes up both in the case of male as well as female respondents.

In terms of occupation, a majority (57.86%) of the respondents' fathers belong to the categories of production and related workers, transport equipment operators and labourers, farmers, fishermen or sales workers.

A majority (nearly 85%) of the respondents' mothers are housewives. A vast majority, 91.29 per cent of the respondents do not have any relative or family member employed abroad.

In terms of annual income of the family, a majority of the respondents (64% of the sample) belonged to either low income (Rs. 8,000-12,000 per annum) or lower middle income (Rs. 12,000-24,000 per annum) groups.

A large majority of the sample (nearly 90%) belonged to families with houses of their own.

A majority of the respondents (63.57% of the sample) belonged to families owning land. By and large, these land holdings are small, i.e. less than 10 cents.

The living standard, in terms of facilities available at the household, was found to be 'lower' (< 25 in the Living Standard Index) in the case of families of a majority (60.86% of the sample) of respondents.

Savings-Investment Credit

A majority of the respondents (more than 66% of the sample) do not have any bank account. More than 79 per cent of them are not members of chit funds organization. More than 82 per cent of them do not hold any share/bond/debentures. A vast majority (89% of the sample) of them are not insurance policy holders. A majority (77.86%) of the respondents have not availed any loan.

Other General Information: Passport

A majority of the respondents (68.43%) do not have passports. Respondents who are passport holders (10.86% of the sample) belong to all levels of education.

Married Respondents

A majority of the respondents (59.14% of the sample) are unmarried.

At all levels of education, a higher proportion of females are married than that of male respondents.

In the case of a majority of the married respondents (76.57%) the source of information in choosing the marriage partner was either relative or marriage broker.

In the case of more than 55 per cent of the married respondents, parents have had the say in the selection of the marriage partner.

A majority (more than 77%) of the currently married male and female respondents got married after attaining the minimum age stipulated by the government.

A vast majority (91.61%) of the married respondents married from within their own caste. Among the married respondents 47.90 per cent reported that they have received/given dowry in the form of cash at the time of marriage. These respondents belonged to all levels of education.

A majority (77.62%) of the married respondents have given/ accepted dowry in the form of gold/cash at the time of marriage. These respondents belong to all levels of education.

A majority of the married respondents (82.52%) have children. Most of them have one or two children.

Birth control was adopted by a sizeable proportion (46.85%) of the currently married respondents. Most of these cases were observed at the lower levels (below SSLC) of education. Among the methods adopted for birth control, sterilization was found to be relatively more frequent.

A vast majority of the currently married respondents had not got triple antigen injections administered to their children.

Among the married respondents, 53.15 per cent reported that they never quarrel with their spouses.

Frequent quarrelling was reported by 3.85 per cent of the currently married whereas 30.42 per cent quarrelled with the spouse 'sometimes'.

Summary of Observations on the Profile of the Sample

Sample selected for the present study is by and large representative of the Indian society which is taking transition from tradition to modernity.

The respondents mostly belong to lower middle class and lower strata of society. A majority of respondents in the sample are non-migrants to Cochin engaged in skilled or unskilled manual labour. They know three or more languages including Malayalam. They are unmarried, non-vegetarians, without any habits. They are without any organised savings and are not members of social and political organizations. They know how to use calculators. A majority of the respondents belong to extended families and their parents have not studied even in the limited cases beyond SSLC. Majority of the respondents have studied in schools/colleges more than their fathers or mothers. Their fathers are skilled or unskilled manual labourers whereas their mothers are mostly housewives. They belong mostly to lower middle or low income households, owning the house in which they live, having small landholdings, belong to lower middle or low category even in terms of 'Living Standard Index'.

The married respondents have got married after they attained the minimum age for marriage and accepted arranged marriages, married within their caste, accepted the custom of dowry, adopted birth control measures and modern child care practices.

5

Levels of Education and Modernity in Terms of Attitudes

In the previous chapter, a general description of the characteristics of respondents in the sample was presented. Demographic particulars, food and nutritional habits, skills, membership in social organisations, family background of the respondents as well as details of married respondents were discussed.

The present chapter discusses the role of formal education in bringing about attitudinal modernity. Illiterates and others with different levels of education are the respondents.

This chapter is organised in three sections. Section I deals with levels of education and modernity in terms of attitudes. In Section II, critical levels of education with reference to modernity in terms of attitudes are examined. In Section III, the relationship between levels of education and modernity in terms of attitudes by different intervening variables is analysed. The plan of analysis followed in this chapter is as follows.

In Section I, relationship between levels of education and modernity in terms of attitudes is subjected to analysis, separately for modernity in 8 areas of life, 5 dimensions, and general modernity.

Using mean and standard deviation, attitudinal modernity scores of different levels of education and illiterate are compared descriptively.

Wherever the mean modernity scores are observed to be different across levels of education, one-way analysis of variance is followed in order to verify the significance of such differences.

Wherever significant mean differences are observed, through one way analysis of variance, multiple range test is followed using Duncan procedure with a purpose of identifying the critical level, if any, of education in the relationship between levels of education and modernity in terms of attitudes. This analysis is presented in Section II of this chapter.

Two-way ANOVA is used to examine the given relationship between levels of education and modernity in terms of attitudes, when one or the other intervening variable is introduced. In the case of three intervening variables—income, occupation, and exposure to mass media—analysis of representative cases is followed. This difference in the analysis is due to the paucity of adequate observations in the appropriate categories of these variables. These analyses are presented in Section III of this chapter.

I. Levels of Education and Modernity in terms of Attitudes

For the present study, data pertaining to modernity in terms of attitudes of the respondents were collected through an attitude scale consisting of 112 statements. Details of the procedure of construction of the scale and methods of scoring have been discussed in Chapter I. However, it is recalled here that modernity is measured in terms of attitudes in the following areas of human life:

1. Education,
2. Employment,
3. Marriage and family,
4. Religious life,
5. Political life,
6. Social life,
7. Health and hygiene, and
8. Economic life.

Modernity is measured with respect to the following Dimensions:

1. Change proneness and openness to new experiences and innovations,
2. Scientific orientation (with an emphasis on rationality),
3. Democratic orientation,

4. Secular orientation, and
5. Achievement orientation.

In a composite way General Modernity is measured covering All Areas of Life and All Dimensions.

Based on the attitude statements, modernity scores were obtained for all the 700 respondents. Each respondent obtained 14 separate modernity scores, i.e. for 8 Areas of life, 5 Dimensions and a 'General Modernity Score' based on all the 112 items in the scale.

General Modernity

The hypothesis set for the present study in the context of general modernity is stated as follows:

"There is no significant relationship between levels of education and general modernity in terms of attitudes of individual respondents."

As a first step towards testing the above hypothesis, mean and standard deviation of modernity scores were calculated for each level of education. The figures thus obtained are presented in Table 5.1.

Table 5.1: Modernity Scores—General Modernity by Levels of Education

Level of Education	*Mean*	*Standard Deviation*	*N*
Illiterate	5.9334	0.8350	100
Lower Primary	6.1385	0.7984	100
Upper Primary	6.2552	0.8579	100
SSLC	7.2392	0.9280	100
PDC	7.5436	0.8956	100
Graduate	7.7294	0.8428	100
PG and Professional	7.9613	0.7889	100
Total Sample	6.9715	1.1506	700

It may be observed from Table 5.1 that among all levels of education, the Illiterate level has the lowest mean score, i.e. 5.9334 on general modernity, whereas the highest mean score of 7.9613 is at the PG and Professional level.

Further, it may be noted that the mean scores gradually increase from Illiterate to PG and Professional level through SSLC.

An important observation to be noted is the sudden spurt in the mean modernity score from 6.2552 at the UP level to 7.2392 at the SSLC level of education.

The mean modernity score for the whole sample is lower than those for the sub-samples at and beyond the SSLC level of education, while it is higher than those for the Upper Primary and lower levels of education.

Since the mean values of modernity scores of all levels of education are found to be different, it is clear that there is difference between levels of education in terms of general modernity.

In order to know whether these observed differences are significant, one way analysis of variance is followed. Figures thus obtained are presented in Table 5.2.

Table 5.2: One way Analysis of Variance—Modernity Score by Level of Education

Source	*DF*	*Sum of Squares*	*Mean Squares*	*F Ratio*	*F Probability*
Between Groups	6	423.7688	70.6281	97.5794	0.0000
Within Groups	693	501.5944	0.7238		
Total	699	925.3632			

It may be observed from Table 5.2 that the calculated value of *F*-ratio is 97.5794. while the table value of *F* qualifying for significance at 6 and 693 degrees of freedom is 3.74, the calculated value is much greater.

Inference

From the above analysis, it may be inferred that the observed differences between different levels of education, with reference to General Modernity are significant.

Hence, the null hypothesis set for the present study is rejected. The alternative hypothesis accepted is as follows:

> "There is significant relationship between Levels of Education and General Modernity in terms of attitudes of individual respondents."

Modernity in terms of Attitudes in the Area of Life 'Education'

The sub-hypothesis set for the present study in terms of attitudes in the Area of Life 'Education' is stated as follows:

> "There is no significant relationship between levels of education and modernity in terms of attitudes in the Area of Life Education of individual respondents."

As a first step towards testing the above hypothesis, mean and standard deviation of modernity scores were calculated for each level of education. Figures thus obtained are presented in Table 5.3.

Table 5.3: Distribution of Modernity Scores in the Area of Education by Levels of Education

Level of Education	*Mean*	*Standard Deviation*	*N*
Illiterate	7.4330	1.2262	100
Lower Primary	7.0661	1.1358	100
Upper Primary	7.2441	1.1836	100
SSLC	8.0182	1.2529	100
PDC	8.5365	0.9724	100
Graduate	8.8689	1.0335	100
PG and Professional	9.1684	0.8415	100
Table Sample	8.0479	1.3404	700

It may be observed from Table 5.3 that among all levels of education, the LP level has the lowest mean score, i.e. 7.0661 on modernity in the Area of Life 'Education' whereas the highest mean score of 9.1684 is at the PG and Professional level.

Further the mean scores gradually increase from LP to PG and Professional level, through SSLC. It is to be noted that the mean score of Illiterate 7.4330 is greater than even that of UP level. It is possible that the illiterates have better expectations from education and thus more favourable attitude regarding the value of education.

An important observation to be noted from Table 5.3 is the sudden spurt in the mean modernity score from 7.2441 at the UP level, to 8.0182 at the SSLC level of education.

Since the mean values of modernity scores of all levels of education are found to be different, it is clear that there is difference between levels of education in terms of modernity in the Area of Life 'Education'.

In order to know whether these observed differences are significant, one way analysis of variance is followed and F ratio is calculated. Figures thus obtained are presented in Table 5.4.

Table 5.4: Oneway Analysis of Variance Modernity Score in the Area of Education by Level of Education

Source	*DF*	*Sum of Squares*	*Mean Squares*	*F Ratio*	*F Probability*
Between Groups	6	415.7201	69.2867	57.1527	0.0000
Within Groups	693	840.1299	1.2123		
Total	699	1255.8501			

The table value of F qualifying for significance at 6 and 693 degrees of freedom is 3.74. The calculated value, as may be observed from Table 5.4 is 57.1527. This is much greater than the table value.

Inference

From the above analysis, it may be inferred that observed differences between different levels of education, with reference to modernity in the area of life education are significant.

Hence, the null hypothesis set for the present study in the context of modernity in terms of attitudes in the Area of Life 'Education' is rejected. The alternative hypothesis accepted is as follows:

> "There is significant relationship between levels of education and modernity in terms of attitudes in the Area of life Education."

Modernity in terms of Attitudes in the Area of Life Employment

The sub-hypothesis in the context of modernity in terms of attitudes in the Area of Life 'Employment' is stated as follows:

"There is no significant relationship between levels of education and modernity in terms of attitudes in the Area of Life 'Employment' of individual respondents."

As a first step towards testing the above hypothesis, mean and standard deviation of modernity scores were calculated for each level of education. Figures thus obtained are presented in Table 5.5.

Table 5.5: Distribution of Modernity Scores in the Area of Employment by Levels of Education

Level of Education	*Mean*	*Standard Deviation*	*N*
Illiterate	5.7400	1.3257	100
Lower Primary	5.8356	1.2879	100
Upper Primary	5.8990	1.1348	100
SSLC	7.3124	1.4470	100
PDC	7.5464	1.4707	100
Graduate	7.7994	1.4952	100
PG and Professional	7.8573	1.2506	100
Total Sample	6.8557	1.6230	700

It may be observed from Table 5.5 that among all levels of education, the illiterate level has the lowest mean score, i.e. 5.7400 on modernity in terms of attitudes in the Area of Life 'Employment' whereas the highest mean score, i.e. 7.8573 is at the PG and Professional level.

Further the mean scores gradually increase from Illiterate to PG and Professional level, through SSLC.

An important observation to be noted is the sudden spurt in the mean modernity score from 5.8990 at the UP level to 7.3124 at the SSLC level of education.

Since the mean values of modernity scores of all levels of education are found to be different, it is clear that there is difference between levels of education in terms of modernity in the Area of Life 'Employment'.

In order to know whether these observed differences are significant, oneway analysis of variance is followed and *F* ratio is calculated. Figures thus obtained are presented in Table 5.6.

Table 5.6: Oneway Analysis of Variance Modernity Score in the Area of Employment by Level of Education

Source	*DF*	*Sum of Squares*	*Mean Squares*	*F Ratio*	*F Probability*
Between Groups	6	578.0353	96.3392	52.8492	0.0000
Within Groups	693	1263.2741	1. 8229		
Total	699	1255.8501			

It may be observed from Table 5.6 that the calculated value of *F*-ratio is 52.8492. While the table value of *F* at 6 and 693 degrees of freedom is 3.74, the calculated value is greater than the latter.

Inference

From the above analysis, it may be inferred that observed differences between different levels of education, with reference to modernity in the Area of Life 'Employment' are significant.

Hence, the null hypothesis set for the present study in the context of modernity in terms of attitudes in the Area of Life 'Employment' is rejected. The alternative hypothesis accepted is as follows.

> "There is significant relationship between levels of education and modernity in terms of attitudes in the Area of Life 'Employment'."

Modernity in terms of Attitudes in the Area of 'Marriage and Family'

The sub-hypothesis in the context of modernity in terms of attitudes in the Area of 'Marriage and Family' is stated as follows:

> "There is no significant relationship between levels of education and modernity in terms of attitudes in the Area of Life, 'Marriage and Family' of individual respondents."

As a first step towards testing the above hypothesis, Mean and Standard Deviation of modernity scores were calculated for each level of education. Figures thus obtained are presented in Table 5.7.

Table 5.7: Distribution of Modernity Scores in the Area of Marriage and Family by Levels of Education

Level of Education	*Mean*	*Standard Deviation*	*N*
Illiterate	4.8654	1.1900	100
Lower Primary	5.2720	1.0295	100
Upper Primary	5.2782	1.0501	100
SSLC	6.1967	1.1312	100
PDC	6.6303	1.3687	100
Graduate	6.7753	1.2551	100
PG and Professional	7.2696	1.4992	100
Total Sample	6.0411	1.4855	700

It may be observed from Table 5.7 that among all levels of education, the illiterate level has the lowest mean score, i.e. 4.8654 on modernity in terms of attitudes in the Area of 'Marriage and Family', whereas the highest mean score, i.e. 7.2696 is at the PG and Professional level. Further the mean scores gradually increase from illiterate to PG and professional level through SSLC.

An important observation to be noted is the sudden spurt in the mean modernity score from 5.2782 at the UP level, to 6.1967 at the SSLC level of education.

Since the mean values of modernity scores of all levels of education are found to be different, it is clear that there is difference between levels of education in terms of modernity in the Area of Life, 'Marriage and Family'.

In order to know whether these observed differences are significant, oneway analysis of variance is followed and *F*-ratio is calculated. Figures thus obtained are presented in Table 5.8.

Table 5.8: Oneway Analysis of Variance Modernity Score in the Area of Marriage and Family by Level of Education

Source	*DF*	*Sum of Squares*	*Mean Squares*	*F-Ratio*	*F Probability*
Between Groups	6	497.5568	82.9261	54.9984	0.0000
Within Groups	693	1044.8987	1.5078		
Total	699	1542.4555			

It may be observed from Table 5.8 that the calculated value of *F*-ratio is 54.9984 while the table value of *F* qualifying for significance at 6 and 693 degrees of freedom is 3.74 the calculated value is much greater.

Inference

From the above analysis, it may be inferred that observed differences between different levels of education, with reference to modernity in terms of attitudes in the Area of Life, 'Marriage and Family' of individual respondents are significant.

Hence the null hypothesis set for the present study in the context of modernity in terms of attitudes in the Area of Life, 'Marriage and Family' is rejected. The alternative hypothesis accepted is as follows:

> "There is significant relationship between levels of education and modernity in terms of attitudes in the Area of Life, Marriage and Family of individual respondents."

Modernity in terms of Attitudes in the Area of 'Religious Life'

The sub-hypothesis in the context of modernity in terms of attitudes in the Area of Religious Life is stated as follows:

> "There is no significant relationship between levels of education and modernity in terms of attitudes in the Area of Life 'Religious Life' of individual respondents."

As a first step towards testing the above hypothesis, mean and standard deviation of modernity scores were calculated for each level of education. Figures thus obtained are presented in Table 5.9.

Table 5.9: Distribution of Modernity Scores in the Area of Religious Life by Levels of Education

Level of Education	*Mean*	*Standard Deviation*	*N*
Illiterate	4.8898	2.2380	100
Lower Primary	5.3561	2.3124	100
Upper Primary	5.2922	2.3735	100
SSLC	7.3414	2.0694	100
PDC	7.4515	2.3503	100
Graduate	7.3580	2.1972	100
PG and Professional	7.9010	1.9513	100
Total Sample	6.5129	2.5020	700

It may be observed from Table 5.9 that among all levels of education, the Illiterate level has the lowest mean score, i.e. 4.8898 on modernity in terms of attitudes in the Area of 'Religious Life', whereas the highest mean score, i.e. 7.9010 is at the PG and Professional level.

Further the mean scores gradually increase from Illiterate to PG and Professional level, through SSLC. However, the mean score of UP level is slightly lower than that of LP.

An important observation to be noted is the sudden spurt in the mean modernity score from 5.2922 at the UP level, to 7.3414 at the SSLC level of education.

Since the mean values of modernity scores of all levels of education are found to be different, it is clear that there is difference between levels of education in terms of modernity, in terms of attitudes, in the Area of 'Religious Life'.

In order to know whether these observed differences are significant, oneway analysis of variance is followed and *F*-ratio is calculated. Figures thus obtained are presented in Table 5.10.

Table 5.10: Oneway Analysis of Variance Modernity Score in the Area of 'Religious Life' by Level of Education

Source	*DF*	*SUM of Squares*	*Mean Squares*	*F-Ratio*	*F Probability*
Between Groups	6	967.1159	161.186C	32.7701	0.0000
Within Groups	693	3408.6562	4.9187		
Total	699	4375.7721			

It may be observed from Table 5.10 that the calculated value of *F*-ratio is 32.7701 while the table value of *F* qualifying for significance at 6 and 693 degrees of freedom is 3.74. The calculated value is much greater.

Inference

From the above analysis, it may be inferred that observed differences between different levels of education, with reference to modernity in terms of attitudes in the Area of 'Religious Life' of individual respondents are significant.

Hence, the null hypothesis set for the present study in the context of modernity in terms of attitudes in the Area of 'Religious Life' is rejected. The alternative hypothesis accepted is as follows:

> "There is significant relationship between levels of education and modernity in terms of attitudes in the Area of 'Religious Life' of individual respondents."

Modernity in terms of Attitudes in the Area of 'Political Life'

The sub-hypothesis in the context of modernity in terms of attitudes in the Area of 'Political Life' is stated as follows:

> "There is no significant relationship between levels of education and modernity in terms of attitudes in the Area of 'Political Life' of individual respondents."

As a first step towards testing the above hypothesis, mean and standard deviation of modernity scores were calculated for each level of education. Figures thus obtained are presented in Table 5.11.

Table 5.11: Distribution of Modernity Scores in the Area of 'Political Life' by Levels of Education

Level of Education	*Mean*	*Standard Deviation*	*N*
Illiterate	7.5708	0.9668	100
Lower Primary	7.3354	0.9786	100
Upper Primary	7.4995	0.9734	100
SSLC	7.9662	1.0136	100
PDC	8.2149	0.8275	100
Graduate	8.1431	0.8325	100
PG and Professional	8.1682	0.7107	100
Total Sample	7.8426	0.96370	700

It may be observed from Table 5.11 that among all levels of education, the Lower Primary level has the lowest mean score, i.e. 7.3354 on modernity in terms of attitudes in the Area of 'Political Life', whereas the highest mean score, i.e. 8.1682 is at the PG and Professional level.

Further, the mean scores gradually increase from LP to PG and

Professional level, through SSLC. Illiterate level has a mean score which is greater than that of LP and UP.

An important observation to be noted is the sudden spurt in the mean modernity score from 7.4995 at the UP level, to 7.9662 at the SSLC level of education. It is also to be noted that the lower levels (below SSLC) of education are clustering together in terms of their mean scores which is also lower than that of the mean score of the total sample. The mean scores at higher levels (including SSLC) are much closer to each other and are higher than the mean score of the total sample. This reflects a 'J' shaped distribution of modernity in the sample.

Since the mean values of modernity scores of all levels of education are found to be different, it is clear that there is difference between levels of education in terms of modernity in the Area of 'Political Life'.

In order to know whether these observed differences are significant, oneway analysis of variance is followed and *F*-ratio is calculated. Figures thus obtained are presented in Table 5.12.

Table 5.12: Oneway Analysis of Variance Modernity Score in the Area of 'Political Life' by Levels of Education

Source	*DF*	*Sum of Squares*	*Mean Squares*	*F Ratio*	*F Probability*
Between Groups	6	79.8990	13.3165	16.2111	0.0000
Within Groups	693	569.2595	0.8214		
Total	699	649.1586			

It may be observed from Table 5.12 that the calculated value of *F*-ratio is 16.2111 while the table value of *F* qualifying for significance at 6 and 693 degrees of freedom is 3.74, the calculated value is much greater.

Inference

From the above analysis, it may be inferred that observed differences between different levels of education, with reference to modernity in terms of attitudes in the Area of 'Political Life' of individual respondents are significant.

Hence, the null hypothesis set for the present study in the context of modernity in terms of attitudes in the Area of 'Political Life' is rejected. The alternative hypothesis accepted is as follows:

> "There is significant relationship between levels of education and modernity in terms of attitudes in the Area of 'Political Life' of individual respondents."

Modernity in terms of Attitudes in the Area of 'Social Life'

The sub-hypothesis in the context of modernity in terms of attitudes in the Area of 'Social Life' is stated as follows:

> "There is no significant relationship between levels of education and modernity in terms of attitudes in the Area of 'Social Life' of individual respondents."

As a first step towards testing the above hypothesis, mean and standard deviation of modernity scores were calculated for each level of education. Figures thus obtained are presented in Table 5.13.

Table 5.13: Distribution of Modernity Scores in the Area of 'Social Life' by Levels of Education

Level of Education	*Mean*	*Standard Deviation*	*N*
Illiterate	4.9114	1.5690	100
Lower Primary	5.1793	1.5450	100
Upper Primary	5.1522	1.7839	100
SSLC	6.7312	1.8131	100
PDC	7.3610	1.8637	100
Graduate	7.6078	1.9777	100
PG and Professional	8.0134	1.8411	100
Table Sample	6.4223	2.1472	700

It may be observed from Table 5.13 that among all levels of education, the Illiterate level has the lowest mean score, i.e. 4.9114 on modernity in terms of attitudes in the Area of Social Life, whereas the highest mean score, i.e. 8.0134 is at the PG and Professional level.

Further the mean scores gradually increase from Illiterate to PG and professional level, through SSLC. However, the mean score at UP level is slightly lower than that of LP. An important observation to be noted is the sudden spurt in the mean modernity score from 5.1522 at the UP level to 6.7312 at the SSLC level of education.

Since the mean values of modernity scores of all levels of education are found to be different, it is clear that there is difference between levels of education in terms of modernity in the Area of 'Social Life'.

In order to know whether these observed differences are significant, oneway analysis of variance is followed and *F*-ratio is calculated. Figures thus obtained are presented in Table 5.14.

It may be observed from Table 5.14 that the calculated value of *F*-ratio is 54.6810 while the table value of *F* qualifying for significance at 6 and 693 degrees of freedom is 3.74. The calculated value is much greater.

Table 5.14: Oneway Analysis of Variance Modernity Score in the Area of 'Social Life' by Levels of Education

Source	*DF*	*Sum of Squares*	*Mean Squares*	*F-Ratio*	*F Probability*
Between Groups	6	1035.4864	172.5811	54.6810	0.0000
Within Groups	693	2187.2056	3.1561		
Total	699	3222.6920			

Inference

From the above analysis, it may be inferred that observed differences between different level of education, with reference to modernity in terms of attitudes in the Area of 'Social Life' of individual respondents are significant.

Hence, the null hypothesis set for the study in the context of modernity in terms of attitudes in the Area of 'Social Life' is rejected. The alternative hypothesis accepted is as follows:

> "There is significant relationship between levels of education and modernity in terms of attitudes in the Area of 'Social Life' of Individual respondents."

Modernity in terms of Attitudes in the Area of 'Health and Hygiene'

The sub-hypothesis in the context of modernity in terms of attitudes in the Area of 'Health and Hygiene' is stated as follows:

> "There is no significant relationship between levels of education and modernity in terms of attitudes in the Area of 'Health and Hygiene' of individual respondents."

As a first step towards testing the above hypothesis, mean and standard deviation of modernity scores were calculated for each level of education. Figures thus obtained are presented in Table 5.15.

Table 5.15: Distribution of Modernity Scores in the Area of 'Health and Hygiene' by Levels of Education

Level of Education	*Mean*	*Standard Deviation*	*N*
Illiterate	6.7788	1.3176	100
Lower Primary	6.9982	1.1781	100
Upper Primary	7.2639	1.1250	100
SSLC	7.8956	1.0659	100
PDC	8.0268	0.9883	100
Graduate	8.2425	0.8435	100
PG and Professional	8.4339	0.7441	100
Total Sample	7.6628	1.2074	700

It may be observed from Table 5.15 that among all levels of education, the Illiterate level has the lowest mean score, i.e. 6.7788, on modernity in terms of attitudes in the Area of 'Health and Hygiene' whereas the highest mean score, i.e. 8.4339 is at the PG and Professional level.

Further the mean scores gradually increase from Illiterate to PG and Professional level, through SSLC. An important observation to be noted is the sudden spurt in the mean modernity score from 7.2639 at the UP level to 7.8956 at the SSLC level of education.

Since the mean values of modernity scores of all levels of education are found to be different, it is clear that there is difference between levels of education in terms of modernity in the Area of 'Health and Hygiene'. In order to know whether these observed differences are significant, oneway analysis of variance is followed and *F*-ratio is calculated. Figures thus obtained are presented in Table 5.16.

It may be observed from Table 5.16 that the calculated value of *F*-ratio is 37.5446 while the table value of *F* qualifying for significance at 6 and 693 degrees of freedom is 3.74. The calculated value is much greater.

Table 5.16: Oneway Analysis of Variance Modernity Score in the Area of 'Health and Hygiene' by Level of Education

Source	*D F*	*Sum of Squares*	*Mean Squares*	*F-Ratio*	*F Probability*
Between Groups	6	249.9730	41.6622	37.5446	0.0000
Within Groups	693	769.00181	1.1097		
Total	699	1018.9748			

Inference

From the above analysis, it may be inferred that observed differences between different levels of education, with reference to modernity in terms of attitudes in the Area of 'Health and Hygiene' of individual respondents are significant.

Hence, the null hypothesis set for the present study in the context of modernity in terms of attitudes in the Area of 'Health and Hygiene' is rejected. The alternative hypothesis accepted is as follows:

> "There is significant relationship between levels of education and modernity in terms of attitudes in the Area of 'Health and Hygiene' of individual respondents."

Modernity in terms of Attitudes in the Area of 'Economic Life'

The sub-hypothesis in the context of modernity in terms of attitudes in the Area of 'Economic Life' is stated as follows:

> "There is no significant relationship between levels of Education and Modernity in terms of attitudes in the Area of 'Economic Life' of individual respondents."

As a first step towards testing the above hypothesis, mean and standard deviation of modernity scores were calculated for each level of education. Figures thus obtained are presented in Table 5.17.

It may be observed from Table 5.17 that among all levels of education, the Illiterate level has the lowest mean score, i.e. 6,1773 on modernity in terms of attitudes in the area of 'Economic Life' whereas the highest mean score, i.e. 8.1321 is at the Graduate level.

Further the mean scores gradually increase from Illiterate to Graduate level through SSLC. The Mean score at the PG and Professional level is smaller than that of Graduate level. This may be because the PG and Professional educated respondents are economically better off and do not run their life on shoestring budgets.

An important observation to be noted is the sudden spurt in the mean modernity score from 6.9750 at the UP level to 7.3904 at the SSLC level of education.

Table 5.17: Distribution of Modernity Scores in the Area of 'Economic Life' by Levels of Education

Level of Education	*Mean*	*Standard Deviation*	*N*
Illiterate	6.1773	2.3007	100
Lower Primary	6.4419	2.6336	100
Upper Primary	6.9750	2.2374	100
SSLC	7.3904	1.9747	100
PDC	7.5361	2.2447	100
Graduate	8.1321	2.0907	100
PG and Professional	7.6967	2.1868	100
Total Sample	7.1928	2.3288	700

Since the mean values of modernity scores of all levels of education are found to be different, it is clear that there is difference between levels of education in terms of modernity in the Area of 'Economic Life'.

In order to know whether these observed differences are significant, oneway analysis of variance is followed and *F*-ratio is calculated. Figures thus obtained are presented in Table 5.18.

Table 5.18: Oneway Analysis of Variance Modernity Score in the Area of 'Economic Life' by Level of Education

Source	*DF*	*Sum of Squares*	*Mean Squares*	*F-Ratio*	*F Probability*
Between Groups	6	293.5603	48.9267	9.6950	0.0000
Within Groups	693	3497.2851	5.0466		
Total	699	3790.8454			

It may be observed from Table 5.18 that the calculated value of *F*- ratio is 9.6950 while the table value of *F* qualifying for significance at 6 and 693 degrees of freedom is 3.74. The calculated value is much greater.

Inference

From the above analysis, it may be inferred that observed differences between different levels of education, with reference to modernity in terms of attitudes in the Area of 'Economic Life' of individual respondents are significant.

Hence, the null hypothesis set for the present study in the context of modernity in terms of attitudes in the Area of 'Economic Life' is rejected. The alternative hypothesis accepted is as follows:

> "There is significant relationship between levels of education and modernity in terms of attitudes in the Area of 'Economic Life' of individual respondents."

Modernity in terms of Attitudes in the Dimension 'Change Proneness'

The sub-hypothesis in the context of modernity in terms of attitudes in the Dimension 'Change Proneness' is stated as follows:

> "There is no significant relationship between levels of education and modernity in terms of attitudes in the Dimension 'Change Proneness' of individual respondents."

As a first step towards testing the above hypothesis, mean and standard deviation of modernity scores were calculated for each level of education. Figures thus obtained are presented in Table 5.19.

It may be observed from Table 5.19 that among all levels of education, the UP level has the lowest mean score, i.e. 9.0875 on modernity in the Dimension 'Change Proneness' whereas the highest mean score, i.e. 9.2768 is at the PDC level. The mean scores, however, do not follow a clear ascending order, from Illiterate to PG and Professional level.

Table 5.19: Distribution of Modernity Scores in the Dimension 'Change Proneness' by Levels of Education

Level of Education	*Mean*	*Standard Deviation*	*N*
Illiterate	9.1515	0.5524	100
Lower Primary	9.1455	0.4863	100
Upper Primary	9.0875	0.3945	100
SSLC	9.2253	0.6416	100
PDC	9.2768	0.4190	100
Graduate	9.1366	1.2530	100
PG and Professional	9.2338	1.2188	100
Total Sample	9.1796	0.7864	700

In order to know whether these observed differences are significant, oneway analysis of variance is followed and *F*-ratio is calculated. Figures thus obtained are presented in Table 5.20.

Table 5.20: Oneway Analysis of Variance Modernity Score in the Dimension 'Change Proneness' by Levels of Education

Source	*DF*	*Sum of Squares*	*Mean Squares*	*F-Ratio*	*F Probability*
Between Groups	6	2.6756	0.4459	0.7193	0.6342
Within Groups	693	429.6485	0.6200		
Total	699	432.3242			

It may be observed from Table 5.20 that the calculated value of *F* ratio is 0.7193 while the table value of *F* qualifying for significance at 6 and 693 degrees of freedom is 3.74. The calculated value is much smaller.

Inference

From the above analysis, it may be inferred that observed differences between different levels of education, with reference to modernity in the Dimension 'Change Proneness' are not significant.

Hence, the null hypothesis set for the present study in the context of modernity in terms of attitudes in the Dimension 'Change Proneness' is accepted, i.e.

> "There is no significant relationship between levels of education and modernity in terms of attitudes in the Dimension 'Change Proneness' of individual respondents."

Modernity in terms of Attitudes in the Dimension 'Scientific Orientation'

The sub-hypothesis in the context of modernity in the Dimension 'Scientific Orientation' is stated as follows:

> "There is no significant relationship between levels of education and modernity in terms of attitudes in the Dimension 'Scientific Orientation' of individual respondents."

As a first step towards testing the above hypothesis, mean and standard deviation of modernity scores were calculated for each level of education. Figures thus obtained are presented in Table 5.21.

Table 5.21: Distribution of Modernity Scores in the Dimension 'Scientific Orientation' by Levels of Education

Level of education	*Mean*	*Standard Deviation*	*N*
Illiterate	4.5070	0.8590	100
Lower Primary	4.6424	1.0410	100
Upper Primary	4.9051	1.1661	100
SSLC	5.7913	1.1443	100
PDC	5.9873	1.3396	100
Graduate	6.0692	1.4748	100
PG and Professional	6.2306	1.3432	100
Total Sample	5.4475	1.3845	700

It may be observed from Table 5.21 that among all levels of education, the Illiterate level has the lowest mean score, i.e. 4.5070 on modernity in the Dimension 'Scientific Orientation' whereas the highest mean score, i.e. 6.2306 is at the PG and Professional level.

Further the mean scores gradually increase from Illiterate to PG and Professional level through SSLC. An important observation to be noted is the sudden spurt in the mean modernity score from 4.9051 at the UP level, to 5.7913 at the SSLC level of education.

Since the mean values of modernity scores of all levels of education are found to be different, it is clear that there is difference between levels of education in terms of modernity in the Dimension 'Scientific Orientation'. In order to know whether these observed differences are significant, oneway analysis of variance is followed and *F*-ratio is calculated. Figures thus obtained are presented in Table 5.22.

Table 5.22: Oneway Analysis of Variance Modernity Score in the Dimension 'Scientific Orientation' by Levels of Education

Source	*DF*	*Sum of Squares*	*Mean Squares*	*F-Ratio*	*F Probability*
Between Groups	6	323.6225	53.9371	36.7839	0.0000
Within Groups	693	1016.1608	1.4663		
Total	699	1339.7833			

It may be observed from Table 5.22 that the calculated value of *F*-ratio is 36.7839 while the table value of *F* qualifying for significance at 6 and 693 degrees of freedom is 3.74. The calculated value is much greater.

Inference

From the above analysis, it may be inferred that observed differences between different levels of education, with reference to modernity in terms of attitudes in the Dimension 'Scientific Orientation' of individual respondents are significant.

Hence, the null hypothesis set for the present study in the context of modernity in terms of attitudes in the Dimension 'Scientific Orientation' is rejected. The alternative hypothesis accepted is as follows:

> "There is significant relationship between levels of education and modernity in terms of attitudes in the Dimension 'Scientific Orientation' of individual respondents."

Modernity in terms of Attitudes in the Dimension 'Demographic Orientation'

The sub-hypothesis in the context of modernity in terms of attitudes in the Dimension 'Democratic Orientation' is stated as follows:

> "There is no significant relationship between levels of education and modernity in terms of attitudes in the Dimension 'Democratic Orientation' of individual respondents."

As a first step towards testing the above hypothesis, mean and standard deviation of modernity scores were calculated for each level of education. Figures thus obtained are presented in Table 5.23.

Table 5.23: Distribution of Modernity Scores in the Dimension 'Democratic Orientation' by Levels of Education

Level of education	*Mean*	*Standard Deviation*	*N*
Illiterate	5.5985	1.2243	100
Lower Primary	6.0238	1.1362	100
Upper Primary	6.0823	1.2064	100
SSLC	7.2727	1.3351	100
PDC	7.6995	1.0753	100
Graduate	7.8628	1.4533	100
PG and Professional	7.9984	1.5703	100
Total Sample	6.9340	1.5903	700

It may be observed from Table 5.23 that among all levels of education, the Illiterate level has the lowest mean score, i.e. 5.5985 on modernity in the Dimension 'Democratic Orientation' whereas the highest mean score, i.e. 7.9984 is at the PG and Professional level.

Further the mean scores gradually increase from Illiterate to PG and Professional level through SSLC.

An important observation to be noted is the sudden spurt in the mean modernity score from 6.0823 at the UP level to 7.2727 at the SSLC level of education.

Since the mean values of modernity scores of all levels of education are found to be different, it is clear that there is difference between levels of education in terms of modernity in the Dimension 'Democratic Orientation'.

In order to know whether these observed differences are significant, oneway analysis of variance is followed and F-ratio is calculated. Figures thus obtained are presented in Table 5.24.

It may be observed from Table 5.24 that the calculated value of F-ratio is 59.8485. While the table value of F qualifying for significance at 6 and 693 degrees of freedom is 3.74. The calculated value is much greater.

Table 5.24: Oneway Analysis of Variance Modernity Score in the Dimension 'Democratic Orientation' by Level of Education

Source	*DF*	*Sum of Squares*	*Mean Squares*	*F-Ratio*	*F Probability*
Between Groups	6	603.3934	100.5656	59.8485	0.0000
Within Groups	693	1164.4726	1.6803		
Total	699	1767.8661			

Inference

From the above analysis, it may be inferred that observed differences between different levels of education, with reference to modernity in terms of attitudes in the Dimension 'Democratic Orientation' of individual respondents are significant.

Hence, the null hypothesis set for the present study in the context of modernity in terms of attitudes in the Dimension 'Democratic Orientation' is rejected. The alternative hypothesis accepted is as follows:

> "There is significant relationship between levels of education and modernity in terms of attitudes in the Dimension 'Democratic Orientation' of individual respondents."

Modernity in terms of Attitudes in the Dimension 'Secular Orientation'

The sub-hypothesis in the context of modernity in terms of attitudes in the Dimension 'Secular Orientation' is stated as follows:

> "There is no significant relationship between levels of education and modernity in terms of attitudes in the Dimension 'Secular Orientation' of individual respondents."

As a first step towards testing the above hypothesis, mean and standard deviation of modernity scores were calculated for each level of education. Figures thus obtained are presented in Table 5.25.

Table 5.25: Distribution of Modernity Scores in the Dimension 'Secular Orientation' by Levels of Education

Level of Education	*Mean*	*Standard Deviation*	*N*
Illiterate	5.0204	1.6289	100
Lower Primary	5.1074	1.3683	100
Upper Primary	5.2206	1.5520	100
SSLC	6.7425	1.3293	100
PDC	7.4170	1.4902	100
Graduate	7.4349	1.7618	100
PG and Professional	7.9580	1.7487	100
Total Sample	6.4144	1.9480	700

It may be observed from Table 5.25 that among all levels of education, the Illiterate level has the lowest mean score, i.e. 5.0204 on modernity in the Dimension 'Secular Orientation' whereas the highest mean score, i.e. 7.9580 is at the PG and Professional level.

Further the mean scores gradually increase from Illiterate to PG and Professional level through SSLC.

An important observation to be noted is the sudden spurt in the mean modernity score from 5.2206 at the UP level to 6.7425 at the SSLC level of education.

Since the mean values of modernity scores of all levels of education are found to be different, it is clear that there is difference between levels of education in terms of modernity in the Dimension 'Secular Orientation'.

In order to know whether these observed differences are significant, oneway analysis of variance is followed and *F*-ratio is calculated. Figures thus obtained are presented in Table 5.26.

Table 5.26: Oneway Analysis of Variance Modernity Score in the Dimension 'Secular Orientation' by Level of Education

Source	*DF*	*Sum of Squares*	*Mean Squares*	*F-Ratio*	*F Probability*
Between Groups	6	961. 3605	160.2267	65.6540	0.0000
Within Groups	693	1691.2479	2.4405		
Total	699	2652.6084			

It may be observed from Table 5.26 that the calculated value of *F*-ratio is 5.6540 while the table value of *F* qualifying for significance at 6 and 693 degrees of freedom is 3.74. The calculated value is much greater.

Inference

From the above analysis, it may be inferred that observed differences between different levels of education, with reference to modernity in terms of attitudes in the Dimension 'Secular Orientation' of individual respondents are significant.

Hence the null hypothesis set for the present study in the context of modernity in terms of attitudes in the Dimension 'Secular Orientation' is rejected. The alternative hypothesis accepted is as follows:

> "There is significant relationship between levels of education and modernity in terms of attitudes in the Dimension 'Secular Orientation' of individual respondents."

Modernity in terms of Attitudes in the Dimension 'Achievement Orientation'

The sub-hypothesis in the context of modernity in terms of attitudes in the Dimension of 'Achievement Orientation' is stated as follows:

> "There is no significant relationship between levels of education and modernity in terms of attitudes in the Dimension 'Achievement Orientation' of individual respondents."

As a first step towards testing the above hypothesis, mean and standard deviation of modernity scores were calculated for each level of education. Figures thus obtained are presented in Table 5.27.

It may be observed from Table 5.27 that among all levels of education, the Illiterate level has the lowest mean score, i.e. 5.4007 on modernity in the Dimension 'Achievement Orientation' whereas the highest mean score, i.e. 7.2382 is at the PG and Professional level.

Table 5.27: Distribution of Modernity Scores in the Dimension 'Achievement Orientation' by Levels of Education

Level of Education	*Mean*	*Standard Deviation*	*N*
Illiterate	5.4007	1.1990	100
Lower Primary	5.4733	1.3478	100
Upper Primary	5.5253	1.1409	100
SSLC	6.7377	1.1258	100
PDC	7.0297	1.3755	100
Graduate	7.1343	1.5973	100
PG and Professional	7.2382	1.5898	100
Total Sample	6.3627	1.5609	700

Further the mean scores gradually increase from Illiterate to PG and Professional level through SSLC.

An important observation to be noted is the sudden spurt in the mean modernity score from 5.5253 at the UP level to 6.7377 at the SSLC level of education.

Since the mean values of modernity scores of all levels of education are found to be different, it is clear that there is difference between levels of education in terms of modernity in the Dimension 'Achievement Orientation'. In order to know whether these observed differences are significant, oneway analysis of variance is followed and *F*-ratio is calculated. Figures thus obtained are presented in Table 5.28.

Table 5.28: Oneway Analysis of Variance Modernity Score in the Dimension 'Achievement Orientation' by Level of Education

Source	*DF*	*Sum of Squares*	*Mean Squares*	*F-Ratio*	*F Probability*
Between Groups	6	436.4998	72.7500	39.8027	0.0000
Within Groups	693	1266.6411	1.8278		
Total	699	1703.1409			

It may be observed from Table 5.28 that the calculated value of *F*-ratio is 39.8027 while the table value of *F* qualifying for significance at 6 and 693 degrees of freedom is 3.74. The calculated value is much greater.

Inference

From the above analysis, it may be inferred that observed differences between different levels of education, with reference to modernity in terms of attitudes in the Dimension 'Achievement Orientation' of individual respondents are significant.

Hence, the null hypothesis set for the present study in the context of modernity in terms of attitudes in the Dimension 'Achievement Orientation' is rejected. The alternative hypothesis accepted is as follows:

> "There is significant relationship between levels of education and modernity in terms of attitudes in the Dimension 'Achievement Orientation' of individual respondents."

Cumulative Observations on the Analysis of the Relationship between Levels of Education and Modernity of the Total Sample in terms of 'Attitudes'

Results of the preceding analyses of the Relationship between Levels of Education and Modernity of the total sample, following oneway Analysis of Variance are summarised in Table 5.29.

Table 5.29: F-Ratios by Category of Modernity

Category of Modernity		*F-ratio*	*Probability*
General Modernity		97.5794	.0000
Areas of Life	1. Education	57.1527	.0000
	2. Employment	52.8492	.0000
	3. Marriage and Family	54.9984	.0000
	4. Religious Life	32.7701	.0000
	5. Political Life	16.2111	.0000
	6. Social Life	54.6810	.0000
	7. Health and Hygiene	37.5446	.0000
	8. Economic Life	9.6950	.0000
Dimensions	1. Change Proneness	0.7193	.6342
	2. Scientific Orientation	36.7839	.0000
	3. Democratic Orientation	59.8485	.0000
	4. Secular Orientation	65.6540	.0000
	5. Achievement Orientation	39.8027	.0000

It may be observed from Table 5.29 that the calculated value of *F*-ratio is greater than the table value of *F*, qualifying for significance at 6 and 693 degrees of freedom, in all cases including General Modernity, Modernity in all Areas of Life and Modernity in all Dimensions, except in the case of Dimension 'Change Proneness'.

The case of 'Change Proneness', therefore, turns out to be a deviation from the general trend. Researcher became curious enough to examine the reasons for the same. What follows is an extended analysis of data in this direction. The distribution of modernity scores, presented earlier in Table 5.19 may be recalled here.

It may be noted from Table 5.19 that the mean scores are different at each level of education and do not follow a clear ascending order from illiterate to PG and Professional levels as found in the case of other components of attitudinal modernity.

However, the mean scores are very close to each other. In fact, the difference between the lowest and highest mean scores is only 0.1893. It is important to understand here that attitudinal modernity in this dimension of 'Change Proneness' is fairly high in the sample as a whole (9.1796). In fact, it is uniform across levels of education as well as among illiterates. Obviously, the observed differences across levels of education are not significant, as found in the ANOVA (Table 5.20). The implication of this may be that increased exposure to formal education does not necessarily make a clear distinction between groups of individuals in terms of their 'Change Proneness'. One may even be tempted to conclude that schooling till the upper primary level of 7 years is likely to bring down 'Change Proneness' since the modernity scores decrease from Illiterate to upper primary level.

At the same time, it is likely that the influence of other modernizing forces like exposure to mass-media is equally strong or even stronger than formal education in developing 'Change Proneness' in individuals. In this context, data in Table 5.30 are of relevance.

It may be noted from Table 5.30 that regular users of radio, TV and Film are concentrated at the Illiterate and lower levels of education including the SSLC level. In other words, those who lack in formal education are the better users of radio, TV and film. Hence it is likely that the cumulative effects of additional years of exposure to formal

Table 5.30: Distribution of Respondents by Level of Education and Regular Use of Mass Media

Level of Education	*Category of Mass Media*		
	Radio	*Television*	*Film*
Illiterate	60	30	47
LP	47	32	39
UP	49	43	44
SSLC	32	24	15
PDC	29	27	5
Graduate	37	34	11
PG and Professional	30	35	13
Total	284	225	174
Percentage out of 700	40.57	32.14	24.86

education in developing 'Change Proneness' among individuals is balanced by regular use of mass media. This might be one possible reason for the proximity of mean modernity scores in 'Change Proneness'.

Another possible reason is that the sample drawn for the study represents a society which is itself characterised by 'Change Proneness'. It may be noted that readiness to accept new ideas and changes in social organisations has been reflected several times in the history of Kerala. Removal of untouchability, redistribution of land, early spread of Western education, free primary education to all children regardless of caste/creed, transition from joint to nuclear family, family planning, inter-caste marriages, etc., are some examples of changes welcomed by Kerala society. Seen in this way, the near parity of mean scores is a micro phenomenon representing a larger social reality.

Another explanation for a high score of modernity among illiterates and lower levels of educated respondents who are comparable with that of middle and higher levels of educated respondents can be traced to the nature of items used for testing 'Change Proneness'. It can be observed that most of the items relate to health and sanitation, marriage, women's status, and child rearing practices. At macro-level it is already observed that women's status in Kerala is high as compared to the rest of the regions in India. Fertility rate is comparable to the ones obtained in the developed parts of the world and health care system has attained a high degree of excellence. Hence the social context in which the respondents pass through their day-to-day existence may be surmised to have a winnowing influence on their attitudes towards the items that go to constitute 'Change Proneness'.

The foregoing explanations for the deviant results in 'Change Proneness' are speculative in nature and based on micro-level perspectives of Keralite society.

Inference

From the above observation, it may be inferred that there is significant difference between levels of education in terms of General Modernity, Modernity in all Areas of Life and Modernity in all the Dimensions, except 'Change Proneness'.

Hence, the null hypothesis is rejected in all the 13 out of 14 cases and alternate hypotheses are formulated. In the case of modernity (in terms of attitudes) for the Dimension 'Change Proneness', the null hypothesis is accepted. The new set of hypotheses accepted are as follows :

1. There is significant relationship between levels of education and 'General Modernity' or in terms of attitudes of individual respondents.
2. There is significant relationship between levels of education and Modernity in the Area of 'Education' in terms of attitudes of individual respondents.
3. There is significant relationship between levels of education and modernity in the Area of 'Employment' in terms of attitudes of individual respondents.
4. There is significant relationship between levels of education and modernity in the Area of 'Marriage and Family Life' in terms of attitudes of individual respondents.
5. There is significant relationship between levels of education and modernity in the Area of 'Religious Life' in terms of attitudes of individual respondents.
6. There is significant relationship between levels of education and modernity in the Area of 'Political Life' in terms of attitudes of individual respondents.

7. There is significant relationship between levels of education and modernity in the Area of 'Social Life' in terms of attitudes of individual respondents.
8. There is significant relationship between levels of education and modernity in the Area of 'Health and Hygiene' in terms of attitudes of individual respondents.
9. There is significant relationship between levels of education and modernity in the Area of 'Economic Life' in terms of attitudes of individual respondents.
10. There is no significant relationship between levels of education and modernity in the Dimension 'Change Proneness' in terms of attitudes of individual respondents.
11. There is significant relationship between levels of education and modernity in the Dimension 'Scientific Orientation' in terms of attitudes of individual respondents.
12. There is significant relationship between levels of education and modernity in the Dimension 'Democratic Orientation' in terms of the attitudes of individual respondents.
13. There is significant relationship between levels of education and modernity in the Dimension 'Secular Orientation' in terms of the attitudes of individual respondents.
14. There is significant relationship between levels of education and modernity in the Dimension 'Achievement Orientation' in terms of the attitudes of individual respondents.

II. Critical Levels of Education with Reference to Modernity in terms of Attitudes of the Total Sample

In the previous section, the relationship between levels of education and modernity in terms of attitudes of the total sample was examined, for all the components (Areas and Dimensions) of modernity. It is recalled that the mean modernity scores were different for all levels of education and Illiterates, by and large following an ascending order from Illiterate to PG and Professional Level of education. The differences observed in the mean modernity scores across levels of education were found to be significant for all components of modernity, except for 'Change Proneness'.

The above findings, however, do not reflect the pattern of differences in the mean modernity scores. It is to be known whether every mean is significantly different from every other. Also it is to be known whether the observed differences between some of the means are significant while others are not. In the context of the present study it is vital to identify whether there is any particular level of education that may turn out to be critical in terms of the significance of mean differences in modernity scores in terms of attitudes. An attempt has been made in this direction in identifying critical levels of education with reference to modernity in terms of attitudes, which is presented in this Section.

In order to examine the differences existing among a set of means, there are different statistical methods available. Among these procedures, for multiple comparisons among the means, it was decided to follow 'Duncan's Multiple Range Test' for the present study.

> "If we wish to determine which of the differences among these means are significant and which are not, the test procedure we suggest is Duncan's multiple range test" (Edwards, 1972 : 131).
>
> "After prolonged investigation of the numerous statistical procedures available, it was the author's opinion that Duncan's Range Test is the most appropriate" (McGuigan, 1965: 172).

By following Duncan's Multiple Range Test, as described by Edwards (1972:131-53), significantly different pairs of mean modernity scores were identified for all cases where the mean differences were significant (as revealed by one-way Analysis of Variance). From this analysis keeping Illiterate as the base, the critical level of education was identified for each component of modernity.

The procedure followed in doing so was to find out the first level of education (in an ascending order from Illiterate) where difference in the mean score on modernity in terms of attitudes begin to attain significance.

In other words, critical level of education is that minimum level of education required for individuals to reflect positively and significantly different score on modernity in terms of attitudes, from that of illiterates.

Critical Level of Education with Reference to 'General Modernity'

It was found through Analysis of Variance that there is significant difference between levels of education, with reference to 'General Modernity' in terms of attitudes of individual respondents. Multiple Range Test, using Duncan Procedure was followed in order to discover a level of education which may be the critical level at which the differences become statistically significant. The result thus obtained in the case of 'General Modernity' is presented in Table 5.31.

Table 5.31: Multiple Range Test: Duncan Procedure 'General Modernity' Score by Levels of Education

Mean	*Levels of Education*		*Levels of Education*						
			1	2	3	4	5	6	7
5.9334	Illiterate	1							
6.1385	LP	2							
6.2552	UP	3	*						
7.2392	SSLC	4	*	*	*				
7.5436	PDC	5	*	*	*	*			
7.7294	Graduate	6	*	*	*	*			
7.9613	PG and Professional	7	*	*	*	*	*		

N = 700

*Denotes pairs of groups significantly different at .05 level.

It may be observed from Table 5.31 that the mean values on 'General Modernity' follow an ascending order from Illiterate to PG and Professional level through SSLC.

As it can be observed from Table 5.31 though the mean value of LP level is greater than that of illiterate, the difference between the two levels is not significant. However, the mean difference between UP level and illiterate is significant. Similarly, all other levels above UP are also significantly different from illiterate level.

The mean difference between UP and LP level is not significant. Whereas all other levels of education above UP are significantly different from LP level in terms of mean score.

It may further be noted that all levels of education above UP are significantly different from UP level in terms of mean score.

It may also be noted that all levels of education above UP i.e. SSLC onwards are significantly different from illiterate, LP and UP levels.

It is clear from Table 5.31 that significant differences in the mean score on 'General Modernity' of different levels of education from that of illiterate begins at the UP level.

However, from SSLC level onwards there is change in the pattern of mean differences. It is observed that all levels of education above SSLC and SSLC are significantly different from that of illiterate, LP and UP levels in terms of mean values on 'General Modernity'.

It is inferred that Upper Primary is the minimum level of education, required for individuals to reflect significant difference from that of illiterate in terms of 'General Modernity'.

Finding

It is observed that Upper Primary is the critical level of education in the case of 'General Modernity'.

Critical Level of Education with reference to Modernity in the 'Area of Education'

Through Analysis of Variance it was found that there is significant difference between levels of education, with reference to modernity in the 'Area of Education'. Multiple range test, using Duncan procedure was followed in order to discover a level of education which may be the 'critical' level at which the differences become statistically significant. Results thus obtained are presented in Table 5.32.

Table 5.32: Multiple Range Test: Duncan Procedure, Modernity Scores in the 'Area of Education' by Levels of Education

Mean	*Levels of Education*		*Levels of Education*						
			2	3	1	4	5	6	7
7.0661	LP	2							
7.2441	UP	3							
7.4330	Illiterate	1	*						
8.0182	SSLC	4	*	*	*				
8.5365	PDC	5	*	*	*	*			
8.8689	Graduate	6	*	*	*	*	*		
9.1684	PG and Professional	7	*	*	*	*	*		

N = 700

*Denotes pairs of groups significantly different at .050 level.

It may be observed from Table 5.32 that the mean scores on modernity in the 'Area of Education' follow an ascending order from L P to PG and Professional level through SSLC. However, it is to be noted that the mean score of illiterate is greater than that of LP and UP levels.

The mean difference between LP and illiterate is significant whereas the mean difference between UP and illiterate is not significant.

Similarly, the mean difference between UP and LP level is not significant. All other levels of education above UP are significantly different from that of LP level in terms of mean score.

It may be noted that all levels of education above UP, i.e. SSLC onwards are significantly different from UP level in terms of mean score on modernity in the 'Area of Education'.

It may also be noted that all levels of education above UP, i.e. SSLC onwards are significantly different from illiterate, LP and UP levels in terms of mean score.

It is clear from Table 5.32 that significant differences in the mean scores on modernity in the 'Area of Education', of different levels of education begins at the SSLC level. All levels of education above SSLC and SSLC are significantly different from Illiterate, LP and UP levels of education in terms of mean scores on modernity in the 'Area of Education'.

It is inferred that SSLC is the minimum level of education, required for individuals to reflect significant difference from that of illiterate in terms of modernity in the 'Area of Education'.

Finding

It is thus clear that SSLC is the critical level of education in the case of modernity in the 'Area of Education'.

Critical Level of Education with reference to Modernity in the 'Area of Employment'

As it was found that levels of education differ significantly with reference to modernity in the 'Area of Employment', Multiple Range Test using Duncan Procedure was followed in order to discover a level of education which may be the critical level at which the differences become statistically significant. The result thus obtained is presented in Table 5.33.

It may be observed from Table 5.33 that the mean scores on modernity in the 'Area of Employment' follow an ascending order from illiterate to PG and Professional level, through SSLC.

As it is revealed in Table 5.33, though the mean score of LP level is greater than that of illiterate, the difference between the two levels is not significant. The mean difference between UP level and illiterate is also not significant. All other levels above UP are significantly different from illiterate level.

Table 5.33: Multiple Range Test: Duncan Procedure, Modernity Scores in the 'Area of Employment' by Levels of Education

Mean	*Levels of Education*		*Levels of Education*						
			1	2	3	4	5	6	7
5.7400	Illiterate	1							
5.8356	LP	2							
5.8990	UP	3							
7.3124	SSLC	4	*	*	*				
7.5464	PDC	5	*	*	*				
7.7994	Graduate	6	*	*	*	*			
7.8573	PG and Professional	7	*	*	*	*			

N = 700

*Denotes pairs of groups significantly different at .050 level.

The mean difference between UP and L P levels is not significant whereas all other levels of education above UP are significantly different from LP level in terms of mean score.

It may further be noted that all levels of education above UP are significantly different from UP level in terms of modernity score in the 'Area of Employment'.

It may also be noted that all levels of education above UP, i.e. SSLC onwards are significantly different from illiterate, LP and UP levels in terms of mean score.

It is clear from Table 5.33 that significant differences in the mean scores on modernity in the 'Area of Employment', of different levels of education from that of illiterate begins at the SSLC level. All levels of education above SSLC and SSLC are significantly different from that of illiterate, LP and UP levels in terms of mean scores on modernity in the 'Area of Employment'.

The SSLC level is followed by Graduate level of education in terms of a shift in the pattern of mean differences. It is inferred that SSLC is the minimum level of education, required for individuals to reflect significant difference from that of illiterate in terms of modernity in the 'Area of Employment'.

Finding

It is thus clear that SSLC is the critical level of education in the case of modernity in the 'Area of Employment'.

Critical Level of Education with Reference to Modernity in the Area of 'Marriage and Family'

Since levels of education were found to be different significantly with reference to modernity in the Area of 'Marriage and Family', Multiple Range Test using Duncan Procedure was followed in order to discover a level of education which may be the critical level at which the differences become statistically significant. The result thus obtained is presented in Table 5.34.

It may be observed from Table 5.34 that the mean scores on Modernity in the Area of 'Marriage and Family' follow an ascending order from illiterate to PG and Professional level through SSLC.

Table 5.34: Multiple Range Test: Duncan Procedure, Modernity Scores in the Area of 'Marriage and Family' by Levels of Education

Mean	*Levels of Education*		*Levels of Education*						
			1	2	3	4	5	6	7
4.8654	Illiterate	1							
5.2720	LP	2	*						
5.2782	UP	3	*						
6.1967	SSLC	4	*	*	*				
6.6303	PDC	5	*	*	*	*			
6.7753	Graduate	6	*	*	*	*			
7.2696	PG and Professional	7	*	*	*	*	*	*	

N = 700

*Denotes pairs of groups significantly different at .050 level.

As it is revealed from Table 5.34, the mean value of LP level is greater than that of illiterate, and the difference between the two levels is significant. The mean difference between UP level and illiterate is also significant. All other levels of education above UP are significantly different from the illiterate level.

It is to be noted that the mean difference between UP and LP levels is not significant. Whereas all other levels of education above UP are significantly different from LP level in terms of mean score.

It may further be noted that all levels of education above UP are significantly different from UP level in terms of mean modernity score.

It is clear from Table 5.34 that significant differences in the mean scores on Modernity in the Area of 'Marriage and Family', of different levels of education from that of Illiterate begins at the LP level.

However, from SSLC level onwards there is a change in the pattern of mean differences. It is observed that all levels of education above SSLC and SSLC are significantly different from that of illiterate, LP and UP levels in terms of mean scores on modernity in the area of 'Marriage and Family'.

It is inferred that lower primary is the minimum level of education required for individuals to reflect significant difference from that of illiterate in terms of Modernity score in the Area of 'Marriage and Family'.

Finding

It is thus clear that Lower Primary is the critical level of education, in the case of modernity in the Area of 'Marriage and Family'.

Critical Level of Education with Reference to Modernity in the Area of 'Religious Life'

Having found that levels of education differ significantly with reference to modernity in the Area of 'Religious Life', Multiple Range Test using Duncan procedure was followed in order to discover a level of education which may be the critical level at which the differences become statistically significant. Result thus obtained is presented in Table 5.35.

Table 5.35: Multiple Range Test: Duncan Procedure, Modernity Scores in the Area of 'Religious Life' by Levels of Education

Mean	*Levels of Education*		*Level of Education*						
			1	3	2	4	6	5	7
4.8898	Illiterate	1							
5.2922	UP	3							
5.3561	LP	2							
7.3414	SSLC	4	*	*	*				
7.3580	Graduate	6	*	*	*				
7.4515	PDC	5	*	*	*				
7.9010	PG and Professional	7	*	*	*				

N = 700

*Denotes pairs of groups significantly different at .050 level.

It may be observed from Table 5.35 that the mean scores on modernity in the Area of 'Religious Life' follow an ascending order from Illiterate to PG and Professional level, through SSLC, except in the case of LP and PDC levels. The mean score of LP is greater than that of UP and the mean score of PDC is greater than that of Graduate level of education.

It may be observed from Table 5.35, though the mean score of LP level is greater than that of Illiterate, the difference between the two levels is not significant. The mean difference between UP level and Illiterate is also not significant. All other levels above UP are significantly different from the Illiterate level.

Similarly, the mean difference between UP and LP levels is not significant, whereas all other levels of education above UP are significantly different from LP level in terms of mean score.

It may be noted that all levels of education above UP are significantly different from UP level in terms of modernity score.

It may also be noted that all levels of education above UP, i.e. SSLC onwards, are significantly different from Illiterate, LP and UP levels in terms of mean score.

It is clear from Table 5.35 that significant differences in the mean scores, on modernity in the Area of 'Religious Life', of different levels of education from that of Illiterate begins at SSLC level.

All levels of education above SSLC and SSLC are significantly different from Illiterate, LP and UP levels, in terms of mean scores on modernity in the Area of 'Religious Life'.

It is inferred that SSLC is the minimum level of education required for individuals to reflect significant difference from that of Illiterates in terms of modernity in the Area of 'Religious Life'.

Finding

It is clear that SSLC is the critical level of education in the case of modernity in the Area of 'Religious Life'.

Critical Level of Education with Reference to Modernity in the Area of 'Political Life'

Having found that levels of education differ significantly with reference to modernity in the area of 'Political Life', Multiple Range Test using Duncan Procedure was followed in order to discover a level of education which may be the critical level at which the differences become statistically significant. Result thus obtained is presented in Table 5.36.

Table 5.36: Multiple Range Test: Duncan Procedure, Modernity Scores in the Area of 'Political Life' by Levels of Education

Mean	*Levels of Education*		*Level of Education*						
			2	3	1	4	6	7	5
7.3354	LP	2							
7.4995	UP	3							
7.5708	Illiterate	1							
7.9662	SSLC	4	*	*	*				
8.1431	Graduate	6	*	*	*				
8.1682	PG and Professional	7	*	*	*				
8.2149	PDC	5	*	*	*				

N = 700

*Denotes pairs of groups significantly different at .050 level.

It may be observed from Table 5.36 that the mean score of Illiterate is greater than UP. However, from LP level onwards the mean scores follow an ascending order till PG and Professional level through SSLC, with an exception of PDC.

As it is revealed in Table 5.36, though the mean value of illiterate level is greater than that of LP, the difference between the two levels is not significant. The mean difference between UP level and illiterate is also not significant. All other levels above UP are significantly different from the illiterate level.

Similarly, the mean difference between UP and LP levels is not significant, whereas all other levels of education above UP are significantly different from LP level in terms of mean score.

It may further be noted that all levels of education above UP are significantly different from UP level in terms of modernity score in the Area of 'Political Life'. It may also be noted that all levels of education above UP, i.e. SSLC onwards are significantly different from illiterate, LP and UP levels in terms of mean score.

It is clear from Table 5.36 that significant differences in the mean scores on modernity in the Area of 'Political Life', of different levels of education from that of Illiterate begins at the SSLC level.

All levels of education above SSLC and SSLC are significantly different from that of illiterate, LP and UP levels in terms of mean scores on modernity in the Area of 'Political Life'.

It is inferred that SSLC is the minimum level of education required for individuals to reflect significant difference from illiterate in terms of Modernity in the Area of 'Political Life'.

Finding

It is clear that SSLC is the critical level of education, in the case of modernity in the Area of 'Political Life'.

Critical Level of Education with Reference to Modernity in the Area of 'Social Life'

As it was found that levels of education differ significantly with reference to modernity in the Area of 'Social Life', Multiple Range Test using Duncan Procedure was followed in order to discover a level of education which may be the critical level at which the differences become statistically significant. The result thus obtained is presented in Table 5.37.

It may be observed from Table 5.37 that the mean scores on modernity in the Area of 'Social Life' follow an ascending order from illiterate to PG and Professional level through SSLC except in the case of LP level. The mean score at the LP level is greater than that of UP.

As it is revealed from Table 5.37, though the mean score of LP levei is greater than that of illiterate, the difference between the two levels is not significant. The mean difference between UP level and illiterate is also not significant. Whereas all other levels above UP are significantly different from the illiterate level.

Table 5.37: Multiple Range Test: Duncan Procedure: Modernity Scores in the Area of 'Social Life' by Levels of Education

Mean	*Levels of Education*		*Levels of Education*						
			1	3	2	4	5	6	7
4.9114	Illiterate	1							
5.1522	UP	3							
5.1793	LP	2							
6.7312	SSLC	4	*	*	*				
7.3610	PDC	5	*	*	*	*			
7.6078	Graduate	6	*	*	•	*			
8.0134	PG and Professional	7	*	*	*	*	*		

N = 700

*Denotes pairs of groups significantly different at .050 level.

Similarly, the mean difference between UP and LP levels is not significant. Whereas all other levels of education above UP are significantly different from LP level in terms of mean score.

It may be noted that all levels of education above UP are significantly different from UP level in terms of modernity score.

It may also be noted that all levels of education above UP, i.e. SSLC onwards, are significantly different from Illiterate, LP and UP levels, in terms of mean score.

It is clear from Table 5.37 that significant differences in the mean scores, on modernity in the Area of 'Social Life', of different levels of education from that of Illiterate begins at the SSLC level.

All levels of education above SSLC and SSLC are significantly different from Illiterate, LP and UP levels in terms of the mean score.

It is inferred that SSLC is the minimum level of education required for individuals to reflect significant difference from that of Illiterate in terms of modernity in the Area of 'Social Life'.

Finding

It is clear that SSLC is the critical level of education in the case of modernity in the Area of 'Social Life'.

Critical Level of Education with Reference to Modernity in the Area of 'Health and Hygiene'

Since levels of education were found to be significantly different with regard to modernity in the Area of 'Health and Hygiene', Multiple Range Test using Duncan Procedure was followed in order to discover a level of education which may be the critical level at which the differences become statistically significant. Result thus obtained are presented in Table 5.38.

It may be observed from Table 5.38 that the mean scores on Modernity in the Area of 'Health and Hygiene' follow an ascending order from Illiterate to PG and Professional level, through SSLC.

As it is revealed in Table 5.38, though the mean score of LP level is greater than that of Illiterate, the difference between the two levels is not significant. Whereas the mean difference between UP level and illiterate is significant and all other levels above UP are significantly different from the Illiterate level.

Table 5.38: Multiple Range Test: Duncan Procedure, Modernity Scores in the Area of 'Health and Hygiene' by Levels of Education

Mean	*Levels of Education*		*Level of Education*						
			1	2	3	4	5	6	7
6.7788	Illiterate	1							
6.9982	LP	2							
7.2639	UP	3	*						
7.8956	SSLC	4	*	*	*				
8.0268	PDC	5	*	*	*				
8.2425	Graduate	6	*	*	*	*			
8.4339	PG and Professional	7	*	*	*	*	*		

N = 700

*Denotes pairs of groups significantly different at .050 level.

While the mean difference between UP and LP levels is not significant at all other levels of education above UP are significantly different from LP level in terms of mean score.

It may be noted that all levels of education above UP are significantly different from UP level in terms of modernity score. It may also be noted that all levels of education above UP, i.e. SSLC onwards are significantly different from illiterate, LP and UP levels in terms of mean score.

It is clear from Table 5.38 that significant differences in the mean scores, on modernity in the Area of 'Health and Hygiene', of different levels of education from that of Illiterate begins at the UP level.

It is inferred that Upper Primary is the minimum level of education required for individuals to reflect significant difference from that of illiterate in terms of modernity in the Area of 'Health and Hygiene'.

Finding

It is clear that Upper Primary is the critical level of education in the case of modernity in the Area of 'Health and Hygiene'.

Critical Level of Education with Reference to Modernity in the Area of 'Economic Life'

In order to discover a level of education which may be the critical level at which the differences become statistically significant between levels of education with reference to modernity in the Area of 'Economic Life', Multiple Range Test using Duncan Procedure was followed. The result thus obtained is presented in Table 5.39.

It may be observed from Table 5.39 that the mean scores on modernity in the Area of 'Economic Life' follow an ascending order from illiterate to PG and Professional level, through SSLC except in the case of Graduate level. The mean score at Graduate level is greater than that of PG and Professional level of education.

As may be observed from Table 5.39, though the mean score of LP level is greater than that of Illiterate, the difference between the two levels is not significant.

Table 5.39: Multiple Range Test: Duncan Procedure Modernity Scores in the Area of 'Economic Life' by Levels of Education

Mean	*Levels of Education*		*Levels of Education*						
			1	2	3	4	5	7	6
6.1773	Illiterate	1							
6.4419	LP	2							
6.9750	UP	3	*						
7.3904	SSLC	4	*	*					
7.5361	PDC	5	*	*					
7.6967	PG and Professional	6	*	*	*				
8.1321	Graduate	7	*	*	*	*			

N = 700

*Denotes pairs of groups significantly different at .050 level.

However, the mean difference between UP level and illiterate is significant and all other levels above UP are also significantly different from the Illiterate level. While the mean difference between UP and LP levels is not significant at all other levels of education above UP are significantly different from LP level in terms of mean score.

It may be noted that only graduate and PG and Professional levels of education are significantly different from UP level in terms of modernity score in the Area of 'Economic Life'.

It may also be noted that only Graduate, and PG and Professional levels of education are significantly different from all the three levels—illiterate, LP and UP—in terms of mean score.

It is clear from Table 5.39 that significant differences in the mean scores, on modernity in the Area of 'Economic Life' of different levels of education from that of Illiterate begins at the UP level.

It is inferred that Upper Primary is the minimum level of education required for individuals to reflect significant difference from that of illiterate in terms of modernity in the Area of 'Economic Life'.

Finding

It is clear that Upper Primary is the critical level of education in the case of Modernity in the Area of 'Economic Life'.

Critical Level of Education with Reference to Modernity in the Dimension 'Change Proneness'

In the case of Modernity in the Dimension 'Change Proneness', it was found that there is no significant difference between levels of education. Therefore, Multiple Range Test was not followed in this case.

Critical Level of Education with Reference to Modernity in the Dimension 'Scientific Orientation'

In the case of Modernity in the Dimension 'Scientific Orientation', it was found that there is significant difference between levels of education. Multiple Range Test using Duncan Procedure was followed in order to discover a level of education which may be the critical level at which the differences become statistically significant. The results thus obtained are presented in Table 5.40.

Table 5.40: Multiple Range Test: Duncan Procedure, Modernity Scores in the Dimension 'Scientific Orientation' by Levels of Education

Mean	*Levels of Education*		*Levels of Education*						
			1	2	3	4	5	6	7
4.5070	Illiterate	1							
4.6424	LP	2							
4.9051	UP	3	*						
5.7913	SSLC	4	*	*	*				
5.9873	PDC	5	*	*	*				
6.0692	Graduate	6	*	*	*				
6.2302	PG and Professional	7	*	*	*	*			

N = 700

*Denotes pairs of groups significantly different at .050 level.

It may be observed from Table 5.40 that the mean scores on modernity in the Dimension 'Scientific Orientation' follow an ascending order from illiterate to PG and Professional level through SSLC.

As can be observed from Table 5.40, though the mean score of LP level is greater than that of illiterate, the difference between the two levels is not significant, whereas the mean difference between UP level and illiterate is significant and all other levels above UP are significantly different from the illiterate level.

The mean difference between UP and LP levels is not significant. Whereas all other levels of education above UP are significantly different from LP level in terms of mean score.

It may be noted that all levels of education above UP are significantly different from UP level in terms of modernity score in the Dimension 'Scientific Orientation'.

Similarly, all levels of education above UP, i.e. SSLC onwards, are significantly different from Illiterate, LP and UP levels, in terms of mean score.

It is clear from Table 5.40 that the significant differences in the mean scores, on modernity in the Dimension 'Scientific Orientation' of different levels of education from that of Illiterate begins at UP level.

It is inferred that Upper Primary is the minimum level of education required for individuals to reflect significant difference from that of Illiterate in terms of modernity in the Dimension 'Scientific Orientation'.

Finding

It is clear that Upper Primary is the critical level of education in the case of Modernity in the Dimension 'Scientific Orientation'.

Critical Level of Education with Reference to Modernity in the Dimension 'Democratic Orientation'

It was found that levels of education differ significantly in the case of modernity in the Dimension 'Democratic Orientation'. Multiple Range Test using Duncan procedure was followed in order to discover a level of education which may be the critical level at which the differences become statistically significant. Results thus obtained are presented in Table 5.41.

Table 5.41: Multiple Range Test: Duncan Procedure, Modernity Scores in the Dimension 'Democratic Orientation' by Levels of Education

Mean	*Levels of Education*		*Levels of Education*						
			1	2	3	4	5	6	7
5.5985	Illiterate	1							
6.0238	LP	2	*						
6.0823	UP	3	*						
7.2727	SSLC	4	*	*	*				
7.6995	PDC	5	*	*	*	*			
7.8628	Graduate	6	*	*	*	*			
7.9984	PG and Professional	7	*	*	*	*			

N = 700

*Denotes pairs of groups significantly different at .050 level.

It may be observed from Table 5.41 that the mean scores on modernity in the Dimension 'Democratic Orientation' follow an ascending order from Illiterate to PG and Professional level through SSLC.

As it is revealed in Table 5.41, though the mean score of LP level is greater than that of Illiterate, and the difference between the two levels is significant. The mean difference between UP level and Illiterate is also significant and all other levels above UP are significantly different from the Illiterate level.

While the mean difference between UP and LP levels is not

significant, all other levels of education above UP are significantly different from LP level in terms of mean score.

It may be noted that all levels of education above UP are significantly different from UP level in terms of modernity score in the Dimension 'Democratic Orientation'.

It may also be noted that all levels of education above UP, i.e. SSLC onwards, are significantly different from illiterate, LP and UP levels, in terms of mean score.

It is clear from Table 5.41 that the significant differences in the mean scores, on modernity in the Dimension 'Democratic Orientation' of different levels of education from that of Illiterate level begins at LP level.

It is inferred that Lower Primary is the minimum level of education required for individuals to reflect significant difference from that of Illiterate in terms of modernity in the Dimension 'Democratic Orientation'.

Finding

It is clear that Lower Primary is the critical level of education in the case of modernity in the Dimension 'Democratic Orientation'.

Critical Level of Education with Reference to Modernity in the Dimension 'Secular Orientation'

In the case of modernity in the Dimension 'Secular Orientation' it was found that levels of education differ significantly. Multiple Range Test using Duncan Procedure was followed to discover a level of education which may be the critical level at which the differences become statistically significant. Results thus obtained are presented in Table 5.42.

It may be observed from Table 5.42 that the mean scores on modernity in the Dimension 'Secular Orientation' follow an ascending order from illiterate to PG and Professional level through SSLC.

As may be observed from Table 5.42, though the mean score of LP level is greater than that of Illiterate, the difference between the two levels is not significant. The mean difference between UP level and Illiterate is also not significant. Whereas all other levels above UP are significantly different from the Illiterate level.

Table 5.42: Multiple Range Test: Duncan Procedure, Modernity Scores in the Dimension 'Secular Orientation' by Levels of Education

Mean	*Levels of Education*		*Levels of Education*						
			1	2	3	4	5	6	7
5.0204	Illiterate	1							
5.1074	LP	2							
5.2206	UP	3							
6.7425	SSLC	4	*	*	*				
7.4170	PDC	5	*	*	*	*			
7.4349	Graduate	6	*	*	*	*			
7.9580	PG and Professional	7	*	*	*	*	*	*	

N = 700

*Denotes pairs of groups significantly different at .050 level.

Similarly, the mean difference between UP and LP levels is not significant. Whereas all other levels of education above UP are significantly different from LP and UP levels in terms of mean score.

Thus, all levels of education above UP, i.e. SSLC onwards, are significantly different from Illiterate, LP and UP levels, in terms of mean score on modernity in the Dimension 'Secular Orientation'.

It is clear from Table 5.42 that the significant differences in the mean scores, on modernity in the Dimension 'Secular Orientation' of different levels of education from that of Illiterate begins at SSLC level.

It is inferred that SSLC is the minimum level of education required for individuals to reflect significant difference from that of Illiterate in terms of modernity in the Dimension 'Secular Orientation'.

Finding

It is clear that SSLC is the critical level of education in the case of modernity in the Dimension 'Secular Orientation'.

Critical Level of Education with Reference to Modernity in the Dimension 'Achievement Orientation'

It was found that levels of education differ significantly in the case of modernity in the Dimension 'Achievement Orientation'.

Multiple Range Test using Duncan Procedure was followed in order to discover a level of education which may be the critical level at which the differences become statistically significant. Results thus obtained are presented in Table 5.43.

It may be observed from Table 5.43 that the mean scores on modernity in the Dimension 'Achievement Orientation' follow an ascending order from Illiterate to PG and Professional level through SSLC.

As may be observed from Table 5.43, though the mean score of LP level is greater than that of Illiterate, the difference between the two levels is not significant. The mean difference between UP level and Illiterate is also not significant. Whereas all other levels above UP are significantly different from the illiterate level.

Similarly, the mean difference between UP and LP levels is not significant. Whereas all other levels of education above UP are significantly different from LP and also UP level in terms of mean score.

Table 5.43: Multiple Range Test: Duncan Procedure, Modernity Scores in the Dimension 'Achievement Orientation' by Levels of Education

Mean	*Levels of Education*		*Levels of Education*						
			1	2	3	4	5	6	7
5.4007	Illiterate	1							
5.4733	LP	2							
5.5253	UP	3							
6.7377	SSLC	4	*	*	*				
7.0297	PDC	5	*	*	*				
7.1343	Graduate	6	*	*	*	*			
7.2382	PG and Professional	7	*	*	*	*			

N = 700

*Denotes pairs of groups significantly different at .050 level.

It is clear from Table 5.43 that the significant differences in the mean scores, on modernity in the Dimension 'Achievement Orientation' of different levels of education from that of Illiterate begins at SSLC level.

It is inferred that SSLC is the minimum level of education required for individuals in reflecting significant difference from that of Illiterate in terms of modernity in the Dimension 'Achievement Orientation'.

Finding

It is thus clear that SSLC is the critical level of education in the case of modernity in the Dimension 'Achievement Orientation'.

Table 5.44: Critical Levels of Education by Category of Modernity

Modernity Category		Levels of Education						
		Illiterate	*LP*	*UP*	*SSLC*	*PDC*	*Graduate*	*PG and Professional*
General Modernity				*				
Areas of Life	1. Education				*			
	2. Employment				*			
	3. Marriage and Family		*					
	4. Religious Life				*			
	5. Political Life				*			
	6. Social Life				*			
	7. Health and Hygiene			*				
	8. Economic Life			*				
Dimensions	1. Change Proneness							
	2. Scientific Orientation			*				
	3. Democratic Orientation		*					
	4. Secular Orientation				*			
	5. Achievement Orientation				*			

* Indicate the critical level of education.

Note: Multiple Range Test using Duncan Procedure was not followed in the case of 'Change Proneness' as it was found that the levels of education do not differ significantly.

Cumulative Observations on Critical Levels of Education with Reference to Modernity in terms of 'Attitudes'

The cumulative observations on critical levels of education, with reference to modernity in terms of 'attitudes' of the total sample, arrived at through Multiple Range Test following Duncan procedure are presented in Table 5.44.

As it may be observed from Table 5.44 Lower Primary is the critical level of education with reference to modernity in terms of 'attitudes' in the Area of 'Marriage and Family' and in the Dimension 'Democratic Orientation' of individual respondents.

From the above observation it is to be understood that even a minimum level of education, i.e. 4 years of lower primary education enables individuals to reflect a higher degree of modernity; in terms of attitudes in the Area of 'Marriage and Family' and in the Dimension 'Democratic Orientation' which is significantly different from that of Illiterates.

It may be noted from Table 5.44 that Upper Primary is the critical level of education with reference to modernity in the case of 'General Modernity', modernity in the Areas of 'Health and Hygiene', 'Economic Life' and in the Dimension 'Scientific Orientation' of individual respondents.

It is to be understood that in terms of modernity in these cases, a minimum of Upper Primary level of education, i.e. 7 years of schooling is required for individuals to reflect a significant difference from that of illiterates.

It may further be observed from Table 5.44 that SSLC is the critical level of education with reference to modernity in terms of attitudes in the Areas of 'Education', 'Employment', 'Religious Life', 'Political Life', 'Social Life' and in the Dimensions 'Secular Orientation' and 'Achievement Orientation' of individual respondents.

In these cases a minimum of 10 years of education is required to enable individuals to reflect a significant difference in modernity from those of Illiterates.

It is clear from the above observations that the critical levels of education are different in the case of different aspects of modernity considered for the present study. The levels observed as critical are LP, UP and SSLC.

Among these three levels of education, while the value of Lower Primary level of education, i.e. 4 years of schooling in promoting modernity of individuals cannot be underestimated, Upper Primary and SSLC are found to be more significant.

It is clear that education at least up to SSLC level (i.e. 10 years of schooling) enables individuals to reach a "take off' level with reference to 'General Modernity', and also modernity in all Areas of Life and in all Dimensions. However, this cannot be definitely inferred with respect to 'Change Proneness'.

III. Intervening Variables in the Relationship between Levels of 'Education and Modernity'

In the previous section, the relationship between levels of education and modernity, in terms of attitudes, was examined. It was found that modernity scores differ significantly across levels of education.

It is necessary to examine whether the variations thus observed in modernity scores can be exclusively attributed to the variations in the levels of education, as there are a number of other variables that are likely to moderate the observed relationship between education and modernity.

A possible line of analysis to understand the interaction of moderator variables on the relationship between levels of education and modernity is to examine the same after statistically controlling for the effect of these variables. This approach is followed here for each moderator variable.

For this purpose the intervening variables considered for the present study are included in the fourth major hypothesis (*vide* p.9): "variables such as sex, marital status, religion, occupation, income, place of residence, migration, type of schooling, and exposure to mass media do not influence the relationship between levels of education and modernity."

The above hypothesis is tested separately for each of the variables, through appropriate sub-hypothesis.

Levels of Education, Sex and Modernity

Modernity is considered to vary between the sexes. For the present study, it has been hypothesised that—

"Sex does not influence the relationship between levels of education and modernity in terms of attitudes of individual respondents."

The above hypothesis is examined through 14 different sub-hypotheses, corresponding to general modernity, modernity in eight areas of life and five dimensions.

Modernity scores of Male and Female respondents are considered for examining the hypotheses. Mean and Standard Deviation have been calculated for Male and Female respondents at all levels of education. Figures thus obtained in the case of 'General Modernity' are presented in the following Table 5.45.

Table 5.45: General Modernity Score by Levels of Education and Sex

Levels of Education	*Male*			*Female*		
	N	*Mean*	*Standard Deviation*	*N*	*Mean*	*Standard Deviation*
Illiterate	48	6.1265	0.8566	52	5.7551	0.7808
LP	48	6.3956	0.8077	52	5.9012	0.7188
UP	48	6.4838	0.8934	52	6.0442	0.7736
SSLC	48	7.4249	0.8974	52	7.0678	0.9312
PDC	48	7.7718	0.9007	52	7.3329	0.8455
Graduate	48	7.7305	0.8590	52	7.7283	0.8360
PG & Professional	48	7.8723	0.8530	52	8.0434	0.7234
Total	336	7.1150	1.1055	364	6.8390	1.1764

It may be observed from Table 5.45 that both in the case of Male and Female respondents, General Modernity score (mean) gradually increases from Illiterate to PG and Professional level of education, through SSLC.

Both in the case of male and female respondents, there is a sharp increment in the mean modernity score from Upper Primary to SSLC level of education.

It may also be observed that the overall mean scores on General Modernity are different in the case of Male and Female respondents. It is higher in the case of Males (7.1150) when compared to that of Females (6.8390). At all levels of education, except at the PG and

Professional level, the mean score is higher in the case of Males than Females. At the PG and Professional level, the mean modernity score of female respondents is slightly higher than that of males.

From the above observations, it appears that mean scores of General Modernity at all levels of education are different for both the sexes. Similarly, there is Male-Female difference in General Modernity scores at all levels of education.

Analysis of Variance

In order to know whether the differences thus observed are significant, analysis of variance has been followed. The figures thus obtained are presented in Tab1e 5.46.

It may be observed from Table 5.46 that the calculated value of *F* for levels of education is greater than the expected value at 0.01 level of probability (2.83).

Table 5.46: General Modernity Scores by Levels of Education and Sex

Source of variation	Sum of squares	df	Mean square	F	Significance of F
A. Between Levels of education	423.769	6	70.628	101.254	**
B. Between sex	13.314	1	13.314	19.087	**
C. Interaction A × B	9.772	6	1.629	2.335	*
Within groups	478.509	686	0.698		
Total	925.363	699	1.324		

* Significant at .05 level.
** Significant at .01 level.

The calculated value of *F* for Sex differences is greater than the corresponding expected value at 0.01 level (6.68).

Similarly, the calculated value of *F* for interaction between levels of education and sex is greater than the expected value for significance at 0.05 level (2.83).

From the above observations it is clear that—

1. General modernity scores of respondents differ significantly in terms of levels of education;
2. There is significant difference between Male and Female respondents in terms of General Modernity; and

3. There is significant interaction between levels of education and Sex in the context of General Modernity scores of respondents at the 95 per cent level of significance.

Thus it may be inferred that sex as a variable does influence the relationship between levels of education and General Modernity measured in terms of attitudes of individual respondents in 95 out of 100 cases.

Likewise, analysis of variance was followed in the case of modernity scores in all Areas of life and all the Dimensions considered for the study. The *F* ratios thus obtained are presented in Table 5.47.

It may be observed from Table 5.47 that the calculated value of *F* for differences in levels of education is greater than the expected value in the case of General Modernity, Modernity in all Areas of Life and in all Dimensions, except Change proneness.

The calculated value of *F* for sex differences is greater than the theoretical value in the case of General Modernity; Modernity in all Areas of Life except in the Areas of 'Education', 'Employment', and 'Economic Life'; Modernity in all 'Dimensions', except 'Change Proneness', 'Democratic Orientation', and 'Achievement Orientation'.

The calculated value of *F* for interaction between Levels of Education and Sex is greater than the expected value in the case of 'General Modernity', Modernity in the Area of 'Education'; Modernity in the Dimensions—'Scientific Orientation', 'Democratic Orientation', 'Secular Orientation', and 'Achievement Orientation'. In the remaining cases the calculated value of *F* is not greater than the expected value.

From the above observations, it is clear that:

1. Levels of education differ significantly in terms of 'General Modernity', Modernity in all 'Areas of Life'; and Modernity in all 'Dimensions', except 'Change Proneness'.
2. There is significant difference between Male and Female respondents in terms of 'General Modernity'; Modernity in all 'Areas of Life', except in the Areas of 'Education', 'Employment' and 'Economic Life'; Modernity in all 'Dimensions' except 'Change Proneness', 'Democratic Orientation' and 'Achievement Orientation'.
3. There is significant interaction between Levels of Education and Sex, in the context of 'General Modernity'; Modernity

Table 5.47: Analyses of Variance Modernity Score by Level of Education and Sex Ratio by Category of Modernity

Category of Modernity		*Analysis of Variance: F-Ratios*					
		Between Levels of Education		*Between Sex*		*Interaction between Levels of Education and Sex*	
		F	*Sig. of F*	*F*	*Sig. F of F*	*F*	*Sig. of F*
General Modernity		101.254	.01	19.087	.01	2.335	.05
Areas of Life	1. Education	57.760	.01	0.745	NS	2.270	.05
	2. Employment	53.044	.01	2.790	NS	1.128	NS
	3. Marriage and family	55.989	.01	8.169	.01	1.885	NS
	4. Religious life	35.135	.01	44.473	.01	2.089	NS
	5. Political life	16.499	.01	10.886	.01	1.403	NS
	6. Social life	55.059	.01	7.684	.01	0.685	NS
	7. Health and Hygiene	39.382	.01	28.387	.01	2.088	NS
	8. Economic life	9.692	.01	0.016	NS	1.124	NS
Dimensions	1. Change proneness	0.721	NS	0.157	NS	1.491	NS
	2. Scientific orientation	38.387	.01	18.897	.01	3.052	.01
	3. Democratic orientation	61.116	.01	1.545	NS	3.356	.01
	4. Secular orientation	71.621	.01	47.154	.01	3.805	.01
	5. Achievement orientation	40.226	.01	0.700	NS	2.279	.05

NS: Not significant.

3. There is significant interaction between Levels of Education and Sex, in the context of 'General Modernity'; Modernity in the Area 'Education'; Modernity in all 'Dimensions' except 'Change Proneness'.

Hence, the null hypothesis is rejected in 6 out of 14 cases of Modernity scores and in the remaining cases the null hypotheses have been accepted and retained.

The new set of hypotheses are as follows:

1. Sex *does* influence the relationship between levels of education and 'General Modernity' in terms of 'attitudes' of individual respondents at 0.05 level of significance.
2. Sex *does* influence the relationship between levels of education and modernity, in terms of attitudes of individual respondents, in the Area of 'Education' at 0.05 level of significance.
3. Sex *does not* influence the relationship between levels of education and modernity in terms of attitudes, of individual respondents, in the Area of 'Employment'.
4. Sex *does not* influence the relationship between levels of education and modernity in terms of attitudes, of individual respondents, in the Area of 'Marriage and Family'.
5. Sex *does not* influence the relationship between levels of education and modernity in terms of attitudes, of individual respondents, in the Area of 'Religious Life'.
6. Sex *does not* influence the relationship between levels of education and modernity in terms of attitudes, of individual respondents, in the Area of 'Political Life'.
7. Sex *does not* influence the relationship between levels of education and modernity in terms of attitudes, of individual respondents, in the Area of 'Social Life'.
8. Sex *does not* influence the relationship between levels of education and modernity in terms of attitudes, of individual respondents, in the Area of 'Health and Hygiene'.
9. Sex *does not* influence the relationship between levels of education and modernity in terms of attitudes, of individual respondents, in the Area of 'Economic Life'.

10. Sex *does not* influence the relationship between levels of education and modernity in terms of attitudes, of individual respondents, in the Dimension 'Change Proneness'.
11. Sex *does* influence the relationship between levels of education and modernity in terms of attitudes, of individual respondents, in the Dimension 'Scientific Orientation' at 0.01 level of significance.
12. Sex *does* influence the relationship between levels of education and modernity in terms of attitudes, of individual respondents, in the Dimension 'Democratic Orientation'.
13. Sex *does* influence the relationship between levels of education and modernity in terms of attitudes, of individual respondents, in the Dimension 'Secular Orientation'.
14. Sex *does* influence the relationship between levels of education and modernity in terms of attitudes, of individual respondents, in the Dimension 'Achievement Orientation' at 0.05 level of significance.

Levels of Education, Marital Status and Modernity

The popular impression about marriage is that after marriage either one or both the spouses are likely to experience a change in their attitudes and life styles. It is essential to know whether or not marital status influences the relationship between levels of education and modernity in terms of attitudes.

In this context the null hypothesis set for the present study is that:

> "Marital Status does not influence the relationship between levels of education and modernity, in terms of attitudes, of individual respondents."

The above hypothesis is examined through 14 different sub-hypotheses, corresponding to General modernity and modernity in eight Areas of life and five Dimensions.

Modernity scores of Unmarried and Married respondents are considered for examining the hypotheses. Mean and Standard Deviation have been calculated for Unmarried and Married respondents at all levels of education. Figures thus obtained in the case of General Modernity are presented in Table 5.48.

As it may be observed from Table 5.48, the mean score on General Modernity gradually increases from Illiterate to PG and Professional level of education, through SSLC both in the case of Unmarried and Married respondents. In both the cases, there is a sudden spurt in the mean modernity score from UP to SSLC level of education.

Table 5.48: General Modernity Score by Levels of Education and Marital Status

Levels of Education	*Unmarried*			*Married*		
	N	*Mean*	*Standard Deviation*	*N*	*Mean*	*Standard Deviation*
Illiterate	32	5.9765	1.0423	68	5.9131	0.7254
LP	37	6.2233	0.7807	63	6.0887	0.8107
UP	43	6.3515	0.8991	57	6.1825	0.8260
SSLC	67	7.2918	0.8694	33	7.1323	1.0430
PDC	68	7.6910	0.9124	32	7.2304	0.7832
Graduate	85	7.7038	0.8733	15	7.8746	0.6483
PG and Professional	78	7.9243	0.8117	22	8.0923	0.7036
Total	410	7.2661	1.1077	290	6.5551	1.0809

It may also be observed that the overall mean scores on General Modernity are different in the case of Unmarried and Married respondents. The mean score on General modernity for the Unmarried respondents (7.2661) is greater than that of Married respondents (6.5551). It is so at all levels of education, except graduate, and PG and professional levels. At these two levels, the Married respondents have an edge over the Unmarried respondents, in terms of General Modernity score.

Analysis of Variance

In order to know whether the observed mean differences are significant, analysis of variance was followed. Figures thus obtained are presented in Table 5.49.

It may be observed from Table 5.49 that the calculated value of F between levels of education is greater than the expected value at 0.01 level of probability.

The calculated value of F for between Marital status is less than the corresponding expected value. Similarly, the calculated value of

F for interaction between levels of education and Marital status is also less than the corresponding expected value.

Table 5.49: General Modernity Score by Levels of Education and Marital Status

Source of variation	*Sum of squares*	*df*	*Mean square*	*F*	*Significance of F*
A. Between levels of education	330.432	6	55.072	76.422	**
B. Between Marital Status	1.175	1	1.175	1.631	
C. Interaction A × B	5.193	6	0.866	1.201	
Within groups	494.350	686	0.721		
Total	925.363	699	1.324		

** Significant at .01 level.

From the above observations it is clear that—

1. Levels of education differ significantly in terms of General modernity scores of respondents;
2. There is no significant difference between Unmarried and Married respondents in terms of General modernity; and
3. There is no significant interaction between levels of education and Marital status in the context of General modernity scores of respondents.

Thus, it is clear that Marital status does not influence the relationship between levels of education and General Modernity in terms of attitudes of individual respondents.

Analysis of Variance

Similar to the above, Analysis of Variance was followed in the case of modernity scores in all areas of life and all the Dimensions considered for the study. The *F*-ratio thus obtained are presented in Table 5.50.

It may be observed from Table 5.50 that the calculated value of *F* for differences between levels of education is greater than the theoretical value in the case of General Modernity, Modernity in all Areas of Life and in all Dimensions, except Change Proneness.

The calculated value of *F* differences between Marital status is less than the theoretical value in the case of General modernity; modernity in all Areas of Life except Religious Life, and modernity in all Dimensions.

The calculated value of *F* for interaction between levels of education and Marital Status is less than the theoretical value in the case of General Modernity; Modernity in all areas of life; and Modernity in all dimensions.

From the above observations, it is clear that—

1. There is significant difference between levels of education in terms of General Modernity; Modernity in all Areas of Life; and Modernity in all Dimensions except Change Proneness. In the case of Change Proneness, there is no significant difference between levels of education in terms of General Modernity.
2. There is no significant difference between unmarried and married respondents in the case of General Modernity; Modernity in all Areas of Life except Religious Life; and Modernity in all Dimensions except Secular Orientation.
3. There is no significant interaction between levels of education and Marital Status in the context of General Modernity; Modernity in all Areas of Life and Modernity in all Dimensions.

Based on the above analyses, the null hypothesis is accepted in all the 14 cases of modernity scores as given below:

1. Marital status does not influence the relationship between levels of Education and General Modernity in terms of attitudes of individual respondents.
2. Marital Status does not influence the relationship between levels of Education and Modernity in terms of attitudes of individual respondents in the area of Education.
3. Marital status does not influence the relationship between levels of Education and Modernity in terms of attitudes of individual respondents in the area of employment.
4. Marital status does not influence the relationship between levels of Education and Modernity in terms of attitudes of individual respondents in the Area of Marriage and Family.

Table 5.50: Modernity Score by Levels of Education and Marital Status (*F* Ratios by Category of Modernity)

Category of Modernity		*Analysis of Variance : F-Ratios*					
		Between levels of education		*Between Marital Status*		*Interaction between levels of Education and Marital Status*	
		F	*Sig. of F*	*F*	*Sig. of F*	*F*	*Sig. of F*
General Modernity		76.422	.01	1.631	NS	1.201	NS
Areas of Life	1. Education	51.144	.01	2.589	NS	1.585	NS
	2. Employment	43.688	.01	0.106	NS	0.444	NS
	3. Marriage and family	43.119	.01	0.182	NS	1.124	NS
	4. Religious life	21.697	.01	19.261	.01	0.970	NS
	5. Political life	13.286	.01	0.137	NS	0.744	NS
	6. Social life	42.666	.01	1.665	NS	0.978	NS
	7. Health and Hygiene	29.256	.01	0.725	NS	1.057	NS
	8. Economic life	8.652	.01	0.291	NS	0.771	NS
Dimensions	1. Change proneness	0.711	NS	0.143	NS	0.983	NS
	2. Scientific orientation	30.140	.01	0.730	NS	1.550	NS
	3. Democratic orientation	54.843	.01	4.770	NS	1.631	NS
	4. Secular orientation	48.351	.01	7.682	.01	0.706	NS
	5 Achievement orientation	33.100	.01	0.052	NS	0.876	NS

NS: Not significant.

5. Marital status does not influence the relationship between levels of Education and Modernity in terms of attitudes, of individual respondents, in the Area of Religious Life.
6. Marital status does not influence the relationship between levels of Education and Modernity in terms of attitudes, of individual respondents in the area of Political Life.
7. Marital status does not influence the relationship between levels of Education and Modernity in terms of attitudes of individual respondents in the area of Social Life.
8. Marital status does not influence the relationship between levels of Education and Modernity in terms of attitudes of individual respondents in the area of Health and Hygiene.
9. Marital status does not influence the relationship between levels of Education and Modernity in terms of attitudes of individual respondents in the area of Economic Life.
10. Marital status does not influence the relationship between levels of Education and Modernity in terms of attitudes of individual respondents in the Dimension Change Proneness.
11. Marital status does not influence the relationship between levels of Education and Modernity in terms of attitudes of individual respondents in the Dimension Scientific Orientation.
12. Marital status does not influence the relationship between levels of Education and Modernity in terms of attitudes of individual respondents in the Dimension Democratic Orientation.
13. Marital status does not influence the relationship between levels of Education and Modernity in terms of attitudes of individual respondents in the Dimension Secular Orientation.
14. Marital status does not influence the relationship between levels of Education and Modernity in terms of attitudes of individual respondents in the Dimension Achievement Orientation.

Levels of Education, Religion and Modernity

In order to know whether religion influences the relationship between Education and Modernity, the null hypothesis set for the present study is that:

> "Religion does not influence the relationship between levels of education and modernity, in terms of attitudes of individual respondents."

The above hypothesis is examined through 14 different sub-hypotheses, corresponding to General Modernity and Modernity in eight Areas of Life and five Dimensions.

Modernity scores of Hindu, Muslim and Christian respondents are considered for examining the hypotheses. Mean and Standard Deviation have been calculated for Hindu, Muslim and Christian respondents at all levels of education. Figures thus obtained in the case of General Modernity are presented in Table 5.51.

It may be observed from Table 5.51 that the mean score on General Modernity gradually increases from Illiterate to PG and Professional level of education, through SSLC in the case of Hindu, Muslim and Christian respondents.

In all the three categories, there is a sharp increment in the mean score on General Modernity from UP to SSLC level of education.

Further it may also be observed from Table 5.51 that the overall mean scores on General Modernity are different for Hindus, Muslims and Christians. Among the three categories, the Hindus have the highest mean score (7.1018), followed by Christians (6.8886) and then by the Muslims (6.6635). This pattern in terms of mean score on General Modernity can be clearly observed at all levels of education.

It is noted that mean scores on General Modernity are different for various levels of education. Similarly, mean scores are different for the three religious groups for various levels of education.

Analysis of Variance

In order to know whether the differences observed are significant, analysis of variance was followed. Figures thus obtained are presented in Table 5.52.

It may be observed from Table 5.52 that the calculated value of *F* for differences between levels of education is greater than the expected value at 0.01 level of probability.

The calculated value of *F* for differences between Religion is also greater than the expected value at less than 0.01 level of probability.

Table 5.51: General Modernity Score by Levels of Education and Religion

Levels of Education	*Religion*								
	Hindus			*Muslims*			*Christians*		
	N	*Mean*	*Standard Deviation*	*N*	*Mean*	*Standard Deviation*	*N*	*Mean*	*Standard Deviation*
Illiterate	60	5.9817	0.7684	20	5.8567	1.1947	20	5.8651	0.5946
LP	60	6.2515	0.8282	20	5.8911	0.7803	20	6.0470	0.6850
UP	60	6.4505	0.8944	20	5.8982	0.7844	20	6.0262	0.6522
SSLC	60	7.4180	0.8354	20	6.5985	1.1953	20	7.3436	0.5891
PDC	60	7.6784	0.8966	20	7.1280	0.9756	20	7.5547	0.7010
Graduate	60	7.9077	0.8095	20	7.4359	0.8276	20	7.4880	0.8541
PG and Professional	60	8.0249	0.8653	20	7.8361	0.7171	20	7.8954	0.6083
Total	420	7.1018	1.1500	140	6.6635	1.1962	140	6.8886	1.0423

However, the calculated value of *F* for interaction between levels of Education and Religion is less than the expected value for significance.

Table 5.52: General Modernity Scores by Levels of Education and Religion

Source of variation	*Sum of squares*	*df*	*Mean square*	*F*	*Significance of F*
A. Between levels of education	323.601	6	53.933	77.444	**
B. Between Religion	21.376	2	10.688	15.347	**
C. Interaction A × B	7.350	12	0.613	0.880	
Within groups	472.868	679	0.696		
Total	925.363	699	1.324		

** Significant at .01 Level.

From the above observations it is clear that:

1. Levels of education differ significantly in terms of General Modernity scores of respondents;
2. There is significant difference between Hindu, Muslim and Christian respondents in terms of General Modernity; and
3. There is no significant interaction between Levels of Education and Religion in the context of General Modernity scores of respondents.

It may be inferred that Religion as a variable does not influence the relationship between Levels of Education and General Modernity, in terms of attitudes of individual respondents.

Analysis of Variance

Similar to the above, analysis of variance was followed in the case of modernity scores in all areas of life and all the dimensions considered for the study. The *F* ratios thus obtained are presented in Table 5.53.

It may be observed from Table 5.53 that the calculated value of *F* for between levels of education is greater than the expected value in the case of General Modernity; Modernity in all Areas of Life and in all Dimensions, except Change Proneness.

The calculated value of *F* for differences between Religion is greater than the expected value in the case of General Modernity; Modernity in all Areas of Life except Education and Employment; Modernity in all Dimensions, except Democratic Orientation.

The calculated value of *F* for interaction between Levels of Education and Religion is lesser than the expected value in the case of General Modernity, Modernity in all Areas of Life except Education, and Modernity in all Dimensions. In the case of Modernity in the Areas of Education, the calculated value of *F* is greater than the theoretical value. The probability is less than .05.

From the above observations, it is clear that:

1. There is significant difference between levels of education in terms of General Modernity, Modernity in all Areas of Life; and Modernity in all Dimensions, except Change Proneness.

Table 5.53: Modernity Score by Levels of Education and Religion (*F*-Ratio by Category of Modernity)

Category of Modernity		*Analysis of Variance: F-Ratio*					
		Between Level of Education		*Between Religion*		*Interaction between Levels of Education and Religion*	
		F	*Sig. of F*	*F*	*Sig. of F*	*F*	*Sig. of F*
General Modernity		77.444	.01	15.347	.01	0.880	NS
Areas of Life	1. Education	48.437	.01	0.622	NS	2.205	.05
	2. Employment	43.165	.01	0.036	NS	1.435	NS
	3. Marriage and family	40.955	.01	6.986	.01	0.326	NS
	4. Religious life	23.469	.01	28.966	.01	1.154	NS
	5. Political life	14.946	.01	6.934	.01	1.271	NS
	6. Social life	41.744	.01	8.076	.01	1.656	NS
	7. Health and Hygiene	28.612	.01	5.813	.01	1.255	NS
	8. Economic life	7.704	.01	8.843	.01	1.486	NS
Dimensions	1. Change proneness	0.812	NS	0.216	NS	0.620	NS
	2. Scientific orientation	29.473	.01	9.123	.01	0.662	NS
	3. Democratic orientation	50.946	.01	2.661	NS	1.416	NS
	4. Secular orientation	51.636	.01	11.299	.01	1.117	NS
	5. Achievement orientation	30.573	.01	7.370	.01	1.301	NS

NS: Not significant.

2. There is significant difference between Hindu, Muslim and Christian respondents in terms of General Modernity; Modernity in all Areas of Life except Education and Employment; and Modernity in all Dimensions except Change Proneness and Democratic Orientation.
3. There is no significant. interaction between Levels of Education and Religion in the context of General Modernity; Modernity in all Areas of Life except Education and Modernity in all Dimensions.

Hence, the null hypothesis is accepted in all the 13 out of 14 cases of modernity scores. In the case of modernity in the Area of Education the null hypothesis has been rejected.

The hypotheses are accepted in the following form:

1. Religion does not influence the relationship between levels of Education and General Modernity in terms of attitudes of individual respondents.
2. Religion does influence the relationship between levels of Education and Modernity in terms of attitudes of individual respondents in the Area of Education.
3. Religion does not influence the relationship between levels of Education and Modernity in terms of attitudes of individual respondents in the Area of Employment.
4. Religion does not influence the relationship between levels of Education and Modernity in terms of attitudes of individual respondents in the Area of Marriage and Family.
5. Religion does not influence the relationship between levels of Education and Modernity in terms of attitudes of individual respondents in the Area of Religious Life.
6. Religion does not influence the relationship between levels of Education and Modernity in terms of attitudes of individual respondents in the Area of Political Life.
7. Religion does not influence the relationship between levels of Education and Modernity in terms of attitudes of individual respondents in the Area of Social Life.
8. Religion does not influence the relationship between levels of Education and Modernity in terms of attitudes of individual respondents in the Area of Health and Hygiene.

9. Religion does not influence the relationship between levels of Education and Modernity in terms of attitudes of individual respondents in the Area of Economic Life.
10. Religion does not influence the relationship between levels of Education and Modernity in terms of attitudes of individual respondents in the Dimension Change Proneness.
11. Religion does not influence the relationship between levels of Education and Modernity in terms of attitudes of individual respondents in the Dimension Scientific Orientation.
12. Religion does not influence the relationship between levels of Education and Modernity in terms of attitudes of individual respondents in the Dimension Democratic Orientation.
13. Religion does not influence the relationship between levels of Education and Modernity in terms of attitudes of individual respondents in the Dimension Secular Orientation.
14. Religion does not influence the relationship between levels of Education and Modernity in terms of attitudes of individual respondents in the Dimension Achievement Orientation.

Levels of Education, Place of Residence and Modernity

In order to know whether Place of Residence influences the relationship between levels of Education and Modernity, the null hypothesis set for the present study is that:

> "Place of residence does not influence the relationship between levels of education and modernity in terms of attitudes of individual respondents."

The above hypothesis is examined through 14 different sub-hypotheses, corresponding to General Modernity and Modernity in different Areas of Life and Dimensions.

Modernity scores of respondents residing in Rural and Urban areas of Cochin taluk are considered for this purpose. Mean and Standard Deviation have been calculated for Rural and Urban respondents at all levels of Education. Figures thus obtained in the case of General Modernity are presented in Table 5.54.

It may be observed from Table 5.54 that General Modernity

Scores are different at all levels of education, both in the case of Rural and Urban respondents. Modernity scores gradually increase from Illiterate to PG and Professional Level through SSLC.

Both in the case of Rural and Urban respondents, there is a sudden spurt in the mean modernity score from UP to SSLC level of education.

Further, it may also be observed that the mean scores on General Modernity are different for Rural and Urban respondents at all levels of education. The mean score for all the Rural respondents (7.0155) is greater than that of Urban respondents (6.9275). A similar pattern is observed at Illiterate, UP, SSLC and Graduate levels whereas at the LP, PDC and PG and Professional levels, the Urban respondents have an edge over their counterparts in terms of General Modernity.

Table 5.54: General Modernity Score by Levels of Education and Place of Residence

Levels of Education	*Rural*			*Urban*		
	N	*Mean*	*Standard Deviation*	*N*	*Mean*	*Standard Deviation*
Illiterate	50	6.0476	0.9205	50	5.8191	0.7313
LP	50	6.1194	0.6653	50	6.1577	0.9190
UP	50	6.3345	0.9364	50	6.1759	0.7728
SSLC	50	7.3802	0.7392	50	7.0982	1.0738
PDC	50	7.4966	0.9462	50	7.5906	0.8488
Graduate	50	7.7962	0.8225	50	7.6626	0.8658
PG & Professional	50	7.9342	0.7691	50	7.9884	0.8151
Total	350	7.0155	1.1229	350	6.9275	1.1776

It appears from the above observations, that in terms of mean scores on General Modernity, all levels of education are different. Similarly, Rural and Urban respondents appear to be different in terms of General Modernity scores at all levels of education.

Analysis of Variance

In order to know whether the differences thus observed are significant, analysis of variance was followed. Figures thus obtained (in the case of General Modernity) are presented in Table 5.55.

Table 5.55: General Modernity Scores by Levels of Education and Place of Residence

Source of variation	*Sum of squares*	*df*	*Mean square*	*F*	*Significance of F*
A. Between levels of education	423.769	6	70.628	97.507	**
B. Between Place of Residence	1.356	1	1.356	1.872	
C. Interaction A×B	3.343	6	0.557	0.769	
Within groups	496.895	686	0.724		
Total	925.363	699	1.324		

** Significant at .01 Level.

It may be observed from Table 5.55 that the calculated value of *F* for differences between levels of education is greater than the expected value at less than 0.01 level of probability.

The calculated value of *F* for differences in place of residence is lower than the expected value. Similarly, the calculated value of *F* for interaction between levels of education and place of residence is also lower than the corresponding expected value for significance.

From the above observations it is clear that:

1. Levels of education differ significantly in terms of General modernity scores of respondents;
2. There is no significant difference between Rural and Urban respondents in terms of General Modernity scores; and
3. There is no significant interaction between levels of education and Place of Residence in the context of General Modernity scores of respondents.

It may be inferred that Place of Residence as a variable does not influence the relationship between Levels of Education and General Modernity in terms of attitudes of individual respondents.

Analysis of Variance

Similar to the above analysis of variance was followed in the case of modernity scores in all Areas of Life and all the Dimensions considered for the study. The *F* ratios thus obtained are presented in Table 5.56.

It may be observed from Table 5.56 that the calculated value of *F* between levels of education is greater than the expected value in the case of General Modernity, Modernity in all Areas of Life and in all Dimensions, except Change Proneness.

The calculated value of *F* for differences between place of residence is lesser than the theoretical value for significance in the case of General Modernity; Modernity in all Areas of Life and Modernity in all Dimensions.

The calculated value of *F* for interaction between Levels of Education and Place of Residence is lower than the expected value for significance in the case of General Modernity, Modernity in all Areas of Life except in the Areas of Political Life and Economic Life; and Modernity in all Dimensions.

From the above observations, it is clear that:

1. Levels of education differ significant in te-ms of General Modernity, Modernity in all Areas of Life; and Modernity in all Dimensions, except Change Proneness.
2. There is no significant difference between Rural and Urban respondents in terms of General Modernity; Modernity in all Areas of Life; and Modernity in all Dimensions.
3. There is no significant interaction between levels of education and place of residence in the context of General Modernity; Modernity in the Areas of Life except in the Areas of Political Life and Economic Life; and Modernity in all Dimensions.

Hence, the null hypothesis is accepted in 12 out of 14 cases of modernity scores. The null hypothesis is rejected in the case of modernity in the Areas of Political Life and Economic Life.

The hypotheses are accepted in the following forms:

1. Place of residence does not influence the relationship between levels of Education and General Modernity in terms of attitudes of individual respondents.
2. Place of residence does not influence the relationship between levels of Education and Modernity in terms of attitudes of individual respondents, in the Area of Education.

Table 5.56: Modernity Scores by Levels of Education and Place of Residence (*F*-Ratios by Category of Modernity)

Category of Modernity		*Analysis of Variance:: F-Ratios*					
		Between levels of education		*Between place of residence*		*Interaction between levels of education & place of residence*	
		F	*Sig. of F*	*F*	*Sig. of F*	*F*	*Sig. of F*
	General Modernity	97.507	.01	1.872	NS	0.769	NS
Areas of Life	1. Education	56.854	.01	2.001	NS	0.230	NS
	2. Employment	52.862	.01	2.051	NS	0.853	NS
	3. Marriage and family	54.994	.01	2.386	NS	0.759	NS
	4. Religious life	32.583	.01	0.042	NS	0.501	NS
	5. Political life	16.449	.01	3.618	NS	2.259	.05
	6. Social life	54.375	.01	0. 137	NS	0.497	NS
	7. Health and Hygiene	37.667	.01	3.517	NS	0.956	NS
	8. Economic Life	9.857	.01	0.466	NS	3.024	.01
Dimensions	1. Change proneness	0.715	NS	0.799	NS	0.317	NS
	2. Scientific orientation	36.632	.01	0. 105	NS	0.672	NS
	3. Democratic orientation	59.962	.01	2.295	NS	1.004	NS
	4. Secular orientation	65.246	.01	1.062	NS	0.273	NS
	5. Achievement orientation	39.909	.01	0. 126	NS	1.456	NS

NS = Not significant.

3. Place of residence does not influence the relationship between levels of Education and Modernity in terms of attitudes of individual respondents in the Area of Employment.
4. Place of residence does not influence the relationship between levels of Education and Modernity in terms of attitudes of individual respondents in the Area of Marriage and Family.
5. Place of residence does not influence the relationship between levels of Education and Modernity in terms of attitudes of individual respondents in the Area of Religious Life.
6. Place of residence does influence the relationship between levels of Education and Modernity in terms of attitudes of individual respondents in the Area of Political Life.
7. Place of residence does not influence the relationship between levels of Education and Modernity in terms of attitudes of individual respondents in the Area of Social Life.
8. Place of residence does not influence the relationship between levels of Education and Modernity in terms of attitudes of individual respondents in the Area of Health and Hygiene.
9. Place of residence does influence the relationship between levels of Education and Modernity in terms of attitudes of individual respondents in the Areas of Economic Life.
10. Place of residence does not influence the relationship between levels of Education and Modernity in terms of attitudes of individual respondents in the Dimension Change Proneness.
11. Place of Residence does not influence the relationship between levels of Education and Modernity in terms of attitudes of individual respondents in the Dimension Scientific Orientation.
12. Place of residence does not influence the relationship between levels of Education and Modernity in terms of attitudes of individual respondents in the Dimension Democratic Orientation.

13. Place of residence does not influence the relationship between levels of Education and Modernity in terms of attitudes of individual respondents in the Dimension Secular Orientation.
14. Place of residence does not influence the relationship between levels of Education and Modernity in terms of attitudes of individual respondents in the Dimension Achievement Orientation.

Levels of Education, Migration and Modernity

In order to know whether Migration influences the relationship between levels of Education and Modernity in terms of attitudes, the null hypothesis set for the present study is that:

> "Migration does not influence the relationship between levels of education and modernity in terms of attitudes of individual respondents."

The above hypothesis is examined through 14 different sub-hypotheses, corresponding to General Modernity and Modernity in eight Areas of life and in five Dimensions.

Modernity scores of Non-migrant and Migrant respondents are considered for this purpose. A migrant is defined as a person whose place of birth is different from his/her place of residence at the time of data collection. The minimum unit considered as a 'place' in this context is a Panchayat.

Mean and Standard Deviation have been calculated for Non-migrant and Migrant Respondents at all levels of Education. Figures thus obtained in the case of General Modernity are presented in Table 5.57.

It may be observed from Table 5.57, that the mean scores on General Modernity are different at all levels of education, both in the case of Non-migrant and Migrant respondents. Modernity scores gradually increase from Illiterate to PG and Professional level through SSLC in both cases.

A sudden spurt in the Mean Modernity score is observed from UP to SSLC level, both in the case of Non-migrants and Migrants.

Table 5.57: General Modernity Score by Levels of Education and Migration

Levels of Education	*Non-migrants*			*Migrants*		
	N	*Mean*	*Standard Deviation*	*N*	*Mean*	*Standard Deviation*
Illiterate	70	6.0207	0.8695	30	5.7296	0.7212
LP	63	6.1334	0.7742	37	6.1472	0.8490
UP	60	6.1750	0.8778	39	6.3706	0.8335
SSLC	72	7.3273	0.8099	27	6.9587	1.1517
PDC	71	7.6367	0.9648	30	7.2846	0.6682
Graduate	70	7.7290	0.8148	30	7.7302	0.9194
PG and Professional	70	8.0031	0.8067	30	7.8637	0.7498
Total	476	7.0365	1.1571	223	6.8252	1.1241

Further, it may also be noted that the overall mean scores on General Modernity are different for Non-migrants and Migrants at all levels of education. The mean score for all the Non-migrants (7.0365) is greater than that of Migrant respondents (6.8252). A similar pattern is observed at the Illiterate, SSLC, PDC, and PG and Professional levels.

However, at the LP, UP and Graduate levels, the Migrant respondents are found to have an edge over their counterparts (Non-migrants) in terms of mean score on General Modernity.

It appears from the Table 5.57 that in terms of mean scores on General Modernity, all levels of education are different. Similarly, the Non-migrant and Migrant respondents appear to be different in terms of General Modernity scores at all levels of education.

Analysis of Variance

In order to know whether the mean differences thus observed are significant, analysis of variance was followed. Figures thus obtained (in the case of General Modernity) are presented in Table 5.58.

It may be observed from Table 5.58 that the calculated value of F for differences between levels of education is greater than the expected value for significance at less than .01 level of probability.

The calculated value of F for differences between Migration is lesser than the expected value for significance.

Similarly the calculated value of F for interaction between Levels of Education and Migration is also lesser than the expected value for significance.

Table 5.58: General Modernity Scores by Levels of Education and Migration

Source of Variation	*Sum of squares*	*df*	*Mean square*	*F*	*Significance of F*
A. Between levels of education	358.648	6	59.775	83.087	**
B. Between migration	2.527	1	2.527	3.513	
C. Interaction A×B	5.750	6	0. 958	1. 332	
Within groups	492.084	684	0.719		
Total	922.956	697	1.324		

** Significant at .01 level.

From the above observations it is clear that:

1. Levels of education differ significantly in terms of General Modernity scores of respondents;
2. There is no significant difference between Non-migrant and Migrant respondents in terms of General Modernity scores;
3. There is no significant interaction between levels of Education and Migration in the context of General Modernity scores of respondents.

It may be inferred that migration as a variable does not influence the relationship between Levels of Education and General Modernity in terms of attitudes of individual respondents.

Analysis of Variance

Similar to the above, analysis of variance was followed in the case of modernity scores in all areas of life and all the dimensions considered for the study. The *F* ratios thus obtained are presented in Table 5.59.

It may be observed from Table 5.59 that the calculated value of *F* for differences between levels of education is greater than the expected value in the case of General Modernity; Modernity in all Areas of Life and in all Dimensions, except Change Proneness.

The calculated value of *F* for differences between Migration is less than the expected value in the case of General Modernity; Modernity in all Areas of Life except Religious Life and Health and Hygiene; and Modernity in all dimensions except Secular orientation.

The calculated value of *F* for interaction between levels of

Education and Migration is lesser than the expected value for significance in the case of General Modernity, Modernity in all Areas of Life and Modernity in all Dimensions.

From the above observations, it is clear that:

1. Levels of education differ significant in terms of General Modernity, Modernity in all Areas of Life; and Modernity in all Dimensions, except Change Proneness.
2. There is no significant difference between Non-migrant and Migrant respondents in terms of General Modernity; Modernity in all Areas of Life except Religious Life and Health and Hygiene; and modernity in all Dimensions except Secular Orientation.
3. There is no significant interaction between levels of education and Migration in the context of General Modernity; Modernity in all Areas of Life and Modernity in all Dimensions. Hence, the null hypothesis is accepted in all the 14 cases of modernity scores.

The accepted hypotheses are as follows:

1. Migration does not influence the relationship between levels of Education and General Modernity in terms of attitudes of individual respondents.
2. Migration does not influence the relationship between levels of Education and Modernity in terms of attitudes of individual respondents in the Area of Education.
3. Migration does not influence the relationship between levels of education and modernity in terms of attitudes of individual respondents in the Area of Employment.
4. Migration does not influence the relationship between levels of Education and Modernity in terms of attitudes of individual respondents in the Area of Marriage and Family.
5. Migration does not influence the relationship between levels of Education and Modernity in terms of attitudes of individual respondents in the Area of Religious Life.
6. Migration does not influence the relationship between levels of Education and Modernity in terms of attitudes of individual respondents in the Area of Political Life.

Table 5.59: Modernity Score by Levels of Education and Migration (*F*-Ratios by Category of Modernity)

Category of Modernity		*Analysis of Variance : F-Ratios*					
		Between levels of education		*Between migration*		*Interaction between levels of education and migration*	
		F	*Sig. of F*	*F*	*Sig. of F*	*F*	*Sig. of F*
	General Modernity	83.087	.01	3.513	NS	1.332	NS
Areas of Life	1. Education	48.321	.01	0.551	NS	1.096	NS
	2. Employment	47.843	.01	0.547	NS	1.832	NS
	3. Marriage and family	48.146	.01	0.645	NS	1.646	NS
	4. Religious life	28.108	.01	13.613	.01	1.216	NS
	5. Political life	13.671	.01	0.008	NS	0.260	NS
	6. Social life	46.400	.01	1.746	NS	1.330	NS
	7. Health and Hygiene	30.729	.01	4.839	.05	0.774	NS
	8. Economic life	6.635	.01	0.009	NS	1.856	NS
Dimensions	1. Change proneness	0.753	NS	0.431	NS	1.239	NS
	2. Scientific orientation	30.629	.01	2.489	NS	0.709	NS
	3. Democratic orientation	51.561	.01	0.051	NS	0.984	NS
	4. Secular orientation	57.425	.01	5.429	.05	1.107	NS
	5. Achievement orientation	33.969	.01	1.985	NS	1.656	NS

NS: Not significant.

7. Migration does not influence the relationship between levels of Education and Modernity in terms of attitudes of individual respondents in the Area of Social Life.
8. Migration does not influence the relationship between levels of Education and Modernity in terms of attitudes of individual respondents in the Area of Health and Hygiene.
9. Migration does not influence the relationship between levels of Education and Modernity in terms of attitudes of individual respondents in the Area of Economic Life.
10. Migration does not influence the relationship between levels of Education and Modernity in terms of attitudes of individual respondents in the Dimension Change Proneness.
11. Migration does not influence the relationship between levels of Education and Modernity in terms of attitudes of individual respondents in the Dimension Scientific Orientation.
12. Migration does not influence the relationship between levels of Education and Modernity in terms of attitudes of individual respondents in the Dimension Democratic Orientation.
13. Migration does not influence the relationship between levels of Education and Modernity in terms of attitudes of individual respondents in the Dimension Secular Orientation.
14. Migration does not influence the relationship between levels of Education and Modernity in terms of attitudes of individual respondents in the Dimension Achievement Orientation.

Levels of Education, Type of Schooling and Modernity

In order to know whether Type of Schooling influences the relationship between levels of Education and Modernity, the null hypothesis set for the present study is that:

Type of schooling does not influence the relationship between levels of education and modernity in terms of attitudes of individual respondents."

The above hypothesis is examined through 14 different sub-hypothesis, corresponding to General modernity and modernity in 8 Areas of life and 5 Dimensions.

Modernity Scores of respondents who studied in government schools and those studied in government schools and those who studied in private schools during V, VI and VII standards, i.e., UP school, are considered for this purpose. Respondent belonging to illiterate and LP level of education are not included in this analysis.

Mean and Standard deviation have been calculated separately for respondent who studied in government schools and those who studied in private schools for all levels of education. Figures thus obtained in the case of general modernity are presented in Table 5.60

Table 5.60: General Modernity Score by Levels of Education and Type of Schooling*

Levels of Education	*Govt. Schools*			*Private Schools*		
	N	*Mean*	*Standard Deviation*	*N*	*Mean*	*Standard Deviation*
UP	36	6.2122	0.8177	64	6.2794	0.8851
SSLC	19	6.9656	0.8756	81	7.3034	0.9334
PDC	16	7.5609	0.8048	82	7.5404	0.9135
Graduate	13	7.6735	0.8798	86	7.7539	0.8334
PG & Professional	24	8.1062	0.7214	75	7.9136	0.8134
Total	108	7.1413	1.0966	388	7.4024	1.0267

* Illiterate and Lower Primary level of education were excluded in this analysis.

It may be observed from Table 5.60 that the mean scores on General modernity gradually increase from UP to PG and professional level through SSLC; both in the case of respondents who studied in government as well as in private schools.

In both the cases a sharp increment in the modernity score is observed from UP to SSLC level of education.

It may further be observed that the overall mean score on General Modernity is different for respondents who studied in Government schools and those who studied in Private schools at all levels of education. The mean score on General Modernity for all the respondents who studied in Private schools (7.4024) is greater than that of the respondents who studied in Government schools (7.1413). A similar pattern is observed at UP, SSLC, and graduate levels of education. However, at the PDC and PG and Professional levels, the mean score of respondents who studied in Government schools is greater than that of their counterparts.

Analysis of Variance

In order to know whether the above observed differences in the mean score are significant, analysis of variance was followed. Figures thus obtained in the case of General Modernity are presented in the Table 5.61.

It may be observed from Table 5.61 that the calculated value of F for differences between levels of education is greater than the expected value at less than 0.01 level of probability.

Table 5.61: General Modernity Score by Levels of Education and Type of Schooling

Source of variation	*Sum of squares*	*df*	*Mean square*	*F*	*Significance of F*
A. Between levels of education	150.145	4	37.536	50.279	**
B. Between type of schooling	0.227	1	0.227	0.304	
C. Interaction A×B	2.427	4	0.607	0.813	
Within groups	362.827	486	0.747		
Total	542.388	495	1.096		

** Significant at 0.01 level.

The calculated values of F for differences between type of schooling as well as for the interaction between levels of education and type of schooling are lesser than expected value for significance.

From the above observations it is clear that:

1. Levels of education differ significantly in terms of General Modernity scores of respondents;
2. There is no significant difference between the respondents who studied in Government schools and those who studied in Private schools in terms of General Modernity scores;
3. There is no significant interaction between levels of education and Type of schooling in the context of General Modernity scores of respondents.

Thus, it is clear that type of schooling does not influence the relationship between levels of Education and General Modernity in terms of attitudes of individual respondents.

Analysis of Variance

Similar to the above analysis of variance was followed in the case of modernity scores in all areas of life and all the dimensions considered for the study. The *F*-ratios thus obtained are presented in the Table 5.62.

It may be observed from Table 5.62 that the calculated value of *F* for differences between levels of education is greater than the expected value in the case of General Modernity, Modernity in all Areas of Life and in all Dimensions except Change Proneness.

The calculated value of *F* for differences between type of schooling is less than the expected value in the case of General Modernity; Modernity in all Areas of Life and Modernity in All Dimensions.

It is further clear from Table 5.62 that the calculated value of *F* for interaction between levels of education and Type of Schooling is less than the expected value for significance in the case of General Modernity, Modernity in all the Areas of Life and Modernity in all Dimensions.

From the above observations, it is clear that:

1. There is significant difference between levels of education in terms of General Modernity, Modernity in All Areas of Life; and Modernity in All Dimensions, except Change Proneness.
2. There is no significant difference between the respondents who studied in government schools and those who studied in private schools in the case of General Modernity; Modernity in all Areas of Life; and Modernity in all Dimensions.
3. There is no significant interaction between levels of education and type of schooling in the case of General Modernity; Modernity in all Areas of Life and Modernity in All Dimensions.

Hence, the null hypothesis is accepted in all the 14 cases of modernity scores. The accepted hypotheses are as follows:

1. Type of schooling does not influence the relationship between Levels of Education and General Modernity, in terms of attitudes of individual respondents.
2. Type of schooling does not influence the relationship between levels of Education and Modernity in terms of attitudes of individual respondents in the Area of Education.
3. Type of schooling does not influence the relationship between levels of Education and Modernity in terms of attitudes of individual respondents in the Area of Ernployment.
4. Type of schooling does not influence the relationship between

Table 5.62: Modernity Score by Levels of Education and Type of Schooling (*F*-Ratios by Category of Modernity)

Category of Modernity		*Analysis of Variance: F-Ratios*					
		Between levels of education		*Between type of schooling*		*Interaction between levels of education and type of schooling*	
		F	*Sig. of F*	*F*	*Sig. of F*	*F*	*Sig. of F*
	General Modernity	50.279	.01	0.304	NS	0.813	NS
Areas of Life	1. Education	40.868	.01	0.246	NS	0.321	NS
	2. Employment	28.947	.01	0.502	NS	0.266	NS
	3. Marriage and family	28.072	.01	0.849	NS	0.219	NS
	4. Religious life	18.794	.01	0.052	NS	0.568	NS
	5. Political life	9.528	.01	0.813	NS	1.460	NS
	6. Social life	30.775	.01	0.570	NS	0.257	NS
	7. Health and Hygiene	18.804	.01	0.526	NS	0.773	NS
	8. Economic life	3.896	.01	0.473	NS	1.838	NS
Dimensions	1. Change proneness	0.289	NS	0.621	NS	0.830	NS
	2. Scientific orientation	13.632	.01	0.061	NS	0.540	NS
	3. Democratic orientation	27.034	.01	0.970	NS	0.689	NS
	4. Secular orientation	37.204	.01	0.033	NS	0.217	NS
	5. Achievement orientation	22.627	.01	0.900	NS	0.994	NS

NS: Not significant.

levels of Education and Modernity in terms of attitudes of individual respondents in the Area of Marriage and Family.

5. Type of schooling does not influence the relationship between levels of Education and Modernity in terms of attitudes of individual respondents in the Area of Religious Life.
6. Type of schooling does not influence the relationship between levels of Education and Modernity in terms of attitudes of individual respondents in the Area of Political Life.
7. Type of schooling does not influence the relationship between levels of Education and Modernity in terms of attitudes of individual respondents in the Area of Social Life.
8. Type of schooling does not influence the relationship between levels of Education and Modernity in terms of attitudes of individual respondents in the Area of Health and Hygiene.
9. Type of schooling does not influence the relationship between levels of Education and Modernity in terms of attitudes of individual respondents in the Area of Economic Life.
10. Type of schooling does not influence the relationship between levels of Education and Modernity in terms of attitudes of individual respondents in the Dimension Change Proneness.
11. Type of schooling does not influence the relationship between levels of Education and Modernity in terms of attitudes of individual respondents in the Dimension Scientific Orientation.
12. Type of schooling does not influence the relationship between levels of Education and Modernity in terms of attitudes of individual respondents in the Dimension Democratic Orientation.
13. Type of schooling does not influence the relationship between levels of Education and Modernity in terms of attitudes of individual respondents in the Dimension Secular Orientation.
14. Type of schooling does not influence the relationship between levels of Education and Modernity in terms of attitudes of individual respondents in the Dimension Achievement Orientation.

Income, Occupation and Exposure to Mass Media

The influence of intervening variables such as Sex, Marital Status, Religion, Place of Residence, Migration and Type of Schooling on the relationship between Levels of Education and Modernity in terms of attitudes was examined, in the preceding sections, following analysis of variance separately for each variable.

In the case of income, occupation and exposure to mass media, such analysis could not be followed due to inadequate data observations. In these cases it was found when the sample is divided across the categories of the variables by levels of education that there were several cells with inadequate observations. Hence, statistical treatment of the available distributions became difficult.

As an alternative, the researcher initially contemplated the slashing of levels of education (where the observations are inadequate) as well as the slashing/clubbing of the categories of intervening variables (where the number of observations were inadequate) for the purpose of analysis. An exercise in this direction revealed that minimum number required for each cell were not available even to them. Instead, a descriptive analysis of representative cases was resorted to. Such analyses are followed in the case of three variables, i.e. Income, Occupation, and Exposure to mass media. They are presented herein.

Income

The distribution of respondents by their annual family income and level of education may be recalled here.

It may be observed from Table 5.63 that a meaningful comparison of all income categories, taking into account all levels of education, is not feasible, as there are many categories (cells) with insufficient observations.

However, within the available distribution comparing income group 2 and 3 (in order to know the variations, if any, in modernity scores, when level of education is controlled) appeared to be meaningful. Since statistical analysis is not justifiable even in this case, a descriptive analysis of representative cases was considered.

For this purpose, two individual cases each from Upper Primary level (representing lower levels of education) and Graduate level (representing higher levels of education) were selected. Modernity

Table 5.63: Distribution of Respondents by Level of Education and Annual Family Income

Level of education	*Family income category*						*Total*
	1	2	3	4	5	NR	
Illiterate	20	50	24	4	—	2	100
LP	13	43	34	7	3	—	100
UP	10	38	39	10	1	2	100
SSLC	16	42	27	9	4	2	100
PDC	6	24	43	16	10	1	100
Graduate	5	24	27	23	21	—	100
PG and Professional	—	1	32	33	34	—	100
Total	70	222	226	102	73	7	700
Percentage	10.0	31.71	32.29	14.57	10.43	1.0	100.0

Note: N R = No response.

1	=	Less than Rs. 6,000	—	Poor
2	=	Rs. 6,001-12,000	—	Low income
3	=	Rs. 12,001-24,000	—	Lower middle income
4	=	Rs. 24,001-36,000	—	Upper middle income
5	=	Above Rs. 36,000	—	High income

scores of the cases representing Upper Primary level are presented in Table 5.64.

It may be observed from Table 5.64 that Raman (whose annual family income is between Rs. 6,001-12,000) and Surendran (whose annual family income is between Rs. 12,001-24,000) are different in their General Modernity, Modernity in all Areas of Life except Education, and in all Dimensions. In the Area of Education, both have equal Modernity Scores.

Comparatively, Surendran (who is from a richer family than that of Raman) is more modern than Raman in General Modernity; in All Areas of Life except Education Health and Hygiene and Economic Life; in all Dimensions except Democratic Orientation and Achievement Orientation. In these cases barring Education, Raman has a negligible edge over Surendaran in the Area of Education both are equal in Modernity.

It is to be noted that both Surendran and Raman are residents of Kumbalanghi—a rural area of Cochin taluk (Surendaran was born in Kanayannur taluk whereas Raman was born in Kumbalanghi itself). Both are male Hindus and are not married at the time of the study.

Table 5.64: Modernity Scores by Income

	Category of Modernity	*Category of Income*	
		* 2	** 3
General	Modernity	7.489130	7.991836
Areas of Life	1. Education	8.72	8.72
	2. Employment	6.692	6.826666
	3. Marriage and Family	5.941818	6.76
	4. Religious life	8.473333	9.765
	5. Political life	8.661666	9.956666
	6. Social life	5.8	10.175
	7. Health and Hygiene	9.35375	8.544444
	8. Economic life	6.665	6.105
Dimensions	1. Change Proneness	8.862	9.335384
	2. Scientific Orientation	7.934285	8.13
	3. Democratic Orientation	7.524444	7.105
	4. Secular Orientation	5.8775	10.33833
	5. Achievement Orientation	5.898571	5.758888

*2 = Annual family income between Rs. 6,001-12,000 (Raman)
**3 = Annual family income between Rs. 12,001-24,000 (Surendran)

Both of them are fishermen. They both studied in government schools where the medium of instruction was Malayalam.

In spite of these and many other similarities, Surendaran and Raman differ in their modernity. While the level of education is same for both, Surendaran who belongs to a richer family than that of Raman is found to be more modern in most of the components of modernity and in General Modernity.

Inference

It appears that the differences between Surendaran and Raman in their Modernity are due to the differences in their family income. Hence, in the context of lower levels of education, income as a variable appears to influence the relationship between levels of education and modernity in terms of attitudes.

In order to know the influence of income on the relationship between levels of education and Modernity in terms of attitudes at the higher levels of education, two individuals, Balakrishnan and Sunil Kumar representing graduate level of education as well as income groups 2 and 3 respectively were selected. Modernity Scores of these individuals are presented in Table 5.65.

Table 5.65: Modernity Scores by Income

		Category of Modernity	*Category of Income*	
			* 2	** 3
General Modernity			6.836607	8.566734
Areas of life	1	Education	7.912857	8.801666
	2	Employment	5.341428	9.115
	3	Marriage and Family	6.183333	7.421
	4	Religious life	8.556666	10.60333
	5	Political life	7.456363	8.13
	6	Social life	4.896	7.283333
	7	Health and Hygiene	7.74625	9.35375
	8	Economic life	7.243333	9.5925
Dimensions	1	Change Proneness	8.856428	9.406
	2	Scientific Orientation	5.320833	8.0525
	3	Democratic Orientation	6.974615	8.704545
	4	Secular Orientation	6.418888	7.444444
	5	Achievement Orientation	5.82125	8.585

*2 = Annual family income between Rs. 6,001-12,000 (Balakrishnan)
**3= Annual family income between Rs. 12,0001-24,000 (Sunil Kumar)

It may be observed from Table 5.65 that Balakrishnan and Sunil Kumar are different in their Modernity Scores in all the components of Modernity as well as in General Modernity.

Relatively Sunil Kumar (whose annual family income is between Rs. 12,001-24,000) is more modern than Balakrishnan (whose annual family income is between Rs. 6001-12,000) in General Modernity and in all components of modernity.

These differences are to be looked at from their backgrounds. Both, Balakrishnan and Sunil Kumar are residents of rural areas of Cochin Taluk. They were also born and brought up in the same place where they reside. They are Hindu men and are not married at the time of study.

Both of them studied in schools where the medium of instruction was Malayalam.

In spite of these and several other commonalities in the background and the common level of education, Sunil Kumar appears to be more modern than Balakrishnan. In all cases, Sunil Kumar having a higher family income than that of Balakrishnan has secured high scores on :nodernity. The variation in the modernity scores of these individuals appear to be related to the difference in their family income. Hence income as a variable appears to influence the relationship between levels of education and modernity in terms of attitudes at higher levels of education.

Inference on Income

Having examined typical cases representing lower as well as higher levels of education, having different income, it appears that income as a variable influences the relationship between levels of education and modernity in terms of attitudes.

Occupation

The distribution of respondents by their Occupation and level of Education may be recalled here.

Table 5.66: Distribution of Respondents by Occupational Category

Level of Education	*Occupational Category**								*Total*
	1	2	3	4	5	6	7-9	NR	
Illiterate	0	1	0	1	3	23	31	41	100
Lower Primary	1	1	0	4	1	13	41	39	100
Upper Primary	0	3	0	3	2	14	33	45	100
SSLC	1	12	0	5	1	7	13	61	100
PDC	6	10	2	9	0	3	6	64	100
Graduate	15	14	4	4	0	4	3	56	100
PG & Professional	13	14	0	5	0	4	5	59	100
Total	36	55	6	31	7	68	132	365	700
Percentage	5.14	7.86	0.86	4.43	1.0	9.71	18.86	52.14	100.0

* Occupational categories (according to the NCO, 1968).
NR = Not response.

1 : Professional, Technical and related workers.
2 : Administrative executive and managerial workers.
3 : Clerical and related workers.
4 : Sales workers.
5 : Service workers.
6 : Farmers, fishermen, hunters, loggers and related workers.
7,8,9 : Production and related workers, transport equipment operators and labourers.

Comparison of occupational categories taking into account all levels of education is not feasible as the concentration of observations is distorted in diagonally opposite directions. A possible way of comparing the occupational categories in order to know the variations in Modernity due to Occupation is to compare groups which are varying in occupation but have common levels of education.

In this regard, comparing occupational categories 6 and 7-9 in the case of lower strata of educational levels and categories 1 and 2 for higher strata of education. Accordingly Upper Primary and Graduate levels of education are considered respectively. Two individual cases each from each of these levels were selected for comparison. Modernity Scores of these cases representing Upper Primary are presented in the following Table 5.67.

Table 5.67: Modernity Scores by Occupation

	Category of Modernity	*Category of Occupation*	
		* 6	** 7-8-9
General Modernity		6.358260	6.725555
Areas of Life	1. Education	7.58	10.44
	2. Employment	4.155	6.26
	3. Marriage and Family	4.403636	6.201818
	4. Religious life	7.423333	5.108
	5. Political life	10.2225	6.906666
	6. Social life	4.315	4.928
	7. Health and Hygiene	8.46	9.35375
	8. Economic life	5.583333	8.775
Dimensions	1. Change Proneness	9.840909	8.402666
	2. Scientific Orientation	6.68625	5.151428
	3. Democratic Orientation	4.384166	6.862222
	4. Secular Orientation	5.111	6.344545
	5. Achievement Orientation	5.404	6.694

*6 = Farmers, fishermen, hunters, loggers and related workers (Dinesan)
**7-8-9 = Production and related workers, transport equipment operators and borrowers (Prasannan).

It may be observed from Table 5.67 that Dinesan and Prasannan differ in Modernity in all Areas of Life, all Dimensions and in General Modernity.

Comparatively Prasannan a production related labourer, is more modern than Dinesan who is an agricultural labourer in most of the components of modernity except Religious Life, Political Life,

Change Proneness, and Scientific Orientation. He is also more modern in General Modernity when compared to Dinesan.

It is to be noted that both Dinesan and Prasannan are residents of Kumbalanghi (Rural area of Cochin taluk).

Both these individuals were born and brought up in Kumbalanghi itself.

Prasannan and Dinesan are male Hindus. Both had their schooling under Christian management.

In spite of these and several other factors in common, these two individuals differ in modernity.

It appears that the differences between Prasannan and Dinesan in their Modernity are due to different Occupations which they have. Hence, Occupation as a variable appears to influence the relationship between levels of education and modernity in terms of attitudes at lower levels of education.

In order to know the influence of Occupation, on the relationship between levels of education and modernity in terms of attitudes, at the higher levels of education, two individuals representing Graduate level of education as well as Occupational categories 1 and 2 were selected. Modernity Scores of these individuals are presented in Table 5.68.

Table 5.68: Modernity Scores by Occupation

Category of Modernity		*Category of Occupation*	
		*1	**2
General Modernity		8.333061	7.601276
Areas of Life	1. Education	9.6075	8.72
	2. Employment	6.076666	9.5
	3. Marriage and Family	8.156666	6.230909
	4. Religious life	10.60333	5.229
	5. Political life	8.878888	9.0325
	6. Social life	9.57	9.57
	7. Health and Hygiene	8.218	9.03875
	8. Economic life	7.482	10.05
Dimensions	1. Change Proneness	9.199285	9.995454
	2. Scientific Orientation	6.455	5.210833
	3. Democratic Orientation	9.201111	7.809
	4. Secular Orientation	9.091428	8.1875
	5. Achievement Orientation	7.945714	6.865

*1 = Professional, technical and related workers (Sasi Kumar).

**2 = Administrative executive and managerial workers (Sunil).

It may be observed from Table 5.68 that Sasi Kumar and Sunil are different in their Modernity Scores in all components of Modernity and in General Modernity. An exception observed is in the Area of Social Life, where both are similar in Modernity.

Comparatively Sasi Kumar, who is a 'Cartoonist' is more modern than Sunil, who is a manager in a factory, in General Modernity, Modernity all Areas of Life except Employment and Political life, Health and Hygiene, and Economic Life; in all Dimensions except Change Proneness. (In Social Life, both of them are equally modern.)

These differences are to be looked at from the backgrounds. It may be noted that both the cartoonist (Sasi Kumar) and the 'Manager' (Sunil) were born and brought up in the same place (i.e., Kumbalanghi—a rural area in Cochin Taluk).

Both are residents of their native place Kumbalanghi. Both of them are male Hindus.

Inference

Having shared several common backgrounds and common level of education, Sasi Kumar and Sunil differ in modernity. This difference appears to be related to their differences in occupation. Hence, occupation as a variable appears to influence the relationship between levels of Education and Modernity in terms of attitudes at higher levels of education.

Inference on Occupation

Having examined typical cases representing lower as well as higher levels of education with different occupations, it appears that Occupation as a variable influences the relationship between levels of Education and Modernity in terms of attitudes.

Exposure to Mass Media

The distribution of respondents by their level of education and exposure to mass media is shown in Table 5.69.

Table 5.69: Distribution of Respondents by Level of Education and Exposure to Mass-Media

Level of education	*Category of exposure to mass-media*	
	Low	High
Illiterate	62	38
Lower Primary	49	51
Upper Primary	28	72
SSLC	27	73
PDC	18	82
Graduate	8	92
PG & Professional	7	93
Total	199	501

It may be observed from Table 5.69 that a meaningful comparison of modernity scores of all categories of exposure to mass-media taking into account all levels of education is not feasible, as there are categories (cells) with insufficient observation in the distribution. Since a statistical analysis may not be justifiable, descriptive analysis of representative cases was considered as a viable alternative. For this purpose, two individual cases each were selected from Upper Primary representing lower levels of educational level and Graduate representing higher levels of educational levels. In each pair one case represents 'low exposure to mass-media', and the other 'high exposure to mass-media'.

Modernity Scores of the cases selected from Upper Primary level representing lower levels of education are presented in Table 5.70.

It may be observed from Table 5.70 that Rameshan and Suresh are different in their Modernity Score in General Modernity in all Areas of life except Education and in all Dimensions.

Suresh, with high exposure to mass-media (scoring more than 50 in the mass-media index) is more modern than Rameshan (who has a low exposure to mass-media) in General Modernity and in most of the components of Modernity. In the Areas of Health and Hygiene, Economic Life; and in the Dimension of Democratic Orientation and Achievement Orientation, Rameshan has an edge over Suresh in the Modernity Score. In the Area of Education both have equal Modernity Scores.

It may be noted that both Suresh and Rameshan are residents of the same village in Cochin taluk. Both are male Hindus and are not married at the time of the study. Both of them are engaged in fishing.

They studied in government schools and learned in Malayalam as medium of instruction.

Table 5.70: Modernity Scores by Mass-Media

	Category of Modernity	*Category of Exposure to Mass-Media*	
		** Low*	*** High*
	General Modernity	7.489130	7.991836
Areas of life	1. Education	8.72	8.72
	2. Employment	6.692	6.826666
	3. Marriage and Family	5.941818	6.76
	4. Religious life	8.473333	9.765
	5. Political life	8.661666	9.956666
	6. Social life	5.8	10.175
	7. Health and Hygiene	9.35375	8.544444
	8. Economic life	6.665	6.105
Dimensions	1. Change Proneness	8.862	9.335384
	2. Scientific Orientation	7.934285	8.13
	3. Democratic Orientation	7.524444	7.105
	4. Secular Orientation	5.8775	10.33833
	5. Achievement Orientation	5.898571	5.758888

*Rameshan
**Suresh

In spite of these and many other similarities, Suresh and Rameshan who have same level of education differ in their Modernity, with Suresh scoring higher in most cases than Rameshan. These differences appear to point towards the difference in the degree of exposure to mass-media that both the individuals have.

It is to be noted that Suresh regularly reads newspapers. '*Desabhimani*, *Malayalamanorama*, *Kerala Koumudi* and *Mathrubhumi*'.

Rameshan on the other hand, reads newspapers only 'sometimes' *Malayalamanorama* and *Mathrubhumi*. (No newspaper is subscribed in either houses of these individuals). While Suresh is regular in reading weeklies, Rameshan never reads weeklies. Suresh reads four weeklies (Malayalam).

Similarly Suresh listens to radio regularly. He listens to the news and film songs whereas Rameshan listens to radio only sometimes he is interested in songs.

Suresh watches TV sometimes particularly the news. Rameshan also reported that he watches TV sometimes, however, he (Rameshan) has no specific programme of interest in TV.

Both Suresh and Rameshan go for films regularly. While the former is interested in films of all languages, the latter sees only Malayalam and Tamil movies.

Inference

From the above comparisons it appears that though there are several commonalities including level of education between Suresh and Rameshan, both of them differ in Modernity in many components. The difference in their Modernity Scores may be due to their differences in the exposure to mass-media. Hence, mass-media as a variable appears to influence the relationship between levels of education and modernity in terms of attitudes at lower levels of education.

In order to know the influence of 'exposure to mass-media' on the relationship between levels of education and modernity in terms of attitudes at higher levels of education, two individuals from graduate level of education, Mohandas (representing low exposure to mass-media) and Prathapan (representing high exposure to mass-media) were selected. Modernity Scores of these individuals are presented in Table 5.71.

It may be observed from Table 5.71 that Mohandas and Prathapan are different in their Modernity Scores in all components of Modernity as well as General Modernity.

Between the two, Prathapan with high exposure to mass-media is more modern than Mohandas who has low exposure to mass-media, in General Modernity and in all components of Modernity, except in the Dimension of Secular Orientation. In Secular Orientation Mohandas has an edge over Prathapan in the Modernity Score.

The above differences, which are in almost all the cases in favour of Prathapan, is to be viewed from the backgrounds of both Mohandas and Prathapan.

Both Mohandas and Prathapan are male Hindus. Both of them are not married at the time of the study. They are residents of two neighbouring villages, Edavanakad and Kuzhupilly respectively in

Table 5.71: Distribution of Modernity Scores by Category of Modernity

	Category of Modernity	*Category of Exposure to Mass-Media*	
		**Low*	*** High*
General	Modernity	6.867948	9.540625
Areas of Life	1. Education	7.456666	8.606
	2. Employment	6.125	8.5
	3. Marriage and Family	3.725	9.193333
	4. Religious life	9.5	10.60333
	5. Political life	7.411666	10.12
	6. Social life	9.57	10.175
	7. Health and Hygiene	8.462857	9.575714
	8. Economic life	3.835	10.16
Dimensions	1. Change Proneness	8.9975	10.067
	2. Scientific Orientation	5.504615	9.62
	3. Democratic Orientation	6.654285	9.795714
	4. Secular Orientation	10.2225	9.083333
	5. Achievement Orientation	5.262857	8.365

* Mohandas
** Prathapan

the rural area of Cochin Taluk. Both have been brought up in the places where they reside. They both studied in Malayalam medium in schools which are aided by the government. It is to be noted that in spite of these and several other similarities in the background Mohandas and Prathapan differ in their modernity.

It is likely that the differences in the modernity between Mohandas and Prathapan are related to differences in their exposure to mass-media.

Prathapan is regular in reading newspaper. He reads three Malayalam dailies (*Malayalamanorama*, *Mathrubhumi*, and *Deshabhimani*). Mohandas on the other hand reads newspaper only 'sometimes'. He reads *Mathrubhumi* and *Manorama*. (While newspaper is subscribed at home in the case of Mohandas, it is not subscribed in the case of Prathapan).

Both of them read weeklies only 'sometimes'. While Prathapan reads two Malayalam weeklies *Kerala Sabdam* and *Malayala- manorama*, Mohandas reads only *Malayalamanorama*. While Prathapan is interested in items on politics, contemporary social issues, sports, and advertisements; and Mohandas is particular about novels and stories only.

Both Mohandas and Prathapan listen to radio only 'sometimes', while Mohandas is interested only in the news. Prathapan is interested in News, announcements of job opportunities, quiz., speeches, dramas, etc.

Both of them watch TV programmes only 'sometimes', while Mohandas watches some serials and news and Prathapan reported that he does not watch any programme regularly.

Mohandas as well as Prathapan go for films 'sometimes', while Mohandas goes for only Malayalam movies but Prathapan goes for Malayalam as well as English.

Inference

From the above comparisons, it appears that in spite of several similarities in their background, Mohandas and Prathapan differ in their modernity. In most of the components Prathapan is more modern.

These differences appear to be related to the differences in their exposure to mass media. It is Prathapan, with better exposure to mass- media, who has secured high on Modernity Scores than Mohandas.

Hence exposure to mass media appears to influence the relationship between levels of education and modernity in terms of attitudes at higher levels of education.

Inference on Exposure to Mass-Media

Having examined typical cases representing lower as well as higher levels of education with different exposures to mass-media, it appears that exposure to mass-media as a variable influences the relationship between levels of education and modernity in terms of attitudes.

Cumulative Observations on the Analyses of Interaction of Intervening Variables on the Relationship between Levels of Education and Modernity in terms of 'Attitudes' of Respondents

Findings on the analyses of interaction of moderator variables on the relationship between levels of education and Modernity in terms of attitudes of respondents are summarised in Table 5.72.

As may be observed from Table 5.72, variables such as Marital Status, Migration, and Type of Schooling do not show any significant

Table 5.72: Interaction of Intervening Variables[1] on the Relationship between Levels of Education and Modernity in terms of Attitudes of Respondents by Category of Modernity

Category of Modernity		*Moderator Variable*					
		Sex	*Marital Status*	*Religion*	*Place of Residence*	*Migration*	*Type of Schooling*
General Modernity		*					
Areas of Life	1. Education	*		*			
	2. Employment						
	3. Marriage and family						
	4. Religious life						
	5. Political life				*		
	6. Social life						
	7. Health and Hygiene						
	8. Economic life				**		
Dimensions	1. Change proneness						
	2. Scientific orientation	**					
	3. Democratic orientation	**					
	4. Secular orientation	**					
	5. Achievement orientation	*					

* Significant at 0.05 level.

** Significant at 0.01 level.

1. Excluding income, occupation, and exposure to mass-media.

interaction on the relationship between Levels of Education and Modernity in terms of attitudes of respondents. Significant interactions are observed in the case of Sex, Religion, and Place of Residence in selected categories of modernity. Of all of them, considerable influence is perceived with regard to the sex status of the respondents.

It may be recalled from Table 5.45 that male-female differences in General Modernity scores are observed at all levels of education as well as illiterates except PG and Professional levels. The differences are in favour of males. The gender differences in modernity scores which cuts across levels of education is likely to be the reflection of the socialisation patterns to which males and females are exposed. The male child in Indian society is taught to be modern and outgoing. A female child, on the other hand, is taught to be traditional and conservative.

Sex as a variable interacts on the relationship between levels of education and modernity in terms of attitudes of respondents in the case of General Modernity; Modernity in the Area of Education; in the Dimension Scientific Orientation, Democratic Orientation, Secular Orientation, and Achievement Orientation. In the remaining cases of modernity, sex differences do not influence the relationship between levels of education and modernity in terms of attitudes.

Significant interaction of Religion as a variable on the relationship between levels of education and modernity in terms of attitudes of respondents is observed only in the Area of Education. In the remaining categories of modernity, Religious differences of individuals do not influence the relationship between levels of education and modernity in terms of attitudes.

Place of residence interacts significantly on the relationship between levels of education and modernity in terms of attitudes of respondents in the Areas of Political Life, and Economic Life. No significant interaction is observed for the remaining categories of modernity.

It is clear from the above observations that variables such as sex, religion, and place of residence influence the relationship between levels of education and some components of modernity in terms of attitudes of respondents whereas Marital Status, Migration, and Type of Schooling do not influence the relationship. Analysis of representative cases indicated that income, occupation, and exposure to mass-media as variables influence the relationship between levels of education and modernity in terms of attitudes.

6

Levels of Education and Modernity in Terms of Behaviour

In the previous chapter, relationship between levels of education and modernity in terms of attitudes was examined.

This chapter deals with the relationship between levels of education and modernity in terms of behaviour.

It is expected that education helps individuals, who receive it in shaping their behaviour in the context of modernisation. It is also expected that differences in levels of education will be reflected in differences in the pattern of behaviour. Further, it is assumed that as levels of education increase, greater will be the movement towards expected behaviour in the context of modernity.

It may be recalled that the null hypothesis formulated in this context is as follows:

> "There is no significant relationship between levels of education and modernity in terms of behaviour of respondents."

The above null hypothesis is examined through percentage analysis of information on selected items pertaining to modernity of the respondents in terms of behaviour in different areas of life.

Levels of Education and Modernity in terms of Behaviour in the Area of Life Education

In order to examine the relationship between levels of education and modernity in terms of behaviour, information on the following items has been considered.

Item 1: Have you ever Studied a Subject which you did not like?

Choice is possible only in regard to the study of language especially second language at UP and SSLC levels, while at higher levels wider choice is possible just as it is in case of subject of specialisation.

Table 6.1: Distribution of Respondents by their Studying of subject which they did not like

Levels of Education	*Category of Response*				*Total*	*%*
	Yes	*%*	*No**	*%*		
UP	53	52.21	43	44.79	96	100.00
SSLC	30	30.61	68	69.39	98	100.00
PDC	27	27.27	72	72.73	99	100.00
Graduate	22	22.22	77	77.78	99	100.00
PG & Professional	36	36.36	63	63.64	99	100.00
Total	168	28.43	323	54.65	591	100.00

* Indicates behaviour considered as modern.

Note: Respondents of illiterate and LP levels are excluded in this analysis.

It may be observed from Table 6.1 that the proportion of respondents who did not study any subject which they did not like is different at different levels of education. While it is only 44.79 per cent at the UP level, it is more than 63 per cent at the higher levels of education i.e., SSLC and above. It is clear from Table 6.1 that as levels of education increases, the proportion at respondents reflecting modern behaviour also increases, with an exception of PG and Professional level.

Thus, it may be observed that levels of education and modernity in terms of behaviour in this case are related positively.

Levels of Education and Modernity in terms of Behaviour in the Area of Life, Marriage and Family

In order to examine the relationship between levels of education and modernity in terms of behaviour in the area of marriage and family of respondents, information on three items have been considered.

Item 2: Have you ever Adopted any Birth Control Measures?

It may be observed from Table 6.2 that the proportion of married respondents who have not adopted any birth control measures is different at different levels of education. A considerable proportion (more than 40 per cent) of respondents at all levels are adopters of birth control measures. More than 60 per cent of the respondents at UP, Graduate, and PG and Professional levels of education have adopted birth control.

Table 6.2: Distribution of Respondents by Adoption of Birth Control

Levels of Education	*Category of Response*				*Total*	*%*
	No	*%*	*Yes**	*%*		
Illiterate	27	46.55	31	53.45	58	100.00
LP	32	57.11	24	42.86	56	100.00
UP	17	34.00	33	66.00	50	100.00
SSLC	16	53.33	14	46.87	30	100.00
PDC	16	59.26	11	40.74	27	100.00
Graduate	5	38.46	8	61.54	13	100.00
PG & Professional	6	31.58	13	68.42	19	100.00
Total	119	47.04	134	52.96	253	100.00

* Indicates behaviour considered as modern.

It is interesting to note that even 53.45 per cent of illiterate respondents have adopted birth control measures.

As may be noted in Table 6.2, differences are there in the proportion of adopters of birth control across levels of education. Still there is no consistent pattern in such adoption.

Hence, it may be inferred that there is no consistent relationship between levels of education and modernity in terms of behaviour with regard to adoption of birth control.

The number of SSLC and PDC educated women who have adopted birth control measures is far lower than that of illiterate women. This may be because the SSLC and PDC educated women belong to middle class homes where traditional practices are still popular. They are mostly housewives. The illiterate women are mostly wage earners and find it convenient to adopt birth control measures. Even otherwise target-oriented measures of the government for birth control concentrate on illiterate women. Hence, education as a variable may not bring out strong differences between illiterate and educated women in regard to birth control measures.

Item 3: Do you Share Household Chores with your Spouse?

As it is clear from Table 6.3, the proportion of married respondents who share household chores with their spouses is different at different levels of education. This proportion is less than 50 per cent at all levels or education below SSLC and SSLC. However, at all levels of education above SSLC there is substantially high per cent, i.e. above 70 of respondents who share or allow to share household chores with their spouses. The highest percentage is observed at the PG and Professional level, i.e. 90.48.

Table 6.3: Distribution of Respondents by their Sharing of Household Chores with Spouse

Levels of Education	*Category of Responses*				*Total*	*%*
	Never	*%*	*Sometimes/ Always**	*%*		
Illiterate	35	55.56	28	44.44	63	100.00
LP	30	52.63	27	47.37	57	100.00
UP	30	56.60	23	43.40	53	100.00
SSLC	19	57.58	14	42.42	33	100.00
PDC	8	26.67	22	73.33	30	100.00
Graduate	2	14.29	12	85.71	14	100.00
PG & Professional	2	9.52	19	90.48	21	100.00
Total	126	46.49	145	53.51	271	100.00

* Indicates behaviour considered as modern

It may be noted that the proportion of respondents who share household chores with their spouse, decreases, though subtly, from illiterate to SSLC level. However, beyond SSLC level the proportion increases till PG and Professional level.

Hence, it appears that levels of education and modernity in terms of behaviour with reference to sharing of household chores with spouse are related negatively at the lower levels till SSLC level of education, and is related positively at the higher levels beyond SSLC.

Item 4: Do you allow your wife to sit along with you and talk to your guests (Do you sit along with your husband and talk to your guests?)

It may be observed from Table 6.4 that the percentage of married respondents who allow their spouse to sit along with them/who sit along with their spouses and talk to their guests is different at different levels of education. While this percentage is quite high at all levels of education and even among illiterates (77.78%), it is relatively lower at the lower levels of education (below SSLC); it is quite high at all levels above SSLC and is highest (100%) at the graduate, and PG and Professional levels.

Table 6.4: Distribution of Respondents by their Sitting or Allowing their Spouse to sit along with them while talking to their Guests

Levels of Education	*Category of Response*				*Total*	*%*
	Never	*%*	*Sometimes/ Always**	*%*		
Illiterate	14	22.22	49	77.78	63	100.00
LP	11	19.30	46	80.70	57	100.00
UP	11	20.75	42	79.25	53	100.00
SSLC	3	9.09	30	90.91	33	100.00
PDC	5	16.67	25	83.33	30	100.00
Graduate	–	–	15	100.00	15	100.00
PG and Professional	–	–	21	100.00	21	100.00
Total	44	16.18	228	83.82	272	100.00

* Indicates behaviour considered as modern.

As the figures in Table 6.4 indicate the percentage of respondents, who allow their spouses while talking to guests by and large increases from illiterate to PG and Professional levels of education, through SSLC. Exceptions to this are UP and PDC levels. It appears that by and large there is a positive relationship between levels of education and modernity in terms of behaviour in this case.

Modernity in terms of Behaviour in the Area of Religious Life

In order to examine the relationship between Levels of Education and Modernity in terms of Behaviour in the Area of Religious Life, information on three items pertaining to the behaviour of respondents have been considered. These items refer to the attendance in church/mosque/temple, beginning of new task/s on Tuesday and observation of 'Rahukala' while starting on any journey.

Item 5: How often do you attend Church/Mosque/Temple

The researcher is aware that one cannot infer a person as modern when he 'never' attends church/mosque/temple. It is possible that a person attending church/mosque/temple may record a high modernity score. This argument will not be pursued further. For this study, however, the stand taken is that the response 'never' for the given question is treated as modern.

Table 6.5: Distribution of Respondents by their Attendance in Church Mosque/Temple and Levels of Education

Levels of Education	*Category of Response*				*Total*	*%*
	*Never**	*%*	*Sometimes/ Regularly*	*%*		
Illiterate	18	18.37	80	81.63	98	100.00
LP	29	29.00	71	71.00	100	100.00
UP	18	18.00	82	82.00	100	100.00
SSLC	17	17.35	81	82.65	98	100.00
PDC	17	17.35	81	82.65	98	100.00
Graduate	15	15.15	84	84.85	99	100.00
PG and Professional	15	15.46	82	84.54	97	100.00
Total	129	18.70	561	81.30	690	100.00

* Indicates behaviour considered as modern.

It may be noted from Table 6.5 that the proportion of respondents who never attend Church/Mosque/Temple is quite low when compared to those who attend either sometimes/regularly.

It may also be noted that the proportion of respondents who never attend Church/Mosque/Temple is quite low among all levels of education. It is relatively higher among those belonging to lower levels of education, i.e. SSLC and below.

By and large the proportion of those who do not attend church/mosque/temple slightly decreases from illiterate to PG and Professional levels. It appears that there is no strong relationship between education and modernity in regard to the religious behaviour of attending Church/Mosque/Temple.

Item 6: Do you begin any new task on Tuesday?

It may be noted from Table 6.6 that the proportion of respondents who 'begin a new task' on Tuesday—sometimes/always—is the highest at the illiterate level.

Table 6.6: Distribution of Respondents by their Beginning of any New Task on Tuesday

Levels of Education	*Category of Responses*				*Total*	*%*
	Never	*%*	*Sometimes/ Always**	*%*		
Illiterate	23	23.23	76	76.77	99	100.00
LP	31	31.31	68	68.69	99	100.00
UP	31	31.63	67	68.37	98	100.00
SSLC	73	73.74	26	26.26	99	100.00
PDC	57	58.16	41	41.84	98	100.00
Graduate	55	57.89	40	42.11	95	100.00
PG & Professional	44	46.81	50	53.19	94	100.00
Total	314	46.04	368	53.96	682	100.00

* Indicates behaviour considered as modern.

From illiterate to UP, this proportion steadily decreases. There is a big slide at the SSLC level. From SSLC onwards, the proportion increases up to PG and Professional level.

With all the education the Matriculate and the Graduate respondents as a group appear to be more superstitious than illiterate and lower levels of educated respondents.

Hence, it appears that levels of education and modernity in terms of behaviour with reference to 'beginning of any new task on Tuesday' are related negatively till SSLC level of education, and is related positively at the higher levels beyond SSLC.

Item 7: Do you observe 'Rahukala' while starting on your Journey?

It may be observed from Table 6.7 that a substantially high per cent (more than 70%) of respondents at all levels of education never observe Rahukala while starting on their journey.

It may also be noted that there is no clear order in the percentage of respondents who do not observe Rahukala, from illiterate to PG and professional level.

An interesting observation to be noted from Table 6.7 is that PDC and Graduate levels of education have relatively lower percentage of respondents who do not observe Rahukala, when compared to all other levels of education as well as illiterates.

Table 6.7: Distribution of Respondents by their Observation of 'Rahukala' while starting on their Journey

Levels of Education	*Category of Responses*						*Total*	*%*
	Always	*%*	*Some-times*	*%*	*Never**	*%*		
Illiterate	13	13.13	6	6.06	80	80.81	99	100.00
LP	12	12.00	8	8.00	80	80.00	100	100.00
UP	8	8.16	7	7.14	83	84.69	98	100.00
SSLC	5	5.10	13	13.27	80	81.63	98	100.00
PDC	6	6.06	20	20.20	73	73.74	99	100.00
Graduate	3	3.03	19	19.19	77	77.78	99	100.00
PG and Professional	–	–	16	16.16	83	83.84	99	100.00
Total	47	6.79	89	12.86	556	80.35	692	100.00

* Indicates behaviour considered as modern.

It appears that education is not necessarily associated with modernity in regard to observance of Rahukala as a higher proportion of even illiterates do not observe it.

Modernity in terms of Behaviour in the Area of Social Life

In order to examine the relationship between levels of education and modernity in terms of behaviour in the Area of Social Life, information on two items pertaining to the behaviour of respondents have been considered. These items refer to (i) the habit of visiting the neighbours and (ii) the nature of response to invitations for functions like marriage.

Item 8: How often do you visit your neighbours?

It may be noted from Table 6.8 that with the exception of LP UP and levels of education, more than 90 per cent of the respondents at other

levels of education visit their neighbours frequently or at least sometimes.

Table 6.8: Distribution of Respondents by their habit of Visiting the Neighbours

Levels of Education	*Category of Responses*				*Total*	*%*
	Never	*%*	*Sometimes/ Frequently**	*%*		
Illiterate	7	7.00	93	93.00	100	100.00
LP	20	20.41	78	79.59	98	100.00
UP	17	17.53	80	82.47	97	100.00
SSLC	9	9.00	91	91.00	100	100.00
PDC	1	1.02	97	98.98	98	100.00
Graduate	8	8.08	91	91.92	99	100.00
PG & Professional	7	7.07	92	92.93	99	100.00
Total	69	9.99	622	90.01	691	100.00

* Indicates behaviour considered as modern.

It may also be noted that there is no clear increase or decrease in the proportion of respondents who visit their neighbours—sometimes/ frequently—as the levels of education increases.

Thus, it appears that education is not necessarily related to modernity in terms of behaviour with regard to habit of visiting neighbours.

Item 9: Whenever invited for functions like marriage, did you respond favourably to all types of invitations.

It may be observed from Table 6.9 that more than 80 per cent of the respondents at all levels of education have responded favourably to all types of invitations to functions like marriage.

Though the differences are not prominent there is by and large an increment in the proportion of respondents from illiterate to PG and Professional level showing a higher incidence of modern behaviour. Exception to this is Graduate level.

Table 6.9: Distribution of Respondents by their Response to Invitations for Functions like Marriage

Levels of Education	Category of Responses				Total	%
	Favourable to all types of invitations*	%	Favourable to only those of higher caste people/only those of own caste people	%		
Illiterate	81	81.82	18	18.18	99	100.00
LP	80	82.47	17	17.53	97	100.00
UP	81	83.51	16	16.49	97	100.00
SSLC	82	83.67	16	16.33	98	100.00
PDC	88	88.89	11	11.11	99	100.00
Graduate	86	88.66	11	11.34	97	100.00
PG & Professional	94	94 00	6	6.00	100	100.00
Total	592	86.17	95	13.83	687	100.00

* Indicates behaviour considered as modern.

Thus, it may be inferred that levels of education and modernity in terms of behaviour in this case are related positively.

Modernity in terms of Behaviour in the Area of Political Life

In order to examine the relationship between levels of education and modernity in terms of behaviour in the area of political life, information on the following item has been considered (see Table 6.10).

Item 10: Have you ever abstained from voting during elections

It is clear from Table 6.10 that more than 85 per cent of the respondents at all levels of education, except SSLC have not abstained from voting during elections. In the case of SSLC it is 79.80 per cent.

It may be noted from Table 6.10 that with regard to the difference in the proportion of non-abstention from voting between different levels of education is not prominent.

Table 6.10: Distribution of Respondents by their Abstention from Voting

Levels of Education	*Category of Responses*				*Total*	*%*
	Yes	*%*	*No**	*%*		
Illiterate	14	14.00	86	86.00	100	100.00
LP	11	11.11	88	88.89	99	100.00
UP	14	14.00	86	86.00	100	100.00
SSLC	20	20.20	79	79.80	99	100.00
PDC	13	13.13	86	86.87	99	100.00
Graduate	13	13.00	87	87.00	100	100.00
PG and Professional	13	13.13	86	86.87	99	100.00
Total	98	14.08	598	85.92	696	100.00

* Indicates behaviour considered as modern.

Thus, it appears that levels of education is not necessarily associated with modernity in terms of behaviour with regard to abstention from voting during elections.

Levels of Education and Modernity in terms of Behaviour in the Area of Health and Hygiene

In order to examine the relationship between levels of education and modernity in terms of behaviour in the area of Health and Hygiene, information on two items pertaining to the behaviour of respondents having children with regard to 'child care practices' have been considered.

Item 11: Were your child/children breastfed ?

It may be observed from Table 6.11 that cent per cent of the respondents at all levels of education have reported that their children were breastfed. Negligible exception to this are LP and PDC levels where 5.56 and 4.00 per cent respectively have not breastfed their children.

It thus appears that level of education is not necessarily associated with regard to modernity in terms of behaviour with regard to breast feeding of children.

Table 6.11: Distribution of Married Respondents by Breast Feeding of their Children

Levels of Education	*Category of Responses*				*Total*	*%*
	No	*%*	*Yes**	*%*		
Illiterate	–	–	57	100.00	57	100.00
LP	3	5.56	51	94.44	54	100.00
UP	–	–	48	100.00	48	100.00
SSLC	–	–	28	100.00	28	100.00
PDC	1	4.00	24	96.00	25	100.00
Graduate	–	–	12	100.00	12	100.00
PG and Professional	–	–	12	100.00	12	100.00
Total	4	1.69	232	98.31	236	100.00

* Indicates behaviour considered as modern.

Item 12: Were your children given triple-antigen injections?

It may be observed from Table 6.12 that more than 90 per cent of respondents at all levels of education have reported that their children were given triple-antigen injections. In the case of SSLC and Graduate levels, this is 100 per cent.

Thus level of education is not necessarily associated with child care practices as even 91.0 per cent of the illiterates have adopted these practices.

Table 6.12: Distribution of Respondents by the Provision of Triple-Antigen Injections to their Children

Levels of Education	*Category of Responses*				*Total*	*%*
	No	*%*	*Yes**	*%*		
Illiterate	5	8.93	51	91.07	56	100.00
LP	5	9.43	48	90.57	53	100.00
UP	3	6.12	46	93.88	49	100.00
SSLC	–	–	29	100.00	29	100.00
PDC	1	3.85	25	96.15	26	100.00
Graduate	–	–	12	100.00	12	100.00
PG and Professional	1	7.69	12	92.31	13	100.00
Total	15	6.30	223	93.70	238	100.00

* Indicates behaviour considered as modern.

Cumulative Observations on the Relationship between Levels of Education and Modernity in terms of Behaviour

Results of the preceding analyses indicate three different patterns in the relationship between levels of education and modernity in terms of behaviour. One of the patterns is characterised by a positive relationship between levels of education and modernity in terms of behaviour. That is, as levels of education increases, modernity in terms of behaviour also increases by and large.

Another pattern is characterised by negative relationship at the lower levels of education up to SSLC and a positive relationship at the higher levels of education, i.e., beyond SSLC. For the present purpose this pattern may be referred to as 'Curvilinear Relationship'.

The third pattern is characterised by the absence of a clear order in modernity, reflecting modernity in terms of behaviour, across levels of education indicating no relationship. Results of the preceding analyses of relationship between levels of education and modernity in terms of behaviour of respondents are summarised in Table 6.13.

It may be observed from Table 6.13 that in the case of items in three areas of life there is a positive relationship between levels of education and modernity in terms of behaviour. These are items No. 1, 4 and 9, belonging to the areas of education, marriage and family, and social life, respectively.

Table 6.13: Distribution of Items Pertaining to Modernity in terms of Behaviour by Areas of Life and their Nature of Relationship with Levels of Education

Areas of Life	*Nature of Relationship*			*Total*
	Positive	*Curvilinear*	*No Relationship*	
Education	1	—	—	1
Marriage and Family	1	1	1	3
Religious Life	—	1	2	3
Social Life	1	—	1	2
Political Life	—	—	1	1
Health and Hygiene	—	—	2	2
Total	3	2	7	12

In the case of items in two areas of life, the relationship observed is curvilinear. It is by and large a 'U' shaped curve. These are item

Nos. 3 and 4, belonging to the areas of marriage and family, and religious life, respectively. This means that without education illiterates and lower levels of educated appear to be modern while respondents at the middle level of education, taken as SSLC and PDC, are not so. Again with increasing levels of education, modernity also increases.

In the remaining cases there is no relationship between levels of education and modernity in terms of behaviour.

It is interesting to note that there is no incidence of steadily increasing inverse relationship between levels of education and modernity.

Inference

It may thus be inferred that modernity in terms of behaviour need not necessarily be associated with levels of education. Incidents of positive and curvilinear relationship are observed.

It is likely that behaviour of individuals are more influenced by factors other than their level of education and are guided by the nature of the given context in which the behaviour is carried out. But it would be worthwhile to examine whether the behaviours observed among the respondents have any bearing with their attitudes in corresponding areas of life. This is attempted in the following Chapter.

7

Consistency between Attitudinal and Behavioural Modernity Across Levels of Education

In the preceding chapters, relationships between levels of education and modernity in terms of attitudes as well as behaviour was examined separately.

This chapter deals with the consistency between attitudes and behaviour reflecting modernity of respondents across different levels of education.

In the context of the present study, it has been hypothesised that:

> "There is no significant relationship between attitudes and behaviour reflecting modernity of respondents with different levels of education."

Relationship between attitudes and behaviour reflecting modernity of respondents is examined by analysing the consistency/inconsistency in the behaviour of respondents with that of their corresponding attitude reflecting modernity. If the expressed attitude and the corresponding behaviour are converging then it is treated as consistency; whereas if the behaviour is divergent from that of the expressed attitude, it is treated as inconsistency. (Divergence of behaviour from that of attitude is referred to as cognitive dissonance).

For the purpose of consistency-inconsistency analysis, information on the response of individual respondents on a selected set of pairs consisting of attitudinal statements and behavioural items is considered. These pairs of items are selected in such a way that both attitudinal statement as well as behavioural items are representing the same component of modernity. Basically the purpose is to identify the levels of education where consistency/inconsistency is observed.

Methodology

Considering only those respondents, who have expressed modernity in their attitude, the number of them reflecting modernity in their corresponding behaviour is worked out. From this, the percentage of divergence in behaviour, from that of attitude is worked out. Based on this consistency/inconsistency is identified at all levels of education.

For operational purposes it was felt that a divergence of up to 25 per cent should be interpreted as consistency. Hence inconsistency is attributed only when the divergence in behaviour exceeds 25 per cent.

Following the above technique, consistency/inconsistency analysis was made at all levels of education for all the selected pairs of items consisting of attitudinal statements as well as behavioural items.

Consistency between Attitudes and Behaviour reflecting Modernity in the Area of Education across Levels of Education

In order to examine the relationship between modernity in terms of attitude and behaviour in the Area of Education, information on the following pair of items is considered:

Attitudinal Statement	—	No child should be forced to study any subject, which the child does not like. Response: Agree/Disagree/No Response
Behavioural Item	—	Have you ever studied a subject which you did not like. Response: Yes/No/No Response

In the above pair, positive (agree) response on attitudinal item is considered modern whereas negative (no) response is treated as modern for the behavioural item.

Consistency-Inconsistency analysis was followed, for the above pair of items, considering only those respondents who have expressed positive response on the attitudinal statement. Respondents belonging to illiterate, LP and UP levels of education are not included in this analysis. Results thus obtained are presented in Table 7.1.

Table 7.1: Distribution of Respondents by Levels of Education and Type of Response in Attitude and Behaviour in the Area of Education

Levels of Education	*Positive Response on Attitudinal Statement*	*Negative Response on Behavioural Item*	*Divergence of Behaviour from Attitude (%)*	*Remarks C/IC*
PDC	88	66	25.00	C
Graduate	86	66	23.26	C
PG and Professional	86	56	34.88	IC
Total	260	188	27.69	IC

C= Consistent
IC= Inconsistent

It may be observed from Table 7.1 that the sample as a whole reflects inconsistency in their behaviour in relation to their attitude reflecting modernity.

It may further be noted that while respondents belonging to PDC and Graduate levels show consistency in their attitudes and behaviour reflecting modernity, those at the PG and Professional level are inconsistent.

While the proportion of divergence is 25 and 23.26 per cent at the PDC and Graduate levels respectively, at the PG and Professional level it is 34.88. (It may be noted that this observation is limited only for PDC, Graduate. and PG and Professional levels of education and, hence, not generalisable for all levels).

It may be thus inferred that at higher levels of education the relationship between behavioural modernity is not a consistent one in the area of education.

Consistency between Attitudes and Behaviour reflecting Modernity in the Area of Marriage and Family across Levels of Education

In order to examine the relationship between modernity in terms of attitudes and behaviour in the area of marriage and family, four pairs of attitudinal and behavioural items are considered.

Pair 1

Attitudinal Statement	:	To practice birth control is against the will of God.
Response	:	Agree/Disagree/No Response
Behavioural item	:	Have you ever adopted any birth control measure?
Response	:	Yes/No/No Response

In the above pair, negative response (disagree) in the case of attitude and positive response on behavioural item (Yes) are considered as modern.

Considering only those married respondents who have reflected modernity in their attitude, consistency/inconsistency analysis was followed for the above pair of items. Results thus obtained are presented in Table 7.2.

Table 7.2: Distribution of Respondents by Levels of Education and Type of Response in Attitude and Behaviour in the Area of Marriage and Family

Levels of Education	*Negative Response on Attitudinal Statement*	*Positive Response on Behavioural Item*	*Divergence of Behaviour from Attitude (%)*	*Remarks C/IC*
Illiterate	33	16	51.52	IC
LP	34	15	55.88	IC
UP	26	17	34.62	IC
SSLC	24	12	50.00	IC
PDC	25	10	60.00	IC
Graduate	12	8	33.33	IC
PG & and Professional	19	13	31.58	IC
Total	173	91	47.40	IC

C = Consistent
IC = Inconsistent

It may be observed from Table 7.2 that the sample as a whole reflects inconsistency in their behaviour in relation to their attitude reflecting modernity. Inconsistency is also observed at all levels of education including illiterate.

It appears that attitude and behaviour reflecting modernity of respondents with regard to the practice of birth control are not related, regardless of the level of education.

Pair 2

Attitudinal Statement	:	One should go on getting children until one gets a son (if he has only daughters).
Response	:	Agree/Disagree/No Response
Behavioural item	:	Have you ever adopted any birth control measure?
Response	:	Yes/No/No Response

In the above pair negative response (Disagree) in the case of attitude and positive response on the behavioural item (Yes) are considered modern.

Considering only those married respondents, who have reflected modernity in their attitude, consistency/inconsistency analysis was followed for the above pair of items. Results thus obtained are presented in Table 7.3.

Table 7.3: Distribution of Respondents by Levels of Education and Type of Response in Attitude and Behaviour in the Area of Marriage and Family

Levels of Education	*Negative Response on Attitudinal Statement*	*Positive Response on Behavioural Item*	*Divergence of Behaviour from Attitude (%)*	*Remarks C/IC*
Illiterate	34	19	44.12	IC
LP	34	13	61.76	IC
UP	32	21	34.38	IC
SSLC	28	14	50.00	IC
PDC	24	10	58.33	IC
Graduate	13	8	38.46	IC
PG and Professional	19	13	31.58	IC
Total	184	98	46.74	IC

C = Consistent
IC = Inconsistent

It may be observed from Table 7.3 that the sample as a whole reflects inconsistency in their behaviour in relation to their attitude reflecting modernity. Similarly inconsistency is observed at all levels of education including illiterate.

From the above observations it may be inferred that attitude and behaviour reflecting modernity of respondents with regard to the 'norm of small family' are not related, regardless of the level of education.

Inference

It appears that there is no relationship between attitude and behaviour reflecting modernity of respondents with ragard to the norm of small family regardless of level of education.

Pair 3

Attitudinal Statement	:	Husband should not do any kitchen work under any circumstance
Response	:	Agree/Disagree/No Response
Behavioural item	:	Do you share household chores with your wife (do you allow your husband to share household chores with you) ?
Response	:	Always/Sometimes/Never/No response

In the above pair negative response (Disagree) on attitudinal statement and positive response (Always/Sometimes) on the behavioural item are considered modern.

Taking only those married respondents, who have reflected modernity in the above attitudinal statement, consistency/inconsistency analysis was followed for the above pair of items. Result thus obtained are presented in Table 7.4.

It may be observed from Table 7.4 that the sample as a whole reflects inconsistency in their behaviour in relation to their attitude reflecting modernity. However, this observation is not uniform across different levels of education

While LP, UP and SSLC levels reflect inconsistency, the remaining levels above SSLC indicate consistency in their behaviour in relation to modernity reflected in their attitude.

Table 7.4: Distribution of Respondents by Levels of Education and Type of Response in Attitude and Behaviour in the Area of Marriage and Family

Levels of Education	*Negative Response on Attitudinal Statement*	*Positive Response on Behavioural Item*	*Divergence of Behaviour from Attitude (%)*	*Remarks C/IC*
Illiterate	17	14	17.65	C
LP	26	19	26.92	IC
UP	21	15	28.57	IC
SSLC	23	14	39.13	IC
PDC	25	20	20.00	C
Graduate	14	12	14.29	C
PG and Professional	20	19	5.00	C
Total	146	113	22.60	C

C = Consistent
IC = Inconsistent

Further it may be noted that in terms of percentage of divergence in the behaviour from that of attitude; the lower levels of education (including SSLC and excluding illiterate) reflect greater degree when compared to high levels of education. This figure increases from LP level to SSLC and decreases from PDC to PG Professional level.

It appears that as levels of education increase beyond SSLC, consistency in behaviour by and large increases and inconsistency decreases.

Inference

From the above observations, it may be concluded that attitude and behaviour reflecting modernity of respondents with regard to 'sharing household chores with spouse' are related at higher levels of education. School education may not lead to consistency in behaviour and attitudes reflecting modernity in family life with regard to sharing household chores with spouse.

Pair 4

Attitudinal Statement	:	Husband should treat his wife as equal to him.
Response	:	Agree/Disagree/No response

Behavioural item : Do you allow your wife to sit along with you and talk to your guests
(Do you sit along with your husband and talk to your guests).

Response : Always/Sometimes/Never/No Response

In the pair mentioned above, positive (agree) response on attitude and behaviour (Always/Sometimes) is considered as modern.

Considering only those married respondents, who have reflected modernity in their attitude, consistency/inconsistency analysis was followed for the above pair of items. Result thus obtained is presented in Table 7.5.

Table 7.5: Distribution of Respondents by Levels of Education and Type of Response in Attitude and Behaviour in the Area of Marriage and Family

Levels of Education	*Positive Response on Attitudinal Statement*	*Positive Response on Behavioural Item*	*Divergence of Behaviour from Attitude (%)*	*Remarks C/IC*
Illiterate	34	27	20.50	C
LP	43	35	18.60	C
UP	35	28	20.00	C
SSLC	29	28	3.45	C
PDC	26	21	19.23	C
Graduate	15	15	0.00	C
PG and Professional	21	21	0.00	C
Total	203	175	13.79	C

C = Consistent.
IC = Inconsistent.

It may be observed from Table 7.5 that the sample as a whole reflects inconsistency in their behaviour in relation to their attitude reflecting modernity. Similarly, consistency is observed at all levels of education including illiterate.

It is apparent from Table 7.5 that regardless of the level of education, there is consistency in terms of modernity as reflected in the attitude and behaviour of respondents.

It may be concluded from the above observations that attitude and behaviour reflecting modernity of respondents with regard to ‘equality of status between spouses’ are related, regardless of the levels of education.

Consistency between Attitudes and Behaviour reflecting Modernity in the Area of Religious Life across Levels of Education

In order to examine the relationship between modernity in terms of attitudes and behaviour in the area of religious life, three pairs of attitudinal and behavioural items are considered.

Pair 1

Attitudinal Statement	:	One can lead a contented life even without attending Church/Mosque/ Temple
Response	:	Agree/Disagree/No Response
Behavioural item	:	How often do you attend Church/ Mosque/Temple
Response	:	Regular/Sometimes/Never/No Response

In the above pair positive response (Agree) on attitudinal statement and negative response (Never) on the behavioural items are considered as modern.

Taking only those respondents, who have reflected modernity in their attitude, consistency/inconsistency analysis was followed for the above pair of items. Results thus obtained are presented in Table 7.6.

Table 7.6: Distribution of Respondents by Levels of Education and Type of Response in Attitude and Behaviour in the Area of Religious life

Levels of Education	*Positive Response on Attitudinal Statement*	*Negative Response on Behavioural Item*	*Divergence of Behaviour from Attitude (%)*	*Remarks C/IC*
Illiterate	44	9	79.55	IC
LP	43	18	58.14	IC
UP	43	6	86.05	IC
SSLC	59	11	81.36	IC
PDC	76	16	78.95	IC
Graduate	53	10	81.13	IC
PG and Professional	70	14	80.00	IC
Total	388	84	78.35	IC

C = Consistent.
IC = Inconsistent.

It may be observed from Table 7.6 that the sample as a whole reflects inconsistency in their behaviour in relation to their attitude reflecting modernity. Inconsistency is also observed at all levels of education including illiterate.

It is clear from Table 7.6 that differences in the levels of education are not reflected in the relationship between attitude and behaviour reflecting modernity (as all levels uniformly show inconsistency).

It appears that there is no relationship between attitude and behaviour reflecting modernity of respondents regarding attending Church/Mosque/Temple and levels of education.

Pair 2

Attitudinal Statement	:	Tuesday is not a good day for auspicious functions
Response	:	Agree/Disagree/No Response
Behavioural item	:	Do you begin any new task on Tuesday
Response	:	Always/Sometimes/Never/No Response

In the above pair, negative response (disagree) on attitude and positive response (Always/Sometimes) on the behavioural items are considered as modern.

Taking only those respondents, who have reflected modernity in their attitude, consistency/inconsistency analysis was followed for the above pair of items. Results thus obtained are presented in Table 7.7.

It may be observed from Table 7.7 that on the whole the sample shows inconsistency in their behaviour in relation to their attitude reflecting modernity.

It may further be noted from Table 7.7 that all levels of education below SSLC, show consistency in terms of attitude and behaviour, whereas SSLC and above levels of education show inconsistency.

Thus, it appears that attitude and behaviour reflecting modernity of respondents with regard to ‘beginning any new task on Tuesday’ are related at lower levels of education and are not related at the higher levels.

Table 7.7: Distribution of Respondents by Levels of Education and Type of Response in Attitude and Behaviour in the Area of Religious Life

Levels of Education	*Negative Response on Attitudinal Statement*	*Positive Response on Behavioural Item*	*Divergence of Behaviour from Attitude (%)*	*Remarks C/IC*
Illiterate	62	57	8.06	C
LP	61	55	9.84	C
UP	57	49	14.04	C
SSLC	74	20	72.97	IC
PDC	74	36	51.35	IC
Graduate	74	35	52.70	IC
PG and Professional	84	49	41.67	IC
Total	486	301	38.07	IC

C = Consistent.
IC = Inconsistent.

Pair 3

Attitudinal Statement	:	One should not start one's journey during Rahukala
Response	:	Agree/Disagree/No Response
Behavioural item	:	Do you observe Rahukala while starting on your journey?
Response	:	Always/Sometimes/Never/No Response

In the above pair, negative response on attitude (Disagree) as well as on behaviour (Never) are considered as modern.

Considering only those respondents, who have reflected modernity in their attitude, consistency/inconsistency analysis was followed for the above pair of items. Results thus obtained are presented in Table 7.8.

It may be observed from Table 7.8 that the sample as a whole shows consistency in their behaviour in relation to their attitude reflecting modernity.

Consistency in attitude and behaviour reflecting modernity is also observed across all levels of education and even illiterates. Thus, it appears that attitude and behaviour reflecting modernity of respondents with regard to 'observing Rahukala while starting on a journey' are related, regardless of levels of education.

Table 7.8: Distribution of Respondents by Levels of Education and Type of Response in Attitude and Behaviour in the Area of Religious Life

Levels of Education	*Negative Response on Attitudinal Statement*	*Negative Response on Behavioural Item*	*Divergence of Behaviour from Attitude (%)*	*Remarks C/IC*
Illiterate	66	63	4.55	C
LP	72	65	9.72	C
UP	76	75	1.32	C
SSLC	81	71	12.35	C
PDC	73	65	10.96	C
Graduate	83	71	14.46	C
PG and Professional	86	78	9.30	C
Total	537	488	9.12	C

C = Consistent.
IC = Inconsistent.

Consistency between Attitudes and Behaviour reflecting Modernity in the Area of Political Life across Levels of Education

In order to examine this relationship between modernity in terms of attitudes and behaviour, in the area of political life, the following pair of attitudinal statement and behavioural item is considered.

Attitudinal Statement : It does not matter even if one abstains from voting
Response : Agree/Disagree/No Response
Behavioural item : Have you ever abstained from voting during elections
Response : Yes/No/No Response

In the above pair, negative response (Disagree) on attitudinal statement and negative response (No) on the behavioural item are considered as modern.

Considering only those respondents, who have reflected modernity in their attitude, consistency/inconsistency analysis was followed for the above pair of items. Results thus obtained are presented in Table 7.9.

It may be observed from Table 7.9 that the sample as a whole shows consistency in their behaviour in relation to their attitude reflecting modernity. Consistency is also observed at all levels of education, including illiterate.

Table 7.9: Distribution of Respondents by Levels of Education and Type of Response in Attitude and Behaviour in the Area of Political Life

Levels of Education	*Negative Response on Attitudinal Statement*	*Negative Response on Behavioural Item*	*Divergence of Behaviour from Attitude (%)*	*Remarks C/IC*
Illiterate	61	55	9.84	C
LP	40	37	7.50	C
UP	47	40	14.89	C
SSLC	71	60	15.49	C
PDC	74	66	10.81	C
Graduate	79	69	12.66	C
PG and Professional	68	63	7.35	C
Total	440	390	11.36	C

C = Consistent.
IC = Inconsistent.

It appears that education is not associated with consistency between attitude and behaviour reflecting modernity with regard to 'abstention from voting during elections'.

Consistency between Attitudes and Behaviour reflecting Modernity in the Area of Social Life across Levels of Education

In order to examine the relationship between attitudes and behaviour reflecting modernity in the area of social life in the context of levels of education, two pairs of attitudinal statement and behavioural items are considered.

Pair 1

Attitudinal Statement : One should have cordial relationship with one's neighbours-
Response : Agree/Disagree/No Response
Behavioural item : How often do you visit your neighbours
Response : Frequently/Sometimes/Never/No Response

In the above pair, positive response (Agree) on attitude as well as behaviour (Frequently/Sometimes) is considered as modern.

Considering only those respondents, who have reflected modernity in their attitude, consistency/inconsistency analysis was followed for the above pair of items. Results thus obtained are presented in Table 7.10:

Table 7.10: Distribution of Respondents by Levels of Education and Type of Response in Attitude and Behaviour in the Area of Social Life

Levels of Education	*Positive Response on Attitudinal Statement*	*Positive Response on Behavioural Item*	*Divergence of Behaviour from Attitude (%)*	*Remarks C/IC*
Illiterate	88	81	7.95	C
LP	92	73	20.65	C
UP	89	73	17.98	C
SSLC	98	89	9.18	C
PDC	96	95	1.04	C
Graduate	96	89	7.29	C
PG and Professional	99	92	7.07	C
Total	658	592	10.03	C

C = Consistent.
IC = Inconsistent.

It may be observed from Table 7.10 that the sample as a whole shows consistency in their behaviour in relation to their attitude reflecting modernity. Consistency is also observed at all levels of education including illiterate.

It is clear from Table 7.10 that attitude and behaviour of respondents are related in this case and consistency does not differ across different levels of education.

It appears that attitude and behaviour reflecting modernity of respondents with regard to their 'relationship with neighbours' are related regardless of levels of education.

Pair 2

Attitudinal Statement	:	It is a shame for anyone to be in the company of a lower caste member
Response	:	Agree/Disagree/No Response
Behavioural item	:	Whenever invited for functions like marriage, you have responded to....?
Response	:	Only those of own caste people/Only those of higher caste people/All types of invitations/None/No Response

In the above pair, negative response (Disagree) on attitude and positive response (All types of invitations) in the case of behaviour is considered modern.

Considering only those respondents, who have reflected modernity in their attitude, consistency/inconsistency analysis was followed for the above pair of items. Results thus obtained are presented in Table 7.11.

Table 7.11: Distribution of Respondents by Levels of Education and Type of Response in Attitude and Behaviour in the Area of Social Life

Levels of Education	*Negative Response on Attitudinal Statement*	*Positive Response on Behavioural Item*	*Divergence of Behaviour from Attitude (%)*	*Remarks C/IC*
Illiterate	62	56	9.68	C
LP	61	50	18.03	C
UP	62	56	9.68	C
SSLC	92	78	15.22	C
PDC	97	86	11.34	C
Graduate	95	85	10.53	C
PG and Professional	99	93	6.06	C
Total	568	504	11.27	C

C = Consistent.
IC = Inconsistent.

It may be observed from Table 7.11 that the sample as a whole shows consistency in their behaviour in relation to their attitude reflecting modernity. Consistency is also observed at all levels of education including illiterate.

It is clear from Table 7.11 that attitude and behaviour of respondents are related in this case and consistency does not differ across different levels of education.

Thus, it appears that attitude and behaviour reflecting modernity of respondents with regard to their 'relationship with people of other castes' are related regardless of levels of education.

Consistency between Attitudes and Behaviour Reflecting Modernity in the Area of Health and Hygiene across Levels of Education

In order to examine the relationship between attitudes and behaviour of respondents reflecting modernity in the area of health and hygiene, two pairs of attitudinal statements and behavioural items are considered.

Pair 1

Attitudinal Statement	:	Breast feeding will affect the health of the mother
Response	:	Agree/Disagree/No Response
Behavioural item	:	Were your child/children breastfed
Response	:	Yes/No/No Response

In the above pair, negative response (Disagree) on attitude and positive response (Yes) on behaviour are considered as modern. (It is confirmed that none of the respondents had any physiological problems in breastfeeding).

Considering only the married respondents having children, and who have reflected modernity in their attitude, consistency/inconsistency analysis was followed for the above pair of items. Results thus obtained are presented in Table 7.12.

Table 7.12: Distribution of Respondents by Levels of Education and Type of Response in Attitude and Behaviour in the Area of Health and Hygiene

Levels of Education	*Negative Response on Attitudinal Statement*	*Positive Response on Behavioural Item*	*Divergence of Behaviour from Attitude (%)*	*Remarks C/IC*
Illiterate	37	37	0.00	C
LP	34	32	5.88	C
UP	33	33	0.00	C
SSLC	23	23	0.00	C
PDC	19	19	0.00	C
Graduate	11	11	0.00	C
PG and Professional	11	11	0.00	C
Total	168	166	1.19	C

C = Consistent.
IC = Inconsistent.

It may be observed from Table 7.12 that the sample as a whole reflects consistency in behaviour in relation to their attitude reflecting modernity. Consistency is observed at all levels of education including illiterate.

It is clear from Table 7.12 that attitude and behaviour of respondents are related in this case and consistency does not differ across different levels of education.

Thus, it appears that attitude and behaviour reflecting modernity of respondents with regard to 'breast feeding of their children' are related, regardless of levels of education.

Pair 2

Attitudinal Statement	:	New born babies should be given triple antigen injections within the stipulated time
Response	:	Agree/Disagree/No Response
Behavioural item	:	Were your child/children given triple antigen injections
Response	:	Yes/No/No Response

In the above pair, positive response (Agree) on attitude and for behaviour (Yes) are considered as modern.

Considering only the married respondents having children, and who have reflected modernity in their attitude, consistency/ inconsistency analysis was followed for the above pair of items. Results thus obtained are presented in Table 7.13.

Table 7.13: Distribution of Respondents by Levels of Education and Type of Response in Attitude and Behaviour in the Area of Health and Hygiene

Levels of Education	*Positive Response on Attitudinal Statement*	*Positive Response on Behavioural Item*	*Divergence of Behaviour from Attitude (%)*	*Remarks C/IC*
Illiterate	51	46	9.80	C
LP	52	48	7.69	C
UP	49	46	6.12	C
SSLC	28	28	0.00	C
PDC	25	25	0.00	C
Graduate	12	12	0.00	C
PG and Professional	12	11	8.33	C
Total	229	216	5.68	C

C = Consistent.

IC = Inconsistent.

It may be observed from Table 7.13 that the sample as a whole shows consistency in behaviour in relation to their attitude reflecting modernity. Consistency is observed at all levels of education, including illiterate.

It is clear from Table 7.13 that attitude and behaviour of respondents are related in this case and consistency does not differ across different levels of education.

Thus, it appears that attitude and behaviour reflecting modernity of respondents with regard to 'immunisation of their children' are related regardless of levels of education.

Cumulative Observations

The results obtained through consistency—inconsistency analyses that were followed for different pairs of items consisting of attitudinal statement and behavioural item are summarised in Table 7.14.

It may be observed from Table 7.14 that there is consistency between attitudes and behaviour reflecting modernity of respondents in different areas of life. It is uniform across levels of education for 7 out or 13 pairs (pairs 5, 8, 9, 10, 11, 12 and 13).

Similarly, inconsistency is observed for different pairs of items belonging to different areas of Life.

Inconsistency is uniform across levels of education in the case of pairs 2 and 3 (Area of Marriage and Family) as well as pair 6 (Area of Religious Life).

Inconsistency is not uniform across levels of education in the case of pairs 1 (Area of Education), 4 (Area of Marriage and Family), and 7 (Area of Religious Life). While inconsistency is observed at higher levels of education in pair 7 and pair 1, the same is found at lower levels of education in pair 4.

Table 7.14: Distribution of Pairs of Items showing Consistency/Inconsistency in Attitude and Behaviour reflecting Modernity of Respondents by Levels of Education and Areas of Life

Levels of Education	*Areas of Life*												
	Education	*Marriage and Family*				*Religious Life*			*Political Life*	*Social Life*		*Health & Hygiene*	
	1	2	3	4	5	6	*7*	8	9	*10*	*11*	*12*	*13*
	C/IC	*C/IC*	*C/IC*	*C/IC*	*C/IC*	*C/IC*	*C/IC*	*C/IC*	*C/IC*	*C/IC*	*C/IC*	*C/IC*	*C/IC*
Illiterate	—	IC	IC	C	C	IC	C	C	C	C	C	C	C
LP	—	IC	IC	IC	C	IC	C	C	C	C	C	C	C
UP	—	IC	IC	IC	C	IC	C	C	C	C	C	C	C
SSLC	—	IC	IC	IC	C	IC	IC	C	C	C	C	C	C
PDC	C	IC	IC	C	C	IC	IC	C	C	C	C	C	C
Graduate	C	IC	IC	C	C	IC	IC	C	C	C	C	C	C
PG and Professional	IC	IC	IC	C	C	IC	IC	C	C	C	C	C	C
Total	IC	IC	IC	C	C	IC	IC	C	C	C	C	C	C

C = Consistent.

IC = Inconsistent.

Conclusion

In general, moderate dissonance is observed across levels of education with regard to attitudes and corresponding behaviour reflecting modernity.

There are many areas of life where formal education is not associated with the relationship between attitude and behaviour reflecting modernity such as on certain items of behaviour under Marriage and Family, Religious Life, Political Life, Social Life and Health and Hygiene, as consonance or dissonance is observed even among illiterates.

8

Summary of the Work Done, Findings and Conclusions

The process of modernisation in India in its crude form began with the advent of the British in the nineteenth century. Initially, as conceived by Lord Macaulay, it was perceived of as an attempt at Westernising the Indian people. However, several dissenting views within the country got crystallised along with the freedom movement. This led to the integration of the rational humane and nobler aspects of indigenous culture with the best traditions of science, technology, and culture of the West. Some of the illustrative dissenting views that may be noted were expressed at different points of time by Dadabhai Naoroji, Raja Ram Mohan Roy, Dayananda Saraswati, Ishwar Chandra Vidyasagar, Annie Besant, Vivekananda, Gokhale, Tilak, Gandhiji, Jawaharlal Nehru, and Sir M. Visveswaraiah. A few movements also came up like the Arya Samaj, Brahma Samaj, Theosophical movement, etc., apart from the freedom movement which had a great potential for the modernisation of Indian society. The later part of the nineteenth century and the early decades of the twentieth century have been referred to as the Renaissance in India. The pervading influence of developments in Europe in the closing stages of eighteenth century and nineteenth century, developments in Russia in the earlier part of the twentieth century as well as the two World Wars which gave rise to the setting up of the United Nations in 1945, had a cumulative effect on the modernisation of Indian society at the time of independence. This is clearly reflected in the blue print of a new society whose framework was defined by the Constitution of India enacted in 1950. Later this was concretised through several instruments of social, economic and political action. Adoption of the Five-Year Planning strategy for development to lift the Indian economy to 'commanding heights', heavy emphasis on industrialisation in the Second Five-Year Plan and the creation of a large network of public sector industries, development of political institutions at the grassroots level through the Panchayati Raj Act, 1959, popularisation of scientific methods of agriculture through green revolution, channelisation of river waters through major hydel and irrigation projects, gold control, nationalisation of banking and development of cooperatives for sugar, milk, and cooperative financial institutions are all illustrations of the modernising process in Indian Society.

Though Indian society has been undergoing a process of modernisation, it was only in 1966 that modernisation as a transparent objective of education came on surface, when education commission headed by Dr. D.S. Kothari considered it as such in the Report entitled 'Education and National Development'. The Indian Parliament adopted this Report in 1968. Since then, modernisation has come to stay as one of the explicitly stated objectives of Indian education.

Modernisation is a macro-level, all-pervading, diffusive process of social change that cuts across the economic, social, and political life of a society. It may include technological changes in the fields of agriculture, industry infrastructural development and support services. It may include the emergence of economic institutions such as those of banking, commerce and trade and the setting up of political institutions for decentralised planning and development of a sophisticated bureaucracy as well as a complex network of institutions for management of the state. There may be changes in social institutions, marriage and kinship, family structure, status of religion in social life, etc. Similarly, large-scale structural changes as well as phenomenal expansion of formal and non-formal educational systems may also be part of this modernising process. It is felt that the end state of these processes of modernisation may be considered to be the creation of a sustainable enlightened civil society, whose tool is 'universal reason' and whose goal is 'human welfare'. The creation of such a society implies a metamorphic change in the lives of the people, a large scale change in their habits of social life, thinking processes, attitudes and values. This contemplated end state of change may be conceived of as 'modernity'. However, for any given point of time modernity can be considered to be a set of attitudes and behaviours that are commensurate with this end state.

Education, then, is one of the chief instruments of development of modernity. Herein heavy reliance is placed on the system of formal education which comprises of schools, colleges, universities and other institutions of higher learning. It is recognised that the very atmosphere in a society, the immediate community environment, the filial influences, the mass media, the religious institutions have all a facilitating or degrading influence on the individual members of a society with regard to the development of modernity. However, formal education as an instrument of promotion of modernity has to be treated differently from these institutions. This is because heavy public investments, investment by the States are made on education in India. It is but natural to expect, apart from other expectations, the development of personalities who have a modern outlook and corresponding behaviour. At the same time, it is also essential to examine whether there is any level of education whose completion should be the basic minimum requirement for the development of modernity. In other words, the relative efficiency of different levels of education in promoting modernity is also of considerable significance. Identification of those 'critical' minimum levels of education for promotion of modernity should have a bearing on future policy decisions on educational investments in India.

This research study has been an attempt to examine the performance of education in promoting modernity. It has also examined the relative performance of different levels of education in the promotion of modernity.

Perspective

For purposes of this study, modernity was conceived at the individual level as consisting of five dimensions, viz., Change Proneness, Scientific Orientation, Democratic Orientation, Secular Orientation, and Achievement Orientation as reflected in eight Areas of life, viz. Education, Employment, Marriage and Family, Religious Life, Political Life, Social Life, Health and Hygiene, and Economic Life.

This conception is holistic in nature as it synthesises two classes of theories, namely (i) the structure function model and the process model as well as (ii) the socio-psychological model. Modernity is a socio-psychological state, in a person, of a network of attitudes and behaviour which has been influenced by the given social structures and the ongoing processes.

Modernity has been studied here as a socio-psychological state in an individual taking into account, in an implicit way, the effect of given social structures and ongoing social processes.

Review of Related Literature

An attempt was made to review the empirical studies related to the study of education and modernity. Based on the review, several insights were drawn which assisted the formulation of hypotheses.

Hypotheses

The following were the hypotheses formulated for the present study:

1. There is no significant relationship between levels of education and modernity in terms of attitudes of respondents.
2. There is no significant relationship between levels of education and modernity in terms of behaviour of respondents.
3. Differences in levels of education do not affect the relationship between education as well as attitudinal and behavioural modernity.
4. Variables such as sex, marital status, religion, place of residence, migration, occupation, income, type of schooling and exposure to mass media do not influence the relationship between levels of education and modernity of respondents.

Objectives

In view of the above hypotheses, the general objectives set for the present study were as follows:

1. To study modernity of individuals with regard to attitudes.
2. To study modernity of individuals with regard to behaviour.

Specific Objectives

The above general objectives have been specified as follows for the present study:

1. To study the relationship between levels of education and modernity in terms of attitudes of respondents.
2. To study the relationship between levels of education and modernity in terms of behaviour of respondents.
3. To study the cognitive dissonance defined as convergence/divergence between attitudes and behaviour of respondents with respect to modernity and in relation to levels of education.
4. To study the relationship between levels of education and modernity in terms of attitudes and behaviour of respondents while accounting for variables such as sex, marital status, religion, place of residence, migration, occupation, income type of schooling and exposure to mass media.

Variables

In this study, Education, defined in terms of levels of completed schooling or higher levels of education was treated as the independent variable.

Modernity defined in terms of attitudes and behaviours (and convergence between the two) was the dependent variable.

Attitudinal modernity was measured in terms of the 'score' obtained by individuals on the Attitudinal Modernity Scale.

Behavioural modernity is understood based on the proportion of respondents who have demonstrated positive or negative behaviour for the behavioural items given in the schedule. Behavioural items correspond to the Areas of Life as in the case of attitudes.

The intervening variables considered are: Sex, Marital Status, Religion, Occupation, Income, Type of Schooling, Place of residence, Migration, and Exposure to mass media.

Methodology

For the present study, normative survey method was adopted. The design followed was as follows:

Sources of Data

Primary data, i.e. qualitative and quantitative, pertaining to the attitudes and behaviour of individual respondents constituted the major data source. In addition to this secondary data from census publications and other literatures were also used at various phases of the study.

Sample

Samples for the study were drawn following quota sampling. The sample selected consisted of male and female adults residing in Cochin taluk of Ernakulam district, who were born between 1962 and 1964. Seven hundred individuals belonging to different levels of education, including illiterates were selected through quota sampling.

Tools

The data required for the present study were collected through a schedule. The schedule had three parts:

Part I : General information schedule for gathering information on independent and intervening variables.

Part II : Attitudinal modernity scale for measuring attitudinal modernity. The attitudinal modernity scale was constructed and standardised for the study following Thurstone technique. It was found to be valid and reliable.

Part III : Items pertaining to behavioural modernity.

Collection of Data

Fieldwork for collection of data for the study was conducted in Cochin taluk of Ernakulam district in Kerala. Fieldwork was carried out in two stages — Pilot and Main study. Pilot study was done in Chellanam Panchayat of Cochin taluk. The insights drawn from the pilot study were incorporated in the main study. For the main study all areas, i.e. rural and urban areas of Cochin taluk except Chellanam were covered. Data were collected by canvassing schedules through household survey.

Analysis

The attitudinal responses were analysed using ANOVA and also Duncan's Multiple Range Test. Case study technique has also been used at certain places. Behavioural items as well as Cognitive dissonance have been analysed using percentages.

Scope of the Study

The study has been essentially interested in the relationship between levels of education and individual modernity. It was confined to the study of modernity in terms of attitudes and behaviour *only* of individuals in the context of their educational levels.

Attitudinal modernity with regard to five dimensions were included in the study. Similarly, eight major Areas of Life were also considered in studying attitudinal modernity.

Behavioural modernity as reflected in selected Areas of life were examined in the study.

An attempt was also made in order to identify whether there was any 'critical level' of education with reference to attitudinal modernity of individuals.

In order to know whether there is any influence of other characteristics and attributes of individuals in the relationship between education and modernity, a set of variables were included in the present study. These were: sex, marital status, religion, place of residence, migration, occupation, income, type of schooling, and exposure to mass media. An analysis of this sort was attempted only in the case of attitudinal modernity.

It was also essential to know whether attitude and behaviour of individuals move in similar directions. An effort is made to this effect in analysing the cognitive dissonance, defined as convergence/divergence of attitudes and behaviour of individuals.

Findings of the Study

Profile of the Sample

Sample selected for the present study is by and large representative of the traditional Indian society exhibiting certain characteristics of a society making a transition from the traditional to the modern.

They mostly belong to lower middle class and lower strata of society. A majority of respondents in the sample are non-migrants to Cochin engaged in skilled or unskilled manual labour. They knew three or more languages including Malayalam. They are unmarried, non-vegetarians without any habits. They are without any organised savings and are not members of social and political organisations. They know how to use calculators. A majority of the respondents belong to extended families and their parents have not studied even in the limited cases beyond SSLC. Their fathers are skilled or unskilled manual labourers whereas their mothers are mostly housewives. They belong mostly to lower middle or low income households, owning the house in which they live, having small land holdings, and belong to lower middle or low category even in terms of 'Living Standard Index'.

The married respondents have got married after they attained the minimum age for marriage and accepted arranged marriages, married within their caste, accepted the custom of dowry, adopted birth control measures and modern child care practices.

Education and Modernity

Attitudinal Modernity

The findings of the study are classified under relationships between education and general modernity as well as between education and components of modernity in various Areas of Life and Dimensions.

(i) There is a significant relationship between education and general modernity. It means that as level of education rises, modernity of a person, in general, also rises.

(ii) This result is also true in case of all the dimensions of modernity except change proneness. It is also true in all areas of life. Differences observed with regard to change proneness among people with different levels of education and no education are not significant. All respondents have recorded a moderately high score on Change Proneness.

(iii) *Critical levels of education*: The level of education which is critical with regard to the degree of modernity of a person in general, appears to be the Upper Primary Level of education. The slowly rising curve of general modernity takes a leap at this stage and is steady thereafter. However, this critical level of education gets shifted when the components of modernity are examined.

The lower primary level of education is observed to be critical with regard to democratic orientation and in the Area of Marriage and Family.

The upper primary level of education is observed to be critical with regard to scientific orientation, health and hygiene as well as economic life apart from general modernity.

For all other areas of life: Education, Employment, Religious Life, Political Life, Social Life as well as for Secular Orientation and Achievement Orientation, it is the secondary level of education which has emerged as the critical level.

(iv) *Intervening Variables:* When the results obtained with regard to the relationship between education and attitudinal modernity were looked at against the background of each of the intervening variables, the following findings emerged:

Marital status, migration and type of schooling did not affect the relationships.

Sex, religion and place of residence were found to influence the relationship between education and some components of attitudinal modernity. Inferences drawn from case studies, indicated that income, occupation, and exposure to mass media influence the relationship between education and attitudinal modernity.

Behavioural Modernity

Three different patterns were observed in the relationship between levels of education and behavioural modernity. Positive relationships were observed in the Areas of Education, Marriage and Family, and Social Life. 'Curvilinear' relationships (like a 'hyperbola') were observed in the Areas of Religious Life, and Marriage and Family. No relationship was observed in some aspects in the Areas of Marriage and Family Religious Life, Social Life, Political Life, and Health and Hygiene. It may, therefore, be inferred that education and behavioural modernity need not necessarily be associated.

Cognitive Dissonance

In general moderate dissonance is observed across levels of education with regard to attitudes and corresponding behaviours relating to modernity.

Conclusions

Several significant and interesting conclusions have emerged from the study. One of the first conclusions that appears on surface is that formal education taken as schooling is not an essential ingredient for the minimum levels of modernity observed in the sample. Modernity score has been derived for each of the 700 respondents using an attitudinal scale of modernity. The score can range from zero to eleven. The average for each group of 100 respondents belonging to various levels of education as well as illiterates have been obtained. Theoretically, it is possible that the average of a particular group can range from zero indicating the total absence of modernity to eleven indicating the end state of total or perfect modernity. The average modernity score on 'General Modernity' even for illiterate is 5.9334. It means that there is modernity among respondents who have not been to a school. The very process of modernisation in a society, the influence of various social institutions in a society, and the immediate community have a modernising influence. Indian social life appears to be caught in a level of modernity. However, it should be useful to examine whether formal education makes a marginal/substantial difference in promotion of people to higher levels of modernity. In this context, it is observed that there are relative differentials in the average modernity scores of respondents belonging to various levels of education. These differences have turned out to be statistically significant. A deeper analysis showed that upper primary level of education appears to be the critical minimum level at which and beyond which the differences from illiterates become significant. This conclusion should act as a strong impetus to the proposal for the provision of a minimum level of seven years of primary education in India.

One may wonder whether lower primary education has no bearing on the promotion of modernity at all. But this is not true. When the relationship between levels of education and modernity was examined for five dimensions and eight areas of life separately, the lower primary education turned out to be the critical minimum level for significance of mean differences for the Dimension Democratic Orientation and in the Area of Life, Marriage and Family. It is also true that upper primary level of education is not sufficient for significant differentials with illiterates in certain Areas of Life and for certain Dimensions. Results have shown that mean differences have turned out to be significant at the secondary level for the Dimensions, Secular Orientation, Achievement Orientation as well as in the Areas of Religious Life, Political Life, Social Life, Education and Employment.

It means that upper primary education may not also be sufficient to guarantee complete modernity in such Dimensions as Secular Orientation. This discovery should be of far-reaching significance for a pluralistic society like India. The long term goal of educational planning should concentrate on minimum levels of secondary education for all the citizens. It is incidentally noted that this is by and large the prevailing achievement in the developed West.

Another important conclusion arising from the study is that though formal education (interpreted as lower primary education for one or two Dimensions/Areas of Life, as upper primary education for several Dimensions/Areas of Life, and secondary education for certain Dimensions/Areas of Life) does have a bearing on levels of modernity, this inference cannot be held good uniformly for all cross-sections of the sample. There are certain other variables which influence the relationship. In other words, variations are observed across sub-groups in the sample with regard to the mean modernity scores, that is, certain variables intervene to disturb the given relationships. The intervening variables thus discovered are sex, religion, place of residence (rural/urban) while certain other variables like respondents' marital status, migration and type of schooling (by management) which were originally hypothesised to influence this relationship did not turn out to be so. Males have recorded a significantly higher mean difference than the females. This is not surprising given the male dominated structure of Indian society where women are socialised to be more conservative than men. This is the result obtained in a region where a high incidence of matriarchal characteristics exists, unlike most other regions of India. However, this finding turned out to be different at the post-graduate and professional level where mean modernity scores between men and women did not significantly differ. This means that there is a need for revamping of the school and college curriculum, especially perhaps the co-curricular experiences in such a way that the male-female differences in mean modernity scores can be absorbed with the passage of time. The curriculum may also be subjected to a content analysis to identify a hidden curriculum which may pass on messages of conservatism for girls/women.

Surprisingly, the mean modernity scores across various levels of education for rural samples turned out to be significantly higher than that of urban samples. One explanation for this is that the demands of urban life such as housing, competitive access to health and other services, greater exposure to a wider cross-section of society may tend to affect adversely the contribution of education to the level of modernity. Hence, a stronger effort towards the promotion of modernity is called for in schools located in urban areas.

In the absence of adequate quota of sub-samples for analysis, a few case studies were made to examine the influence of income, occupation, and exposure to mass media on their relationship between education and modernity. Contrasting cases were taken for the intervening variables and for the same level of education. A qualitative analysis showed that all the three variables are significant. Still it is felt that this analysis would not be adequate to draw meaningful conclusions.

Plato said long ago that 'knowledge is virtue'. On the other hand, his disciple, Aristotle said that 'virtue is a matter of habits' implying that it is subject to rigorous socialising practices and not just instruction. These diverging contentions have been a subject of debate all through history. Even this study was curious to know whether attitudinal changes that can be exclusively attributed to education can have corresponding overtones with regard to behaviours of individual respondents. As such cognitive dissonance analysis is made to examine the relationship between certain behaviours as corresponding to the attitudes in certain Dimensions/Areas of Life, across levels of education. The study has revealed that the given levels of dissonance/consonance are moderate. Dissonance has been observed in certain Areas of Life/Dimensions such as Marriage and Family, Religious Life. Perhaps education/schooling cannot by itself bring about modernity in both behaviour and attitudes. Schooling can only bring about the desired changes in attitudes. In order to enlist the support of family in bringing about corresponding modern behaviours in marriage and family one may have to depend upon adult education, voluntary social action, etc. However, the schools have to be aware of the incidence of dissonance and teachers have to be orientated towards the same.

Finally, one question that remains is whether education can lead Indian society to greater and higher heights of modernity in the years to come. The reply is a definite 'Yes'. This is based on the discovery that the average Indian is 'change-prone'. The mean modernity score on change-proneness is 9.1796 (out of 11) for all the 700 respondents in the sample including that of illiterates whose mean modernity score is 9.1515. This is a redeeming discovery of the study. Whatever differences in modernity appear across levels of education are with regard to the direction of 'change' such as Democratic Orientation. Secular Orientation, Achievement Orientation, and Scientific Orientation across various Areas of life. Hence, a well-planned system of education intended to promote modernity would be successful. The long term goal should be the minimum provision of secondary education for all the citizens, while the immediate and compelling plan should be for the universalisation of 7 years of primary education which should be treated as 'on top priority'.

Bibliography

Abraham, M. Francis, 1973. *Dynamics of Leadership in Village India.* India International, Allahabad.

Abraham, M. Francis, 1977. "Modernisation or Social Change — A Redefinition of Concepts". *The Indian Journal of Social Work,* 37 (4) (January): 421-33.

Acheampong, Konadu. 1988. "Structural Change, Individual Modernity and Fertility Preference in Taiwan". *Dissertation Abstracts International,* (A) 48(7) (January): 1892.

Agyei, William Kwaku Addey, 1976. "The Effects of Modernisation on Fertility in Jamaica". *Dissertation Abstracts International* (A) 37(6) (December): 3938.

Albornoz, Orlando, 1989. "Education and Development Revisited: A Sociological Perspective". *International Sociology,* 4(3) (September): 273-91.

Al-Khazraji, M.G., 1979. Expansive Attitudes Influencing Modernisation and their Sociological Correlates: An Exploratory Study in a Developing Nation. *Indian Psychological Abstracts,* 13 December: 9.

Altbach, Philip G., 1976. "Higher Education and Modernisation: The Indian Case". In Giri Raj Gupta (Ed.), *Main Currents in Indian Sociology-I Contemporary India: Some Sociological Perspectives.* Vikas Publishing House Pvt. Ltd., Delhi: 200-20.

Anand, C.L. and Sudhir Kumar, M.A., 1986. "Development and Standardisation of a Modernity Attitude Scale (MAS)" in M.B. Buch (Ed.), *Third Survey of Research in Education 1978-1983.* NCERT, New Delhi: 474.

Apter, David E., 1965. *The Politics of Modernisation*, Chicago University Press, Chicago.

Armer, Michael, 1971, "Formal Education and Individual Modernity in an African Society". *American Journal of Sociology*, 76: 604-26.

Armer, Michael, 1977. "Reply to Cohen and Till". *American Sociological Review*, 42(2) (April): 378-82.

Armer, Michael and Robert Youtz. 1971. "Formal Education and Individual Modernity in an African Society", in *American Journal of Sociology,* 76: 604-26.

Atal, Yogesh, 1976. "Political Participation and Modernisation" in S.K. Srivastava (Ed.), *Tradition and Modernisation: Processes of Continuity and Change in India*. India International Publications, Allahabad: 153-67.

Ben-Bakr, Khaled Abdallah, 1987. "Modernization as if People Mattered: Toward A New Indigenous and Non-ethnocentric Theory of Modernisation". *Dissertation Abstracts International*, (A) 48(2), (August): 477.

Beran, Janice Ann, 1977. "The Effect of Modernisation on Attitudes Toward Play Among Filipino Children of Negros Oriental, Philippines". *Dissertation Abstracts International*, (A) 37(11), (May): 7019.

Beriot, Colette, 1973. Attitude Towards Modernisation: Activism, Theoretical Discussion and Experimental Attempt to Avoid Cultural Subjectivity (Preliminary Study), *Journal of Psychological Researches,* 17 (2) (May): 54-58.

Bhattacharya, Debika, 1986. "Educational Policy for Modernisation and National Development", *Journal of Indian Education,* (September): 6-14.

Black, Cyril E., 1966. *The Dynamics of Modernisation: A Study in Comparative History*, Harper & Row, New York.

Black, Cyril E., 1974. "The Dynamics of Modernisation" in Frank Tachau (Ed.) *The Developing Nations: What Path to Modernisation*? Dodd, Mead & Company, New York, pp. 22-41.

Boudon, Raymond, 1973. *Education, Equality and Social Opportunity*, Wiley, New York.

Bourdieu, P., 1972. *Current Research*. Centre for European Sociology, Paris.

Breese, Gerald, 1966. *Urbanisation in Newly Developing Countries*. Prentice-Hall, Englewood Cliffs.

Broines, Guillermo and F.B. Waisanen, 1966. "Educational Aspirations, Modernisation and Urban Integration". *Paper presented at the American Sociological Association*, Miami Beach, Fla.

Brookover, Wilbur B. and Gottlieb, David, 1964. *A Sociology of Education* (II ed.). Van Nostrand Reinhold Company, New York.

Buss, Andreas, 1985. "Max Weber's Contributions to Questions of Development in Modern India", *Journal of Developing Societies* 1 (December): 130-49.

Buch, M.B. (ed.), 1991. *Fourth Survey of Research in Education* 1983-1988, Vols. I & II, NCERT, New Delhi.

Census of India, 1981. (1989). *Census Atlas*, Series 10, Kerala, Government of India Publications, New Delhi.

Census of India, 1981. (1990). *District Census Handbook*: Ernakulum District, Series 10, Kerala, Part XIII A & B, Government of India Publications, Government Press, Trivandrum.

Census of India, 1991, (1991). *Provisional Population Totals*, Series 12, Kerala. Government of India Publications, Government Press, Koratty.

Chatterjee, Lipi, 1982. "Attitudinal Modernity of Factory Workers and Farmers". *Social Change* 12, (2) (June): 24-28.

Cochran, Thomas C., 1959. *The Puerto Rican Businessman*, University of Pennsylvania Press, Philadelphia.

Cohen, Jere and Till, Amnon, 1977. "Another Look at Modernity Scales: Reanalysis of the Convergent and Discriminant Validities of Armer Kahl, Smith and Inkeles, and Schnaiberg Scales" (Comment on Armer and Schnaiberg, ASR June 1972. *American Sociological Review*, 42 (2) (April): 373-78.

Coleman, James S., 1974. "Education" in Frank Tachau (Ed.) *The Developing Nations: What Path to Modernisation*? Dodd, Mead & Company, New York: 98-105.

Conklin, George H., 1977, "Family Modernisation Values and Factory Employment: An example from South India", *Journal of Comparative Family Studies*, 8, (3 Autumn): 315-26.

Cormack, Margaret L., 1961. *She Who Rides a Peacock*, Asia Publishing House, Bombay.

Dalwai, Mehrunnisa H., 1979. "Religion and Modernity". *Philosophy and Social Action*, 5 (1-2): 39-41.

Damle, Y.B., 1966. *College Youth in Poona: A Study of Elite in the Making*. Mimeographed, Deccan College, Poona.

Damle, Y.B., 1974. "Perception of Modernisation by College Youth in India", *Assignment Children*, 27 (July-September): 33-43.

Damle, Y.B., 1976. "Educated Youth as Promoters of Modernisation" in S.K. Srivastava (Ed.) *Tradition and Modernisation: Processes of Continuity and Change in India*, India International Publications, Allahabad: 108-20.

Desai, A.R., 1971. *Essays on Modernisation of Underdeveloped Societies*, I & II, Thacker & Co. Ltd., Bombay.

Deutschmann, Paul J., 1963. "The Mass Media in an Underdeveloped Village" in *Journalism Quarterly*, 40: 27-35.

District Statistical Hand Book, 1986. Ernakulam, Department of Economics and Statistics, Trivandrum.

Di Tella, Torcuato, 1969. "Populism and Reform in Latin America" in Claudio Velis (Ed.), *Obstacles to Change in Latin America*, Oxford University Press, New York.

Doob, Leonard W., 1961, *Communication in Africa*, Yale University Press, New Haven

Dube, Leela and Dube, S.C., 1976. "Barriers to Modernisation" in S.K. Srivastava (Ed.) *Tradition and Modernisation: Processes of Continuity and Change in India*, India International Publications, Allahabad: 79-82.

Dube, S.C., 1967. "Modernisation and its Adaptive Demands on Indian Society" in M.S. Gore, *et al.* (Eds.), *Papers in the Sociology of Education*, NCERT, New Delhi: 33-51.

Dube, S.C., 1976. "Modernisation and Education" in S.K. Srivastava (Ed.) *Tradition and Modernisation: Processes of Continuity and Change in India*. India International Publications, Allahabad: 102-107.

Dube, S.C., 1976. *Modernisation and Development: The Search for Alternative Paradigms*. Vistaar Publications, New Delhi.

Dubey, S.M., 1976. "Modernisation among the Tribes of North-Eastern India (Assam)" in S.K. Srivastava (Ed.), *Tradition and Modernisation: Processes of Continuity and Change in India*. India International Publications, Allahabad: 168-78.

Edwards, Allen L., 1989. *Techniques of Attitude Scale Construction*. Vakils, Feffer and Simons Pvt. Ltd., Bombay.

Edwards, Allen L., 1972. *Experimental Design in Psychological Research*, Holt Rinehart Winston, Inc., New York.

Eisenstadt, S.N., 1966. *Modernisation: Protest and Change*, Prentice-Hall, Englewood Cliffs.

Elarabi, Ali Mohamed Ali, 1985. "Education and Bureaucratic Modernisation in Sudan". *Dissertation Abstracts International*, (A) 46 (6) (December): 1456.

Fals Borda, Orlanda, 1962. *Facts and Theory of Socio-Cultural Change in a Rural Social System*, National University of Columbia, Bogota.

Farrell, William Timothy, 1977. "Community Development and Individual Modernisation in San Lucas Toliman, Guatemala". *Dissertation Abstracts International*, (A) 38(5) (November): 2881-82.

Ferguson, George A., 1976. *Statistical Analysis in Psychology and Education*, McGraw-Hill Kogakusha Ltd., Tokyo.

Fillol, Thomas Roberto, 1961. *Social Factors in Economic Development: The Argentina Case*, MIT Press, Cambridge.

Fliegel, Frederick C. *et al.*, 1968. *Agricultural Innovations in Indian Villages*, National Institute of Community Development, Hyderabad.

Freire, Paulo, 1972. *Pedagogy of the Oppressed*, Penguine, London.

Frey, Frederick W., 1966 (Quoted in Abraham, 1977). "The Mass Media and Rural Development in Turkey". *Rural Development Research Report*. MIT Centre for International Studies, Cambridge.

Galfo, Armand J., 1975. *Interpreting Educational Research.*, W.M.C. Brown Company Publishers, Iowa.

Gandhi, P.K., 1986. "Youth Culture – A Study of Rural Youth in Urban-based Institutions", in M.B. Buch (Ed.) *Third Survey of Research in Education*, 1978-1983, NCERT, New Delhi: 126.

Garrett, Henry E., 1985. *Statistics in Psychology and Education.* Vakils, Feffer and Simons Ltd., Bombay.

Ghaban, Mahroos Ahmed, 1987. "Education and Individual Modernity among Saudi Students: A Study of the Impact of Formal and Cross Cultural Education on Modernizing Attitudes and Values". *Dissertation Abstracts International*, 47(9) (March): 3295.

Goodman, Paul, 1974. *Compulsory Miseducation*, Penguine, London.

Ghose, Sisirkumar, 1968. Tradition and Modernity. *Bulletin of the Ramakrishna Mission Institute of Culture*, XIX (10) (October): 279-87.

Gore, M.S. *et al.*, (Ed.), 1967. *Papers in the Sociology of Education*, NCERT, New Delhi.

Gore, M.S., I.P. Desai and Suma Chitnis, 1970. *Field Studies in the Sociology of Education*. NCERT, New Delhi.

Gore, M.S., 1982. *Education and Modernisation in India*, Rawat Publications, Jaipur.

Government of Kerala, 1988. *Statistics for Planning 1988*, Department of Economics & Statistics, Trivandrum.

Gusfield, Joseph R., 1966-67. Tradition and Modernity Misplaced Polarities in the Study of Social Change, *American Journal of Sociology,* 72 (July-May): 351-62.

Halpern, Manfred, 1963. "The Character and Scope of the Social Revolution in the Middle East" in William R. Polk (Ed.), *Developmental Revolution*, The Middle East Institute, Washington DC, pp. 7-23.

Haldipur, R.N., 1973. (Book Reviewed) "Pedagogy of the Oppressed" by Paulo Freire in *Social Change*, 3(1-2) (March-June): 46-49.

Hasan, Munch Zaini, 1987. "Individual Development Oriented Modernity and Forces Prompting it among Students as Four Teacher Training Colleges in Malang, Indonesia". *Dissertation Abstract: International*, (A) 47(12) (June): 4277.

Hoselitz, Bert and Wilbert M. Moore, 1963. *Industrialization and Society*, UNESCO, Paris.

Holsinger, D.B., 1987. "Modernization and Education" in George Psacharopoulos (Ed.), *Economics of Education Research and Studies*. Pergamon Press, Oxford: 107-10.

Hunter, Guy., 1969. *Modernising Peasant Societies*, Oxford University Press, New York.

Huntington, Samuel P., 1968. *Political Order in Changing Societies*. Yale University Press, New Haven.

Illich, Ivan, 1971. *Deschooling Society*. Calder and Boyars, London.

Inkeles, Alex, 1969-70. Making Men Modern: On the Causes and Consequences of Individual Change in Six Developing Countries. *American Journal of Sociology* 75 (July-May): 208-25.

Inkeles, Alex, 1969-70. Comments on John Stephenson's "Is Everyone Going Modern?" *American Journal of Sociology*, 75 (July-May): 146-51.

Inkeles, Alex, 1983. *Exploring Individual Modernity.* Columbia University Press, New York.

Inkeles, Alex, and Holsinger, D.B, 1974. *Education and Individual Modernity in Developing Countries*, Brill, Leiden.

Inkeles, Alex and Smith, David H., 1974. *Becoming Modern: Individual Changes in Six Developing Countries.* Harvard University Press, Cambridge, Massachusetts.

Jayaswal, Meera, 1985. Health Modernity and its Correlates in Women of South Bihar, *Social Change* 15(2) (June): 7-14.

Jayaswal, Meera and Singh, Amar Kumar, 1989. "Health Modernity in Tribals of South Bihar", *Social Change*, 19(1) (March): 13-29.

Jindal, B.L., 1986. "Schooling and Modernity" in M.B. Buch (Ed.) *Third Survey of Research in Education 1978-1983.* NCERT, New Delhi: 141-42.

Junadi, Purnawan, 1987. "The Effect of Village Modernisation and the Family Planning and Nutrition Programme on Household Knowledge and Behaviour in East Java and Bali, Indonesia". *Dissertation Abstracts International*, (A) 48(2) (August): 491.

Kahl, Joseph A., 1968. *The Measurement of Modernism*, University of Texas Press, Austin and London.

Kama, Raju, Malyala, S.S, 1984. The Paradigm of Modernity, *Social Change*, 14(1) (March): 31-34.

Kamat, A.R., 1982. Education and Social Change: A Conceptual Framework. *Economic and Political Weekly*, XVII (July 31): 1237-44.

Karabel, Jerome and Halsey, A.H., 1977. "Educational Research: A Review and an Interpretation" in Jerome Karabel and A.H. Halsey (Ed.) *Power and Ideology in Education*, Oxford University Press, New York: 1-85.

Kazan, Fayad El-Abd., 1987. "Relations between Mass-Media and attitudes toward Modernity and Psychological stress of University Students and Civil Servants in four Arabian Gulf Countries (Vols. I & II)". *Dissertation Abstracts International*, (A) 48(2) (August): 242-3.

Khatun, R., 1991. "Education and Modernisation (A Comparative Study of Two Villages of Bangladesh) in M.B. Buch (Ed.), *Fourth Survey of Research in Education 1983-1988,* Vol. I, NCERT, New Delhi: 162-63.

Kim, Doo Sik, 1987. "A Cross-National Study on Economic Development, Economic Dependency, Cultural Dependency and Internal Structural Mechanisms: Modernisation or Dependency". *Dissertation Abstracts International,* (A) 48(1) (July): 229-30.

Kim, Jim Young, 1987. "The Role of Christianity in the Economic Modernisation of South Korea", *Dissertation Abstracts International*, (A) 48(5) (November): 1288.

Korllos, Thomas Stephen, 1977. "Values and Education in Modernising Greece: The Case of Athens", *Dissertation Abstracts International*, (A) 37(8) (February): 5383.

Kumar, Krishna, 1970 (Quoted in Abraham, 1977). "Ritual Caste Ranking and Modernisation in India: A Study of Peasants in Six Villages", *Unpublished Master's Thesis*, Michigan State University, East Lansing.

Kuthiala, Sudharsan Kumar, 1979. "Industrial Workers in India: A Case Study in Modernisation". *Indian Psychological Abstracts*, 13 (December): 34-35.

Lachman, Ran, 1977. "Effects of Industrialisation and Socialisation on "Core" and "Periphery" Values in Personal Modernity". *Dissertation Abstracts International*, (A) 37(11) (May): 7329.

Larner, Daniel, 1958, 1963. *The Passing of Traditional Society, Modernising the Middle East*, Free Press, Glenco, Illinois.

Lerner, Daniel and Wilbur Schramm (Eds.), 1967. *Communication and Change in Developing Countries*, East West Centre Press, Honolulu.

Levy, Marion, 1966. *Modernisation and the Structure of Societies*. Princeton University Press, Princeton.

Levy, Marion, 1972. *Modernisation: Latecomers and Survivors*. Basic Books, New York.

Levy, Marion, 1986. "Modernisation Exhumed". *Journal of Developing Societies*, 11 (April): 1-11.

Lipset, Seymour Martin, 1967. "Values, Education and Entrepreneurship" in Martin Lipset and Aldo Solari (Eds.) *Elites in Latin America*, Oxford University Press, New York: 3-60.

Lulu, Li, 1989. "Theoretical Theses on Modernisation". *International Sociology* 4(4) (December): 365-77.

Mahajan, Harinder Nanda, 1989. "Education and Modernity". *Indian Journal of Social Sciences*, 2(3): 339-416.

Mahanta, K.C., 1991. "Modernisation and the Problem of Rural Development in North-East India" in H.C. Upadhyay (Ed.), *Modernisation and Rural Development*. Anmol Publications, New Delhi: 49-61.

Malik, Yogendra K. and Jese F. Marquete, 1974. "Changing Social Values of College Students in the Punjab", *Asian Survey*, 14(9): 795-806.

Mansur, Salim Syed, 1988. "Modernisation and Islam: The Experience and Lesson of Pakistan", *Dissertation Abstracts International*, (A) 48(11) (May): 2972.

Mathur, H.M., 1971. Modernising Educational Management. *NIE Journal*, V (4) (March): 1-4.

McCleland, David C., 1961. *The Achieving Society*. Van Nostard, Princeton.

Mehdi, Abbas Salih, 1988. "Modernisation in Three Egyptian Communities". *Dissertation Abstracts International*, (A) 48(9) (March): 2468.

Misra, Bhaskar D., 1976. "Demographic Factors and Modernisation" in S.K. Srivastava (Ed.), *Tradition and Modernisation: Processes of Continuity and Change in India*, India International Publications, Allahabad: 179-91.

Mishra, Vishwa Mohan, 1979. Mass-Media Use Patterns and Modernisation Process in the Indian Slums: A Study of four *basties* in Greater Delhi. *Indian Psychological Abstracts*, 13 (December): 15-16.

Moore Jr., Barrington, 1966. *Social Origins of Dictatorship and Democracy*, Beacon Press. Boston.

Moore, Wilbert E., 1965. *Impact of Industry*. Prentice Hall, Englewood Cliffs.

Moore, 1975. *Social Change* (2nd Ed.), Prentice Hall India Pvt. Ltd., New Delhi.

Morse, Richard M., 1958. *From Community to Metropolis*, University of Florida Press, Grainesville.

Murty, K. Radhakrishna and Rao, N. Umamaheswara, 1983. "Female Education, Modernity and Fertility: A Study in the Indian Context", *Demography India*, 12 (1): 86-96.

Murty, K. Satchidananda, 1987. Values and Modernity. *University News*, (January 12th): 7-8.

Nair, P. and R. Gopinathan, 1984. "How Kerala became Literate", *Future*, 11-12 (Summer-Autumn): 50-55.

Natarajan, Janaki, 1979. Social Transition and Modernisation: Case Studies in Urban South India. *Indian Psychological Abstracts*, 13 (December): 10.

National Commission on "Education and National Development", Ministry of Education, Government of India, 1966.

National Commission on "Education and National Development", Ministry of Education, Government of India, 1992. Fifth All-India Educational Survey, Vols. I & II, NCERT, New Delhi.

Nehru, Jawaharlal, 1972. "Democratic Collectivism and Socialism" in Frank Tachau (Ed.), *The Developing Nations: What Path to Modernisation*? Dodd, Mead & Company, New York: 169-72.

Nettl, J.P. and Roland, Robertson, 1968. *International Systems and the Modernisation of Societies*. Basic Books, New York.

Pandey, A.N., 1976. "Modernisation of a Complex Society: Some Theoretical and Methodological Issues" in S.K. Srivastava (Ed.), *Tradition and Modernisation: Processes of Continuity and Change* in India. India International Publications, Allahabad: 1-19.

Pandey, Rajendra, 1988. "Education and Society: Review of Perspectives". *Indian Educational Review*, 23(2) (April): 120-29.

Pareek, U. and Kothandapani, V., 1969. "Modernisation and Attitude Toward Family Size and Family Planning: Analysis of Some Data from India". *Social Biology* 16(1): 44-48.

Pavichevich, Hellen A., 1976. "Education and Modernisation in Montenegro, 1831-1918. *Dissertation Abstracts International*, (A) 37(5) (November): 2686.

Phimphisut, Tipaporn, 1987. "Modernisation and Political Instability in Thailand". *Dissertation Abstracts International*, (A) 48(1) (July): 213.

Pillai, P. Gopinathan, 1991. "Ernakulam: The First Total Literacy District in India". *Indian Journal of Adult Education*, 52(3) (July-September): 58-65.

Pool, Ithel de Sola, 1967. "The Mass-Media and Politics in the Modernisation Process" in Daniel Learner and Wilbur Schramm (Eds.), *Communication and Change in the Developing Countries*, East-West Centre Press, Honolulu.

Portes, Alejandro, 1973. The Factional Structure of Modernity: Empirical Replications and A Critique, *American Journal of Sociology*, 79(1) (July): 15-43.

Praprutidee, Borvorn, 1987. "The Military and Modernisation in Thailand, 1960-1984". *Dissertation Abstracts International*, (A) 48(1) (July): 213.

Premi, Mahendra K., 1991. India's Population: Heading Towards a Billion, an Analysis of 1991 *Census Provisional Results*, B.R. Publishing Corporation, New Delhi.

Psacharopoulos, George (Ed.), 1987. *Economics of Education Research and Studies*, Pergamon Press, Oxford.

Pye, Lucien, 1963. *Communication and Political Development*, Princeton University Press, Princeton.

Pye, Lucian W. and Daniel, Lerner, 1974. "Communications" in Frank Tachau (Ed.), *The Developing Nations: What Path to Modernisation*?, Dodd, Mead & Company, New York: 84-98.

Ramana, P.V.L., 1991. "Modernist Orientation and Role Performance of Lady Teachers of Visakhapatnam Municipal Schools" in M.B. Buch (Ed.), *Fourth Survey of Research in Education 1983-1988*. Vol. I, NCERT, New Delhi: 187.

Rayappa, P. Hanumantha, 1979. "Economic Costs and Benefits from Children" in K. Srinivasan *et al. Demographic and Socio-economic Aspects of the Child in India*. Himalaya Publishing House, Bombay: 221-34.

Reddy, G.P., 1988. "Socialisation for Modernisation in the Tribals". *Social Change*, 18(1) (March): 30-40.

Reed, Fred W., 1970. Migration and Modernisation. *Indian Journal of Sociology*, 1(2) (September): 104-27.

Reimer, Everett, 1971. *School is Dead*. Penguin Harmondsworth.

Rogers, Everett M., 1969. *Modernisation Among Peasants: The Impact of Communication*. Holt, Rinehart and Winston Inc., New York.

Rostow, Walter W., 1960. *Stages of Economic Growth*. Cambridge University Press, New York.

Roy, Bina, 1976. "Perception of Modernisation" in S.K. Srivastava (Ed.) *Tradition and Modernisation: Processes of Change and Continuity in India*. India International Publications, Allahabad: 72-78.

Roy, Prodipto *et al.*, 1968. *Agricultural Innovation among Indian Farmers*. National Institute of Community Development, Hyderabad.

Rudolph, Lloyd I. and S.H. Rudolph, 1974. "The Modernity of Tradition" in Frank Tachau (Ed.), *The Developing Nations: What Path to Modernisation*? Dodd, Mead & Company, New York: 41-51.

Sachidananda, 1976. "Tradition, Modernity and Modernisation in India" in S.K. Srivastava (Ed.), *Tradition and Modernisation: Processes of Continuity and Change in India*. India International Publications, Allahabad: 38-52.

Sahay, Manoranjan and Singh, Amar Kumar, 1989. "Modernity in Tribal Hindus", *Social Change* 19(4) (December): 74-92.

Sainath, P., 1986. "Unconventional Wisdom: The Anarchy of Education". *Imprint* (February): 45-48.

Saksena, R.N., 1972. Modernisation and Development: Trends in India. *Sociological Bulletin* 21(2) (September): 91-102.

Saksena, R.N., 1976. "Some Thoughts on Tradition and Modernisation" in S.K. Srivastava (Ed.), *Tradition and Modernisation: Processes of Continuity and Change in India*. India International Publications, Allahabad: 200-05.

Sams, Bert F., 1987. "Tradition and Modernity in a Lao Song Village of Central Thailand", *Dissertation Abstracts International*, (A) 48(6) (December): 1488.

Saunders, John V.D., 1969. "Education and Modernisation in Brazil" in Eric N. Barklanoff (Ed.) *The Shaping of Modern Brazil*, Louisiana University Press, Baton Rogue.

Schnaiberg, Allen, 1970. "Modernising Modernism: Theoretical and Empirical Explorations", *American Journal of Sociology*, 76: 399-425.

Schramm, Wilbur, 1964. *Mass Media and National Development*, Stanford University Press, Stanford.

Seetharamu, A.S., 1992. Optimising Efficiency of Resource Use in Indian Education: A Normative Framework in Jandhyala B.G. Tilak (Ed.), *Effective Utilisation of Resources in Education*, (Seminar Volume), NIEPA, New Delhi, 1992, pp. 72-89.

Shah, B.V., 1964. *Social Change and College Students of Gujarat*. Maharaj Shivaji Rao University, Baroda.

Shah, B.V., 1971. "Problems of Modernisation of Education in India", in A.R. Desai (Ed.), *Essays on Modernisation of Underdeveloped Societies*, Vol. 2., Thacker & Co., Ltd., Bombay: 240-53.

Sharma, Satish Chander, 1975a. "Psycho-Social Modernism in Indian Villages and its Implications for Programmes for Planned Social Change", *Dissertation Abstracts International*, (A) 35 (11) (May): 7409-10.

Sharma, Satish Chander, 1975b. "Psycho-Social Modernism Indian Villages and its Implications for Programmes for Planned Social Change", *Indian Psychological Abstracts*, 13 (December): 11.

Sharma, S.L., 1979. *Modernising Effects of University Education*, Indian Council of Social Science Research, New Delhi.

Sharma, S.L. 1979. The Modernising Effects of University Education on the Value Orientations of Students, *ICSSR Research Abstracts Quarterly*, 5(3-4): 97-103.

Shukla, S., 1976. "Modernisation and Education" in S.K. Srivastava (Ed.) *Tradition and Modernisation: Processes of Continuity and Change in India*. India International Publications, Allahabad: 83-101.

Shukla, P.D., 1990. *The New Education Policy in India*, Sterling Publishers Private Limited, New Delhi.

Singh, Amar Kumar, 1983. Health Modernity Education in India. *Social Change*, 13(2) (June): 27-34.

Singh, Amar Kumar, 1984A. "Socio-psychological Pre-requisites of Rural Development". *Social Change*, 14(2) (June): 41-47.

Singh, Amar Kumar, 1984B. Health Modernity: Concept and Correlates. *Social Change*, 14(3) (September): 3-16.

Singh, Amar Kumar, 1985. "Education and Development in India: The God that Failed", *Social Change*, 15(3) (September): 3-16.

Singh, Amar Kumar, *et al.* 1988. "Population–Health Education in the Tribals of South Bihar". *Social Change*, 18(1) (March): 3-28.

Singh, Yogendra, 1976. "Historicity of Modernisation" in S.K. Srivastava (Ed.), *Tradition and Modernisation: Processes of Continuity and Change in India*. India International Publications, Allahabad: 53-71.

Singer, Milton, 1985. "Max Weber and the Modernisation of India". *Journal of Developing Societies*, (December): 150-67.

Singh, R., 1986. "Impact of Education on Social Change among Tribals of Ranchi" in M.B. Buch (ed.), *Third Survey of Research in Education 1978-1983*, NCERT, New Delhi: 215.

Singh, R.G., 1982. Measurement of Rural Modernisation, *Rural India*, 47 (June): 84-87.

Singh, Satvir *et al.*, 1982. Psychometric Correlates of Modernity, *Social Change*, 12(2) (June): 29-33.

Sinha, Anand Mohan Prasad, 1977. "Communication Theory of Modernisation: An Empirical Exploration in Two Indian Villages". *Dissertation Abstracts International,* (A) 38(5) (November): 2398.

Smelser, Neil J., 1966. "The Modernisation of Social Relations" in Myron Weiner (Ed.), *Modernisation.* Basic Books, New York.

Smith, David Horton and Alex Inkeles. 1966. "The OM Scale: A Comparative Socio-Psychological Measure of Individual Modernity", *Sociometry*, 29(4) (December): 353-77.

Soepangat, *Soeharini*, 1987. "Indonesian School as Moderniser: A Case Study of the Orang Lembah Ballem Encultivation". *Dissertation Abstracts International,* (A) 47(12) (June): 4353.

Soni, H.S., 1969. Education and Modernity. *NIE Journal*, 4(2) (November): 3-4.

Srinivas, M.N., 1966, *Social Change in Modern India*, University of California Press, Berkeley.

Srinivas, M.N., 1976. "Tradition and Modernisation" in S.K. Srivastava (Ed.), *Tradition and Modernisation: Processes of Continuity and Change in India.* India International Publications, Allahabad: 206-11.

Srivastava, H.C., 1976. "Idea Systems of Indian Intellectuals: A model approach to tradition and modernisation" in S.K. Srivastava (Ed.), *Tradition and Modernisation: Processes of Continuity and Change in India*, India International Publications, Allahabad: 135-152.

Srivastava, L.R.N., 1971. The Role of Education in Modernisation of Two Tribes of Chotanagpur, *Indian Educational Review*, 6(1) (January): 162-82.

Srivastava, P.C., 1986. "The Process of Modernisation Among Educated Rural Youth" in M.B. Buch (Ed.) *Third Survey of Research in Education*, 1918-1983. NCERT, New Delhi: 223-24.

Srivastava, S.K. (Ed.), 1976. *Tradition and Modernisation: Processes of Continuity and Change in India*, India International Publications, Allahabad.

Srivastava, S.K. *et al.*, 1976. "Tradition and Modernisation Concepts and Processes" in S.K. Srivastava (Ed.), *Tradition and Modernisation: Processes of Continuity and Change in India.* India International Publications, Allahabad: 20-33.

Stephenson, John B., 1968-69. Is Everyone Going Modern? A Critique and a Suggestion for Measuring Modernism, *American Journal of Sociology,* 74 (July 1968-May 1969): 265-75.

Stephenson, John B., 1969-70. "The Author Replies", *American Journal of Sociology*, 75 (July-May): 151-56.

Sudhir Kumar, M.A., 1986. "Impact of Education on Social Attitudes of People in Some Backward Villages of Malabar" in M.B. Buch (ed.), *Third Survey of Education 1918-1983.* NCERT, New Delhi: 226.

Sullivan, Edward Eugene. 1968. *Education in Social Change*, Asia Publishing House, Bombay.

Tachau, Frank (Ed.), 1974. *The Developing Nations: What Path to Modernisation*? Dodd, Mead & Company, New York.

Tharakan, P.K. Michael, 1990. *The Ernakulam District Total Literacy Programme: Report of the Evaluation*, Centre for Development Studies, Trivandrum.

Thorat, S.S. *et al.*, 1978. "Change Proneness, Educational Levels, Aspirations and Achievement Motivations of Farmers", *Social Change,* 8(1) (March): 16-19.

Tilak, Jandhyala B.G., 1978. "Poverty Inequality and Education", *Social Change,* 8(2) (June): 25-28.

Toffler, Alvin, 1984. *Previews and Premises.* Pan Books, London.

Tripathi, Satyendra, 1976. "Role of Elites in Modernisation, in Context to Value and Ideology", in *Tradition and Modernisation: Processes of Continuity and Change in India.* India International Publications, Allahabad: 121-34.

Vajpeyi, Dhirendra Kumar. 1971. "The Role of Political Participation, Mass-Media and Empathy in Modernisation: A Case Study of Uttar Pradesh (India)". *Dissertation Abstracts International*, (A) 32(6) (December): 3396.

Varma, Baidya Nath, 1982. Modernisation, *Seminar 271* (March): 26-29.

Varma, V.P., 1976. "Conceptual Framework for the Study of Tradition and Modernisation" in S.K. Srivastava (Ed.) *Tradition and*

Modernisation: Processes of Continuity and Change in India. India International Publications, Allahabad: 34-37.

Venkatarangaiya, M., 1970. Communication. *Seminar 129*, (May): 46-47.

Venugopal, C., 1991. "Kerala Attains Total Literacy", *Sunday Herald* (*Deccan Herald*) 44 (April 28): 1-4.

Venugopal, P., 1990. "Ernakulam Makes History: First District in Country to Achieve Total Literacy". *Express Magazine: Indian Express* (Sunday Edition) 58 (February 4): 1-4.

Verghese, S., 1991. "Modernisation and Alienation, their Empirical Structure and Relationship with Education" in M.B. Buch (ed.), *Fourth Survey of Research in Education 1983-1988*, Vol. I, NCERT, New Delhi: 212-13.

Vlassoff, C., 1978. "Educating Female Adolescent: Possibilities and Limitations for Social Change and Population Learning in Rural India". *Demography India*, 7(1-2) (January): 175-93.

VVD and CGG., 1970. "Statistical Measurement of Modernisation". *Economic and Political Weekly*, 5 (November 14): 1850-52.

Waisanen, F.B. and Hideya, Kumata, 1972. "Education, Functional Literacy and Participation in Development", *International Journal of Comparative Sociology*, 13(1): 21-35.

Watson, Keith, 1988. "Forty Years of Education and Development: From Optimism to Uncertainty", *Educational Review*, 40(2): 137-74.

Weber, M. 1958. *The Protestant Ethic and the Spirit of Capitalism* (T. Parsons, Trans.), Charles Scribner's Sons, New York.

Willems, Emillo, 1953. "The Structure of the Brazilian Family". *Social Forces*, 31:343.

Williamson, Robert C., 1970. "Modernism and Related Attitudes: An International Comparison among University Students". *International Journal of Comparative Sociology*, 11(2): 130-45.

Yamboonruang, Wichid, 1977. "The Influence of Some Aspects of Modernisation on Fertility: A Time-Series and Cross-Sectional Analysis of the Thai Data". *Dissertation Abstracts International*, (A) 38(5) (November): 3079.

Index